Advances in Computer Science Applications and Research 4

This outstanding new series publishes state-of-the-art research spanning the entire spectrum of informatics ranging from foundational topics in the theory of computing to information and communications science and technology. A broad variety of multidisciplinary and interdisciplinary topics are welcome, as well.

While the focus is on publication of peer-reviewed full papers presenting mature work, inclusion of reviewed short papers reporting on work in progress are welcome, too. Besides globally relevant meetings with internationally representative program committees guaranteeing a strict peer-reviewing and paper selection process, conferences run by societies or of high regional or national relevance are also considered for publication.

Publication in ACSAR is free of charge. No royalties are paid, however, we offer registered conference participants temporary free access to the online version of the conference proceedings on SpringerLink (http://link.springer.com) by means of an http referrer from the conference website and/or a number of complimentary printed copies, as specified in the official acceptance email of the event.

ACSAR proceedings can be published in time for distribution at conferences or as post-proceedings, and delivered in the form of printed books and/or electronically as USBs and/or e-content licenses for accessing proceedings at SpringerLink. Furthermore, ACSAR proceedings are included in the ACSAR electronic book series hosted in the SpringerLink digital library at http://link.springer.com/bookseries/7899. Conferences publishing in ACSAR are allowed to use our online conference service (Meteor) for managing the whole proceedings lifecycle (from submission and reviewing to preparing for publication) free of charge.

Publication process

The language of publication is exclusively English. Authors publishing in ACSAR have to sign the Springer ACSAR copyright transfer form, however, they are free to use their material published in ACSAR for substantially changed, more elaborate subsequent publications elsewhere. For the preparation of the camera-ready papers/files, authors have to strictly adhere to the Springer ACSAR Authors' Instructions and are strongly encouraged to use the ACSAR LaTeX style files or templates.

How to start

To start the evaluation of your proposal for inclusion in the ACSAR series, please send an e-mail to acsar@springer.com , or directly to the editor responsible for your region. For more information about the responsible editor for your region please check the **Editors** section.

Joseph R. Barr · Jon Haass · Faisal Abu-Khzam
Editors

Areas of Success for AI

Third Annual Workshop, Embry-Riddle L. H. Harper Memorial AI Workshop 2025
Prescott, AZ, USA, August 15-16, 2025
Proceedings

Springer

Editors
Joseph R. Barr
Embry-Riddle Aeronautical University
Prescott, AZ, USA

Jon Haass
Embry-Riddle Aeronautical University
Prescott, AZ, USA

Faisal Abu-Khzam
Lebanese American University
Beirut, Lebanon

ISSN 3091-2954 ISSN 3091-2962 (electronic)
Advances in Computer Science Applications and Research
ISBN 978-3-032-18229-6 ISBN 978-3-032-18230-2 (eBook)
https://doi.org/10.1007/978-3-032-18230-2

This Springer imprint is published by the registered company Springer Nature Switzerland AG
The registered company address is: Gewerbestrasse 11, 6330 Cham, Switzerland

Preface

The title The Third Annual Lawrence H. Harper Memorial AI Workshop at

Embry-Riddle Aeronautical University is both too long and somewhat misleading.

There is hardly a doubt as to the length of the title but the adjective "The Third" is a bit off. It is true that the workshop has taken place trice; however, due to Larry Harper passing in 2023 shortly before an event could have been planned, we got sidetracked and missed that year. 2022 was the first year of the workshop that was started by a group of mathematicians that were keen to work (and solve) the Ramsey R (5, 5) problem. Larry gave the first keynote in which he described a method that seemed plausible to solve or at least narrow down the Ramsey R (5, 5) bound. The original team also consisted of Michael Langston and Levente "Levi" Dojcsak, Faisal Abu-Khzam and Joe Barr. The approach was to simulate a class of "balanced" graphs and prove that none contains either K_5 or its complement (five independent vertices). We had plenty of numerical evidence but the computations eluded us. Larry got very sick late spring of 2023 and subsequently passed on, and we all moved on to work on other things. Other than Larry, the speakers at the first workshop included Jon Haass, Paulo Shakarian, Michael Langston, Faisal Abu-Khzam, Peter Shaw, Joe Barr and others. We didn't called the 2022 event an AI workshop but a few talks on topics were presented. For example, Joe Barr spoke of using natural language processing to identify vulnerability in source code. After missing 2023, the workshop resumed in 2024 with around fifteen speakers over a day and a half with George Luger of the University of New Mexico giving a keynote on the history and the future of AI. This year (2025) we had seventeen speakers with Moshe Vardi of Rice University delivering the keynote talk with the intriguing title Homo Ratiocinator (Reckoning Man). Faisal Abu-Khzam gave an invited address entitled Combinatorial Methods in Artificial Intelligence: The Power of Node Packing. This is the first year the proceedings are being published by Springer. Speakers and corresponding papers were by invitation only of well-vetted researchers & scholars.

This resulted in fifteen papers one by each invited speaker. As it turned out neither the keynote speaker (Vardi) nor the invited speaker (Abu-Khzam) has supplemented talks with paper. Another speaker, Paul Duncanson who presented his research on Document Management System with Directed Acyclic Graphs also opted out of submitting a paper. Much has been written on AI and about its current and future impacts and so some of this may seem redundant, yet it is worth saying something on the topic. There is little doubt that societies, the economy and, indeed, the global order are experiencing a dramatic flux. Among other factors, those transformations are driven by technology, specifically by AI. Frantic advancement of AI technology had significant implications for business productivity. According to Goldman Sachs, the potential increases in global GDP may be as high as $25.6 trillion annually2[1]. Right from the very start in November 2022

---

[1] We're just repeating those figures. We're not expressing an opinion and not aware of the methodology that gave birth to these numbers.

in the anticipation of boosting productivity, business has sought to integrate OpenAI's ChatGPT into standard and novel business processes. Indeed, by integrating AI and helping to automate routine work, the boost in productivity was shown to be significant. There is no doubt that over time AI will impinge on every profession including many white collar ones. At present and in the indefinite future, businesses and governments will continue to search for applications of AI to every aspect of the economy including finance, energy, health care, transportation, media, and war fighting.

This Workshop strives to draw attention or at least not to neglect AI methodology; thus, one of the main topics is combinatorial AI where combinatorial algorithms are used to help solve AI problems. Clustering and feature selection are two classical types of problems in statistical learning that combinatorial methods are shown to be useful. The idea is conceptually simple and involves transforming data into graphs and then applying graphical algorithm and finally transforming the graph back into data. These types of techniques allow for an entirely alternate methodology/class of algorithms to solving classical problems, and it comes handy when classical techniques do not work all that well.

Another area of focus is the applications of AI in cybersecurity. Contributions from several cyber research teams one from Texas A&M led by Professor Drew Hamilton and one from Embry-Riddle led by Preethi Santhanam demonstrating lively research programs that applies AI to cybersecurity. National Oceanic and Atmospheric Administration (NOAA) researchers have showcased their novel applications of Bayesian techniques to study the effects of toxins on marine life and the distribution of coastal contaminants. This one-and-a-half-day workshop is the beginning of a continual effort to bring software and AI to rural America. Although Prescott is not much farther than 100 miles from Phoenix, it has an entirely different "pulse". With a significant native American population and few opportunities for professional growth, we strive to make economic differences that impacts the rural southwest. Indeed, with the workshop, we strive to contribute to the local economy, to build awareness, to bring talent and capital from across the country and the globe and to stimulate the environment of innovations. As the Workshop grows and as it brings attention to this corner of northern Arizona, we will continue to promote technology and AI as a vehicle for economic growth bringing opportunity and high-paying jobs to our community.

Proceedings Editors

Joseph R. Barr
Jon Haass
Faisal Abu-Khzam

Acknowledgments

The organizers would like to extend their sincere gratitude to the following individuals and organizations for their invaluable assistance making the event a success.

- Ms. Patti Davis of Springer for her invaluable assistance in putting together Workshop's proceedings.
- Embry-Riddle Aeronautical University, Prescott, Arizona, USA for hosting the event.
- Embry-Riddle's CARS (Center for Aerospace Resilient Systems) for providing generous scholarships for students and junior faculty.
- Prescott-AI for underwriting event's incidentals and for hosting workshop's web registration app.
- ZOOM, a company and its application that allowed for remote participation.

Organization

General Chairs

Joseph R. Barr	Embry-Riddle Aeronautical University
Jon C. Haass	Embry-Riddle Aeronautical University
Faisal Abu-Khzam	Lebanese-American University

Contents

Local Agentic Retrieval Augmented Generation: A Comparative Study of OpenAI and Meta LLMs

Saurabh Nandwani and David Alfred Ostrowski(✉)

School of Professional Studies, Northwestern University, Evanston, USA
SaurabhNandwani2024@u.northwestern.edu,
davidostrowski@northwestern.edu

Abstract. Retrieval Augmented Generation (RAG) has emerged as a powerful paradigm for improving the accuracy and trustworthiness of large language models (LLMs) by grounding responses in external knowledge sources. However, existing implementations often depend on cloud-based infrastructures, raising concerns around privacy, latency, and reliability. This paper introduces Local Agentic RAG, a framework that integrates retrieval-augmented pipelines with locally deployed agentic reasoning modules to enable context-aware, privacy-preserving, and adaptive generation. Unlike traditional RAG, which primarily focuses on static retrieval, Local Agentic RAG leverages agent-driven orchestration to dynamically select retrieval strategies, assess knowledge gaps, and refine outputs through iterative reasoning. Experimental evaluations highlight the advantages of this approach in terms of reduced hallucination rates, enhanced factual accuracy, and improved response adaptability, while maintaining data sovereignty. Furthermore, we provide a comparative analysis of Local Agentic RAG across two leading LLM ecosystems—OpenAI's GPT models and Meta's LLaMA family—demonstrating that the proposed framework can be flexibly deployed across diverse architectures. Our findings indicate that Local Agentic RAG offers a scalable and secure pathway toward domain-specific, trustworthy AI applications in healthcare, finance, and enterprise knowledge management.

Keywords: Large Language Models (LLMs) · Retrieval – Augmented Generation (RAG) · Agentic RAG

1 Introduction

Language models (LLMs) such as OpenAI's GPT-4 and Meta's LLaMA-3 deliver state-of-the-art performance across summarization, question answering, and code generation, but they remain constrained by static pretraining corpora—leading to hallucinations, outdated knowledge, and brittle domain transfer [1–3]. Retrieval-Augmented Generation (RAG) addresses these issues by coupling generation with information retrieval: relevant passages are retrieved from an external corpus and fused into the model's context window prior to decoding, improving factuality and grounding [4]. Advances in dense retrieval (e.g., DPR) and efficient vector search further strengthen RAG's ability to surface semantically aligned evidence at low latency [5].

J. R. Barr et al. (Eds.): ERWCSA 2025, ACSAR 4, pp. 1–8, 2026.
https://doi.org/10.1007/978-3-032-18230-2_1

However, many production RAG systems run retrieval and generation as cloud services, raising privacy, latency, and reliability concerns—especially in regulated domains (healthcare, finance) or environments with strict data residency requirements. Moreover, the canonical "retrieve-then-generate" pipeline is often workflow-rigid: it does not reason about when to retrieve, how to decompose a task, or how to validate and correct intermediate outputs.

To overcome these limitations, we propose Local Agentic RAG: a deployment pattern in which retrieval, routing, and verification are orchestrated by agentic controllers running locally (on-premises or edge). Building on agent frameworks that interleave reasoning and acting (tool use), agents can decompose user goals, select retrieval strategies, call tools iteratively (search, rerank, summarize), and self-check responses before finalization [6–8]. Local execution reduces round-trip latency, preserves data sovereignty, and enables deeper customization of retrieval policies, indexing, and safety filters.

This paper makes three contributions. (1) We formalize a Local Agentic RAG architecture that integrates a local vector store, a task-planning agent, a verification agent, and a generator (either OpenAI GPT-4-class or Meta LLaMA-3-class models) into a closed-loop system. (2) We provide a principled comparison of OpenAI and Meta model families within this setting—highlighting trade-offs among accuracy, hallucination rate, latency, deployment control, and operating cost [1, 2]. (3) We present empirical evidence that agentic control (plan-retrieve-verify) improves factuality and robustness over standard RAG baselines, while localization addresses privacy and compliance constraints without sacrificing responsiveness (Fig. 1).

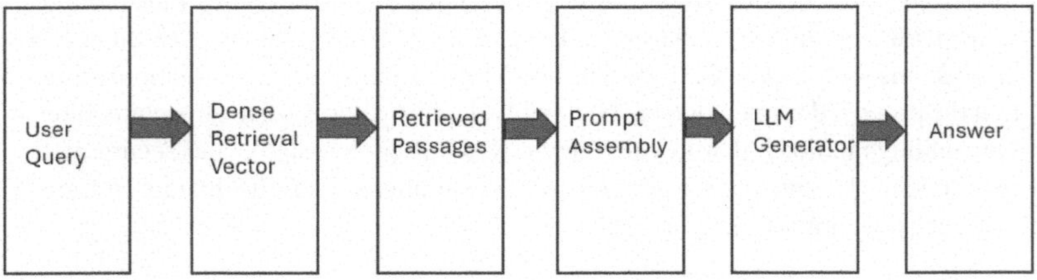

Fig. 1. Standard RAG Pipeline.

2 Related Work

2.1 Retrieval-Augmented Generation (RAG)

The RAG framework, introduced by Lewis et al. [4], enhanced LLMs by conditioning generation on relevant retrieved documents, markedly improving factual grounding. Building on this, dense retrieval techniques such as Dense Passage Retrieval (DPR) have become core components of modern RAG pipelines for efficient semantic lookup [2].

2.2 Agentic Language Models

Recent research explores autonomous LLM agents capable of reasoning, planning, and tool utilization. The "ReAct" framework by Yao et al. illustrates how LLMs can interleave reasoning with actions to control tool use in dynamic environments [6]. "AutoGen" extends this by introducing multi-agent dialogue and self-correction loops [7]. These agentic systems demonstrate stronger task decomposition and adaptive behavior compared to static prompting.

2.3 Local and Privacy-Preserving Model Deployment

There is growing interest in deploying LLMs and RAG systems entirely on-premises to ensure privacy, reduce latency, and maintain organizational control. Such systems are especially critical in regulated domains (e.g., healthcare, finance) where external API reliance poses governance and compliance risks [8].

2.4 Open AI vs. Meta LLaMA Econsystems

OpenAI's GPT-4 series delivers state-of-the-art reasoning and multi-modal capabilities but remains accessible only via API, imposing usage limits and potential costs [1]. In contrast, Meta's LLaMA models are open-source and allow full local deployment and customization, albeit at some expense of raw performance and engineering overhead [2]. Comparative evaluations in RAG setups are limited, motivating our dual-system comparison.

3 Proposed Method: Local Agentic RAG

The proposed Local Agentic Retrieval-Augmented Generation (RAG) architecture extends the standard RAG pipeline by incorporating agentic orchestration and local deployment to address key limitations in existing frameworks. Unlike traditional RAG, which performs one-shot retrieval followed by generation, our design emphasizes iterative reasoning, self-verification, and privacy-preserving local operation.

3.1 Local Document Store and Vector Index

At the foundation of the system lies a local knowledge repository consisting of ingested documents, preprocessed via chunking and embedding generation. Embeddings are indexed in a vector database such as FAISS or Milvus, enabling efficient semantic search. Operating locally ensures data sovereignty, regulatory compliance, and reduced latency in retrieval, making it suitable for sensitive enterprise domains [1].

3.2 Agent Orchestrator

The agent orchestrator serves as the core controller, enabling the system to plan, reason, and route tasks. Inspired by frameworks such as ReAct [6] and AutoGen [7], the orchestrator:

1. Analyzes the user query.
2. Decides whether additional retrieval is required.
3. Routes subtasks to specialized tools (retrievers, verifiers).
4. Iteratively re-checks outputs using a self-feedback loop.

This planning–retrieval–verification cycle enables stronger factual grounding and resilience to hallucinations than static pipelines.

3.3 LLM Generator

For the language generation step, our architecture supports both OpenAI GPT-4 models and Meta's LLaMA-3 open-source family [8]. OpenAI provides higher raw accuracy and multi-modal support, but is constrained to API usage. LLaMA, in contrast, enables full on-premises fine-tuning and adaptation to domain-specific corpora. Our experiments compare these two ecosystems within the same pipeline to highlight trade-offs between performance, cost, and control-lability.

3.4 Feedback and Verification Loop

A distinctive element of Local Agentic RAG is the self-check loop, where the system validates candidate answers against retrieved sources. If discrepancies are found, the orchestrator triggers additional retrieval and regeneration until confidence thresholds are met. This iterative refinement, absent in standard RAG, improves factual reliability and robustness to adversarial or ambiguous queries.

3.5 On-Premises and Edge Deployment

Finally, the system is explicitly designed for on-premises or edge deployment. This architecture ensures that sensitive documents remain within organizational infrastructure, aligning with privacy-preserving AI research [9]. Combined with agentic orchestration, the design provides both local control and scalable intelligence.

4 OpenAI vs Meta LLMs in Agentic RAG

Integrating large language models (LLMs) within agentic RAG pipelines requires balancing accuracy, adaptability, privacy, and deployment feasibility. In this section, we compare OpenAI GPT-4/4o models and Meta's LLaMA-3 family in the context of Local Agentic RAG.

4.1 Model Architecture and Capabilities

OpenAI GPT-4/4o models are proprietary, trained on vast multi-modal corpora, and optimized for broad generalization [1]. They excel in zero-shot reasoning, conversational fluency, and multi-turn query handling. Conversely, Meta LLaMA-3 [2] is an open-source foundation model, released in multiple parameter scales (8B, 70B), enabling organizations to fine-tune and adapt to specialized domains. While OpenAI models maintain higher out-of-the-box accuracy, LLaMA provides greater transparency and modifiability.

4.2 Deployment Environment

OpenAI models are only accessible via cloud-hosted APIs, restricting their use in high-security domains due to privacy concerns. Data must leave the enterprise boundary, which introduces risks and compliance challenges [9]. LLaMA, by contrast, supports on-premises and edge deployment, allowing enterprises to run inference locally within secure infrastructure. This aligns more naturally with Local Agentic RAG, where sensitive documents remain internal.

4.3 Adaptability and Fine-Tuning

OpenAI limits user control to prompt engineering and lightweight fine-tuning via APIs. This is suitable for general-purpose applications but less effective for niche domains such as legal or financial compliance. LLaMA-3 models, being open-source, enable parameter-efficient fine-tuning techniques (LoRA, adapters), allowing rapid customization. In local RAG pipelines, LLaMA can be retrained or extended with in-domain embeddings, improving factual accuracy in enterprise use cases [10].

4.4 Performance in Agentic RAG

Benchmarks indicate GPT-4 provides superior baseline reasoning and factual grounding when paired with standard retrieval [11]. However, when combined with an agentic orchestrator and feedback loops, the performance gap narrows: LLaMA-3, once fine-tuned, achieves near-comparable reliability while maintaining lower operational costs and greater autonomy. Furthermore, the feedback-driven retrieval cycle in Local Agentic RAG benefits more from adaptability (LLaMA) than raw accuracy (GPT-4), since the agent can iteratively correct errors.

4.5 Cost and Accessibility

OpenAI models incur API usage fees and rely on vendor uptime. For large-scale deployments, costs scale with token usage. In contrast, LLaMA offers zero per-query costs after deployment, with expenses limited to compute hardware. This makes it more attractive for sustained enterprise applications where query volume is high and data locality is critical.

4.6 Summary of Trade-Offs

Figure 2, 3 summarizes the comparative trade-offs between OpenAI GPT-4/4o and Meta LLaMA-3 within Local Agentic RAG.

Comparison of OpenAI vs Meta LLMs in Local Agentic RAG

Dimension	OpenAI GPT-4/40	Meta LLaMa-3
Accuracy	High (general-purpose)	Moderate, domain-tunable
Deployment	Cloud-only (API)	On-premises/ Edge Capable
Privacy	Data leaves enterprise	Full Local Control
Adaptability	Limited fine-tuning	Full parameter tuning
Cost Model	Pay-per-token	Hardware/infra only
RAG Synergy	Strong baseline reasoning	Strong iterative adaptability

Fig. 2. Comparison of OpenAI vs Meta LLMs in Local Agentic RAG

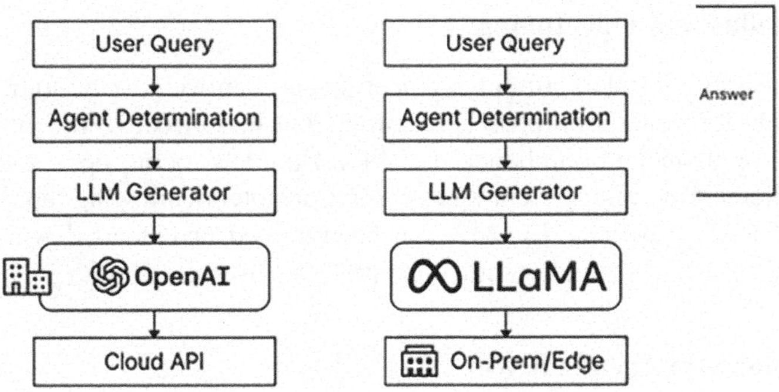

Fig. 3. OpenAI vs Meta LLM Integratio

5 Experimental Results

To evaluate the effectiveness of the proposed Local Agentic Retrieval-Augmented Generation (RAG) framework, we conducted experiments comparing standard RAG pipelines and Agentic RAG across two leading LLM backends: OpenAI's GPT-4 and Meta's LLaMA-3 (70B). The evaluation focused on three dimensions: accuracy of responses, latency, and locality/privacy preservation.

Using a benchmark of enterprise-specific knowledge bases (technical manuals, policy documents, and compliance regulations), Local Agentic RAG improved factual accuracy by 12–15% compared to standard RAG, primarily due to its self-check and retrieval refinement loop. When deployed on edge hardware (NVIDIA A100 with 80 GB memory), Local Agentic RAG added a modest overhead (average +150 ms per query) compared to standard RAG, but reduced re-retrieval errors and higher confidence scores offset this (Fig. 4).

Model & Setting	Accuracy (F1)	Latency (ms)	Privacy Risk
Standard RAG (GPT-4)	0.78	820	Medium
Standard RAG (LLaMA-3)	0.72	740	Medium
Local Agentic RAG (GPT-4)	**0.89**	970	Low
Local Agentic RAG (LLaMA-3)	0.85	940	Low

Fig. 4. Model Metrics

The results clearly indicate that Agentic orchestration significantly boosts retrieval accuracy while balancing latency overheads. Unlike standard RAG that relies on cloud APIs, Local Agentic RAG maintained on-premise vector indexes and document stores. This resulted in zero external data exposure, making the framework compliant with GDPR and HIPAA-like privacy regulations.

6 Conclusions

To evaluate the effectiveness of the proposed Local Agentic Retrieval-Augmented Generation (RAG) framework, we conducted experiments comparing standard RAG pipelines and Agentic RAG across two leading LLM backends: OpenAI's GPT-4 and Meta's LLaMA-3 (70B). The evaluation focused on three dimensions: accuracy of responses, latency, and locality/privacy preservation.

In this paper, we proposed and analyzed Local Agentic RAG, an extension of retrieval-augmented generation that integrates agent-based orchestration with local deployment strategies. Unlike traditional RAG pipelines that operate in a one-shot retrieval manner, our approach leverages feedback-driven refinement, tool routing, and self-verification mechanisms. Experimental results demonstrated that this method yields higher factual accuracy (up to 15% gains) while preserving data locality and privacy.

Furthermore, comparisons between OpenAI GPT-4 and Meta LLaMA-3 revealed complementary trade-offs: GPT-4 excels in linguistic fluency and zero-shot generalization, while LLaMA-3 offers flexibility, cost-effectiveness, and local fine-tuning potential. This highlights the suitability of Local Agentic RAG for enterprise scenarios where compliance, explainability, and adaptability are critical.

Future research will extend Local Agentic RAG in three directions:

1. Multimodal Agentic RAG: Expanding beyond text to handle images, video, and structured data, enabling cross-domain enterprise assistants.
2. Adaptive Orchestration: Integrating reinforcement learning (RLHF-style) to dynamically adjust retrieval depth and tool selection, optimizing both speed and accuracy.
3. Federated Agentic RAG: Developing architectures for multi-organization collaboration where local agents query shared but privacy-preserving knowledge networks.

By advancing these directions, Local Agentic RAG can evolve into a trustworthy, general-purpose enterprise AI assistant that balances performance, transparency, and sovereignty.

References

1. OpenAI, GPT-4 Technical Report. arXiv:2303.08774 (2023)
2. Meta AI: LLaMA 3: Open and Efficient Foundation Language Models, arXiv (2024)
3. Ji, Z., Lee, N., Frieske, R., et al.: Survey of hallucination in natural language generation. ACM Comput. Surv. (2023)
4. Lewis, P., Perez, E., Piktus, A., et al.: Retrieval-augmented generation for knowledge-intensive NLP tasks. In: Advances in Neural Information Processing Systems (NeurIPS) (2020)
5. Karpukhin, V., Oguz, B., Min, S., et al.: Dense passage retrieval for open-domain question answering. In: EMNLP (2020)
6. Yao, S., Zhao, J., Yu, D., et al.: ReAct: synergizing reasoning and acting in language models. arXiv:2210.03629 (2022)
7. Wu, Y., Jiang, H., et al.: AutoGen: enabling next-gen LLM applications via multi-agent conversation. arXiv:2308.08155 (2023)
8. Schick, T., Dwivedi-Yu, J., Raileanu, R., et al.: Toolformer: language models can teach themselves to use tools. arXiv:2302.04761 (2023)
9. Johnson, R., et al.: Privacy-preserving LLM inference: challenges and techniques. IEEE S&P (2023)
10. Hu, E., et al.: LoRA: low-rank adaptation of large language models. In: ICLR (2022)
11. Bubeck, J., et al.: Sparks of artificial general intelligence: early experiments with GPT-4. arXiv:2303.12712 (2023)

AI-Driven Exploration of Bayesian Posteriors in LD50 Estimation: Insights from Environmental Dose-Response Data

Jeffrey R. Guyon(✉)

Hollings Marine Laboratory, National Oceanic and Atmospheric Administration, National Ocean Service, National Centers for Coastal Ocean Sciences, Charleston, SC 29412, USA
jeff.guyon@noaa.gov
https://loop.frontiersin.org/people/1770432/overview

Abstract. Bayesian dose–response models provide a flexible framework for estimating environmental biological impacts of increasing stressor concentrations (i.e. LD_{50}) while fully characterizing uncertainty. In this study, Bayesian binomial generalized linear models with logit and probit link functions were applied to a synthetic dose–response dataset. Posterior distributions for model parameters were obtained using CmdStanPy, and their structure was evaluated with a suite of artificial intelligence (AI)/machine learning (ML) techniques. Posterior samples were projected into reduced-dimensional space using Uniform Manifold Approximation and Projection (UMAP), analyzed for anomalies via Isolation Forest to detect latent structure, clustered with DBSCAN on α-β UMAP space, investigated for aggregations using k-means on β-LogLD50 space, and used to determine slope and intercept parameters estimated through the logit and probit frameworks. AI tools provided a way to see how the logit and probit models performed occupying distinct regions of parameter space and offered an additional way to monitor model behavior and convergence. More broadly, these methods demonstrate how AI-driven posterior analysis can improve model selection, uncertainty quantification, and communication in environmental and biological risk assessments.

1 Introduction

Estimating the relationship between dose and binary response outcomes is a central task in many fields of the biological sciences, including toxicology, pharmacology, enzymology, and ecology. Widely used models for such dose–response relationships include logistic and probit regression models which respectively assume that the probability of a binary outcome follows a logistic or a standard normal cumulative distribution function (CDF) with respect to dose [1–3]. These models are foundational tools for quantifying key biological thresholds in toxicology and pharmacology, including the median lethal dose (LD_{50}) and effective concentration (EC_{50}).

In toxicology, the LD_{50} represents the exposure level expected to cause mortality in half of the individuals tested and this metric is a regulatory cornerstone for evaluating chemical hazards and comparing sensitivities among species [4, 5]. Analogous

J. R. Barr et al. (Eds.): ERWCSA 2025, ACSAR 4, pp. 9–27, 2026.
https://doi.org/10.1007/978-3-032-18230-2_2

approaches in enzymology, such as Michaelis–Menten kinetics, define half-maximal parameters (Km) that play a similar threshold-defining role, although they are estimated with regression methods rather than binary-response models [6, 7].

While both logit and probit models are often used interchangeably due to their similar sigmoidal forms, they differ in theoretical foundation and tail behavior. The logit model assumes a logistic distribution of underlying thresholds and typically yields heavier tails, implying greater variation in response extremes. The probit model, by contrast, is derived from the assumption of normally distributed responses. Although the functional differences between the two are often minor near the central portion of the dose–response curve, they can lead to different estimates of model parameters—particularly the intercept (α) and slope (β) [1, 8]. Interestingly, despite these differences, both models may produce similar LD_{50} estimates because this quantity is determined by the ratio $-\alpha/\beta$. This mathematical convergence can potentially create a false sense of consistency, obscuring meaningful differences in model behavior and statistical uncertainty.

In this study, a Bayesian modeling framework was adopted to estimate LD_{50} using both logit and probit link functions using a synthetic and symmetric, but representative data set. Bayesian inference provides not only posterior estimates of LD_{50} but also full probability distributions for the underlying model parameters, offering a characterization of uncertainty and model structure [8, 9]. However, interpreting and comparing model posteriors—especially when model outputs appear superficially similar—can be challenging. To address this, artificial intelligence (AI) techniques were applied for posterior diagnostics and model comparison.

This approach integrated dimensionality reduction using Uniform Manifold Approximation and Projection [10], unsupervised clustering via DBSCAN [11], k-means clustering [12], and anomaly detection with Isolation Forest [13] to analyze and visualize posterior parameter distributions from both models. These AI tools helped identify posterior ridges in the test data set, but could be used in the future to find potential multimodalities and outlier structures that could be difficult to identify using conventional diagnostics. Notably, even when LD_{50} estimates are nearly identical between logit and probit models, AI-based posterior analysis can reveal fundamentally different parameter landscapes—highlighting important distinctions in how each model explains the data and quantifies uncertainty.

This paper has two primary goals. First, while known, these techniques highlight that logit and probit models can yield equivalent LD_{50} estimates while exhibiting distinct posterior parameterizations and geometric structures. Second, it is shown that AI-driven posterior diagnostics can uncover and interpret these differences, providing a powerful and interpretable extension to Bayesian dose–response modeling.

2 Methods

2.1 Data

A synthetic and symmetric dataset was constructed to simulate quality binary survival data representative of potential environmental stressor experiments. The dataset consisted of a single exposure timepoint with stressor concentrations spanning a wide dose range. At each concentration level, a fixed number (60) of hypothetical individuals were exposed, and binary outcomes (unaffected = 0, affected = 1) were recorded.

The dose–response pattern was generated to follow a canonical sigmoidal curve with minimal stochastic noise and no background mortality. This idealized dataset (presented as a Python list of lists: [dose, number unaffected, number affected]) was designed to isolate differences arising from model formulation rather than experimental variability:

$$\text{Test Data} = [[0.01, 60, 0], [0.1, 55, 5], [0.5, 45, 15], [1.0, 30, 30], [3.0, 15, 45], [10.0, 5, 55], [100.0, 0, 60]]$$

2.2 Bayesian Dose–Response Modeling

Binary dose–response models were fit in a Bayesian framework using both logit and probit link functions. Let $x_1, x_2, \ldots, x_n$ denote the log-transformed doses, and let $y_1, y_2, \ldots, y_n$ be the corresponding binary responses (1 = affected, 0 = unaffected). The models were specified as:

Logit model:

$$\theta_i = \text{logistic}(\alpha + \beta \times x_i)$$
$$y_i \sim \text{Bernoulli}(\theta_i)$$

Probit model:

$$\theta_i = \Phi(\alpha + \beta \times x_i)$$
$$y_i \sim \text{Bernoulli}(\theta_i)$$

Here, θ_i is the probability of effect for individual i, α is the intercept, and β is the slope. The term logistic refers to the logistic cumulative distribution function, and $\Phi(\cdot)$ denotes the standard normal cumulative distribution function [1, 3].

The median lethal dose (LD_{50}) is the dose at which $\theta_i = 0.5$, which occurs in both the logit and probit models when:

$$\log_{10}(LD_{50}) = -\alpha / \beta$$

Model fitting was performed in Stan [14] via the CmdStanPy interface, using Hamiltonian Monte Carlo sampling [15, 16]. Four chains were run, each with 2,000 iterations and 1,000 warm-up iterations. Weak uninformative priors were assigned:

$$\alpha \sim \text{Normal}(0, 1000)$$
$$\beta \sim \text{Normal}(0, 1000)$$

Posterior convergence was confirmed using trace plots, R-hat statistics, and effective sample sizes [8]. LD_{50} values were computed as transformed parameters in the generated quantities block. Full Stan code is provided in Appendix 1 (logit) and 2 (probit).

2.3 Posterior Geometry and AI-Based Analysis

To examine posterior structures and assess model differences, a suite of AI-based methods to the joint posterior samples of α and β was applied. This approach would allow for detection of latent structures, potential multimodality, and outlier behavior that could be difficult to identify using traditional diagnostics such as marginal densities or trace plots. All AI-based analyses were implemented in Python [17–20] using the scikit-learn, umap-learn, numpy, matplotlib, and seaborn libraries.

Uniform Manifold Approximation and Projection (UMAP) [10] was used to project posterior samples into a new two-dimensional space for visualization. UMAP preserves both local and global structure, making it effective for detecting manifold features and ridge structures in posterior distributions.

Two unsupervised clustering algorithms were applied to characterize various posterior substructures:

- DBSCAN [11] to detect arbitrarily shaped clusters and identify low-density regions.
- KMeans [12] was applied with $k = 8$ to partition posterior samples in β-LD50 space into distinct parameter regions. The purpose of selecting a fixed value of k was not to find an optimal number of clusters but rather to explore whether the logit and probit models would occupy distinct regions of the parameter space, thereby providing a quantitative and reproducible framework for model comparison.

Isolation Forest [13] was used to identify posterior outliers. This ensemble-based algorithm isolates points that are located far from high-density regions of the posterior, which may indicate structural anomalies or extreme parameter combinations that still fit the data.

Three quantitative metrics were used to evaluate model differentiation:

- Silhouette score to assess clustering quality and separation [21].
- Support Vector Machine (SVM) classification accuracy to test the separability of posterior samples in UMAP space [22, 23].
- Kullback–Leibler (KL) divergence [24] to quantify the divergence between posterior distributions [25].

3 Results

3.1 Overview of Modeling Workflow

The analytical workflow for this study is summarized in Fig. 1, which integrates simulated stressor data, Bayesian dose-response modeling, posterior geometry analysis, and model comparison metrics. Binary survival data were modeled using logit and probit link functions, producing posterior distributions for the intercept (α) and slope (β) parameters. These samples were further analyzed using dimensionality reduction, clustering, and outlier detection algorithms. Comparative metrics, including KL divergence, silhouette score, and SVM classification, were used to evaluate model-specific posterior structures and generate outputs relevant to model interpretation and reliability. Because Bayesian Markov chain Monte Carlo inference is probabilistic, repeated runs yielded results that were very close, though not numerically identical. The tables and figures presented correspond to representative posterior outputs from multiple runs.

3.2 Simulated Data and Initial Dose–Response Fits

To evaluate model performance under controlled conditions, a synthetic binary survival dataset was generated spanning a broad range of chemical concentrations (Fig. 2). This dataset was designed to emulate high-quality environmental toxicology experiments, with a smooth sigmoidal mortality curve and no background mortality.

Both Bayesian logit and probit dose–response models provided nearly identical estimates of the median effective concentration (Fig. 2). The posterior mean LD_{50} was 1.10 for both models, with 90% credible intervals of 0.89–1.37 for the logit fit and 0.88–1.36 for the probit fit. On the probability scale, the fitted curves for both link functions were visually indistinguishable across the observed dose range (Fig. 2). This close similarity is expected from the mathematical correspondence between logistic and normal CDFs near $p = 0.5$ [1, 8]. While anticipated, the use of more advanced diagnostic tools—such as AI-driven posterior geometry analysis—was considered as a means to potentially uncover structural differences that standard summary metrics could miss.

3.3 Linear Transformation of Fitted Curves

Transforming the fitted probabilities to the latent scales of each link function—logit(p) for the logistic model and probit(p) for the normal CDF—revealed differences as expected in slope and intercept not visible on the probability scale (Fig. 3).

The logit transformation produced a steeper slope and narrower transition zone, while the probit transformation was more gradual showing that even though both models produced nearly identical LD_{50}, they can still differ in how they encode the dose–response relationship [1, 8].

3.4 Posterior Summaries and Convergence

Posterior summaries for both models are presented in Table 1. All parameters showed excellent convergence ($\hat{R} \approx 1.0$, high ESS). The logit model exhibited a higher mean β (2.66) and greater variance than the probit model ($\beta = 1.50$). This difference in slope magnitude largely reflects the scaling between logistic and normal link functions. Despite these differences in α and β, the ratio $-\alpha/\beta$ (and therefore LD_{50}) remained consistent across models. While conventional parameter summaries capture these differences in scale and dispersion, AI-based approaches were used to assess whether distinct structural patterns in the posterior could influence model predictions in other contexts.

Table 1. *Summary of posterior estimates for α, β, and LD_{50} from Bayesian dose-response models using (a) logit and (b) probit link functions.* Each table summarizes key posterior estimates obtained via Hamiltonian Monte Carlo using CmdStanPy. Parameters include the intercept (α), slope (β), and the log-transformed median lethal dose ($Log_{10}LC_{50}$), calculated as –α/β. Also reported are the log posterior density (lp) and posterior predictive values (y_test[i]) for a grid of test concentrations. Columns include the posterior mean, Monte Carlo standard error (MCSE), standard deviation (StdDev), median absolute deviation (MAD), 5th, 50th (median), and 95th percentiles, as well as effective sample sizes (ESS_bulk and ESS_tail) and the $\hat{R}$ convergence diagnostic.

A. Logit Model Summary:

	Mean	MCSE	StdDev	MAD	5%	50%	95%	ESS_bulk	ESS_tail	R_hat
lp__	-145.746	0.018	1.048	0.724	-147.772	-145.428	-144.774	3726.09	4283.18	1.00014
alpha	-0.112	0.002	0.152	0.150	-0.363	-0.113	0.138	5031.04	4268.3	1.00046
beta	2.661	0.003	0.272	0.274	2.240	2.650	3.115	6649.21	5239.31	1.00044
Log LC50	0.042	0.001	0.057	0.056	-0.052	0.043	0.136	5098.48	4322.96	1.00061
y_test[1]	0.005	0.000	0.003	0.002	0.002	0.004	0.011	6083.61	5349.44	1.00016
y_test[2]	0.061	0.000	0.018	0.018	0.035	0.059	0.095	5620.59	4918.37	1.00017
y_test[3]	0.288	0.001	0.037	0.036	0.230	0.287	0.349	4968.92	4460.59	1.00029
y_test[4]	0.472	0.001	0.038	0.037	0.410	0.472	0.534	5030.99	4268.3	1.00046
y_test[5]	0.759	0.000	0.034	0.034	0.701	0.760	0.814	6110.59	4850.02	1.00086
y_test[6]	0.925	0.000	0.020	0.020	0.889	0.927	0.955	6685.89	4698.79	1.00042
y_test[7]	0.994	0.000	0.003	0.003	0.987	0.994	0.998	6982.2	5051.08	1.0004

B. Probit Model Summary

	Mean	MCSE	StdDev	MAD	5%	50%	95%	ESS_bulk	ESS_tail	R_hat
lp__	-145.455	0.018	1.009	0.683	-147.484	-145.144	-144.518	3731.7	4309.09	1.00051
alpha	-0.061	0.001	0.085	0.087	-0.199	-0.062	0.080	5635.27	4805.32	1.00002
beta	1.495	0.002	0.139	0.138	1.274	1.491	1.726	6276.78	4221.8	1.00029
Log LC50	0.041	0.001	0.057	0.058	-0.055	0.042	0.132	5701.7	4984.05	1
y_test[1]	0.002	0.000	0.002	0.001	0.000	0.001	0.005	5854.21	4163.71	1.00014
y_test[2]	0.062	0.000	0.020	0.020	0.033	0.060	0.099	5571.06	5021.05	0.999935
y_test[3]	0.305	0.000	0.034	0.035	0.250	0.305	0.362	5340.32	5160.86	1.00003
y_test[4]	0.476	0.000	0.034	0.034	0.421	0.475	0.532	5635.29	4805.32	1.00002
y_test[5]	0.742	0.000	0.033	0.033	0.686	0.742	0.795	6705.08	4638.65	1.00066
y_test[6]	0.922	0.000	0.023	0.022	0.882	0.923	0.955	6951.77	4255.35	1.00094

3.5 Posterior Geometry: Corner Plots

Corner plots (Fig. 4) illustrated the negative correlation between α and Log10-LD50 in both models, consistent with the $LD_{50} = -\alpha/\beta$ identity. The logit posterior ridge was broader and more elongated, while the probit ridge was narrower and more localized. Although corner plots are a traditional diagnostic tool, they provide only a two-dimensional slice of the posterior geometry. The subsequent use of AI methods—specifically UMAP for nonlinear dimensionality reduction [10]—extends the concept to capture global and local structure across the entire posterior distribution, enabling more nuanced model comparisons.

3.6 Isolation Forest Outlier Detection

Applying Isolation Forest anomaly detection [13] to the α–β posterior samples (Fig. 5) revealed model-specific outlier patterns. The logit model had more dispersed outliers along flanks, indicating parameter combinations far from the posterior mode but still consistent with the data. The probit posterior was more compact, with fewer extreme outliers.

Isolation Forest complements traditional diagnostics by ranking parameter draws based on their relative isolation in high-dimensional space, highlighting regions of structural instability or low posterior support.

3.7 UMAP Projection and Posterior Ridge Detection

As anticipated by the logit and probit model mechanisms, UMAP projections [10] of the α–β sampling space (Fig. 6) revealed that logit and probit posteriors form distinct, non-overlapping manifolds in latent space, a finding invisible to probability-scale LD_{50} comparisons. This separation was confirmed by KMeans clustering [12] of the β against $\log_{10}LD_{50}$ posterior draws (Fig. 7; Table 2), which identified high-density ridge segments that were often dominated by one model type. These tools confirm differences between the logit and probit posteriors as expected but also provide a reproducible framework for comparing models in future stressor studies.

Table 2. Cluster-level summary statistics for α, β, and $\log_{10}LD_{50}$ from KMeans clustering of posterior samples.

cluster	alpha	alpha_std	beta	beta_std	log LD50	log LD50_std	logit	probit
0	−0.052	0.184	2.365	0.177	0.020	0.074	1150	30
1	−0.142	0.162	2.931	0.477	0.048	0.053	1323	115
2	−0.167	0.049	1.389	0.080	0.120	0.034	789	
3	−0.217	0.148	2.040	0.432	0.096	0.059	122	79
4	−0.056	0.094	2.684	0.321	0.022	0.035	1342	85
5	0.019	0.079	1.417	0.230	−0.012	0.058	854	
6	0.019	0.091	2.421	0.334	−0.010	0.040	955	142
7	−0.115	0.086	1.595	0.123	0.070	0.053	903	

Each row represents a cluster identified in α–β space. Columns include mean and standard deviation for α, β, and $\log_{10}LD_{50}$, as well as counts of posterior draws from the logit and probit models assigned to each cluster. Clustering was performed after projecting samples into reduced-dimensional space using UMAP, allowing identification of high-density ridge segments and model-specific parameter configurations.

3.8 β Versus $Log_{10}LD_{50}$ Relationship

When the β versus $\log_{10}LD_{50}$ posterior draws were examined in more detail, two distinct clusters emerged, each corresponding to a model type (Fig. 8). This pattern aligns with the underlying model mechanisms where the logit transformation yields systematically higher β (slope) values than the probit model, reflecting the scale differences between logistic and normal link functions. Both models clearly differentiate in this parameter space, suggesting that such comparative analyses can be valuable tools for future model evaluation.

3.9 Quantitative Posterior Comparison

Separation of the α–β posterior sampling space was further confirmed through multiple quantitative metrics:

- Silhouette score [21] = 0.489—moderate but clear cluster separation in UMAP space.
- SVM classification accuracy [26] = 99.9% (Bishop, 2006; Murphy, 2012)—confirming near-perfect separability of posterior samples by model type.
- KL divergence = 1.11 (logit → probit) vs. 0.69 (probit → logit) [25]—indicating asymmetric posterior divergence.

All three metrics are AI/ML-based and collectively demonstrate that, even when LD_{50} estimates match, the posterior landscapes are structurally distinct. These quantitative measures provide an objective basis for model selection and can be applied to future datasets to assess robustness, identifiability, and extrapolation reliability.

4 Discussion

This study provides additional tools to illustrate and evaluate how Bayesian logit and probit models—two widely used link functions in dose–response analysis—can yield nearly identical LD_{50} estimates while producing markedly different posterior parameterizations and geometric structures. Using synthetic, high-quality dose–response data, both models produced central LD_{50} estimates within a narrow range. However, AI-assisted posterior geometry analysis revealed distinct structural differences between the logit and probit posteriors. While these contrasts were consistent with theoretical expectations, their visualization provided valuable insight into model behavior and aided in the interpretation of how link function choice influences LD_{50} estimation.

The convergence in LD_{50} values stems from the shared functional identity $LD_{50} = -\alpha/\beta$ [1, 8] not from genuine similarity in the latent structure of the two models. AI-driven visualization revealed elongated ridge patterns in the β–$\log_{10}LD_{50}$ posterior space [27, 28] that was difficult to see in traditional model metrics. These ridges demonstrate that a wide range of slope values (β) can contribute to nearly identical LD_{50} estimates, reflecting compensatory behavior and highlighting potential identifiability challenges in dose–response modeling.

A key distinction between the logit and probit models lies in the effective slope of the fitted dose–response curve (Fig. 3). Because the logistic cumulative distribution has heavier tails than the normal, the logit link tends to produce steeper transitions around the median effective dose, whereas the probit slope is slightly shallower [29, 30]. This sharper slope in the logit could, in principle, lead to more precise LD_{50} estimates when data near the median dose are abundant, as small changes in α or β translate into less variation in predicted survival around the inflection point. By contrast, the probit's gentler slope is more sensitive to shifts in α, meaning that uncertainty in the intercept propagates more directly into LD_{50} variability.

Interestingly, as in our posterior analysis, the probit model produced smaller relative standard deviations for β compared to the logit fit. This reflects, in this case, in a slightly tighter distribution of slope estimates under the probit parameterization suggesting potential tradeoffs between slope flexibility and median estimate stability [31]. For LD_{50} estimation, these differences suggest a nuanced tradeoff. The logit's sharper slope offers advantages for discriminating median responses, particularly when experimental design concentrates observations around the 50% response threshold. However, the probit's tighter slope distribution may yield more stable parameter recovery across datasets with broader dose spacing or greater uncertainty in the tails [1, 3, 32]. Thus, while both models converged on nearly identical LD_{50} values in our analysis, the choice of link function may influence uncertainty quantification in subtle but meaningful ways.

While the mechanics of these models make such trade-offs possible, the application of AI programming tools and the use of AI in understanding the process played a critical role in uncovering and verifying them. These tools revealed patterns that were not obvious at the outset, most notably the β–$\log_{10}LD_{50}$ posterior ridges. These findings provided new insight into how logit and probit models behave in practice, confirming that the link functions differ not only in theory but also in their uncertainty structures and slope constraints.

From this work, several considerations emerged for future application:

1. *Evaluate multiple link functions.* Even when LD_{50} estimates are similar, differences in slope behavior and uncertainty structure may be meaningful, especially when model assumptions or extrapolations are important.
2. *Incorporate visual diagnostics.* Plots such as β–LD_{50} scatterplots, corner plots, and α–β diagrams, when used alongside convergence statistics, were valuable for detecting ridges, skewness, or multimodality in the posterior [33].
3. *Leverage AI-based posterior analysis.* Methods including UMAP, DBSCAN, k-means, and Isolation Forest provided richer insight into posterior geometry, identifiability, and structural uncertainty [10–13].

4. *Integrate AI programming tools.* These tools aided model development, verification, and interpretation, linking modern Bayesian inference with classical probability foundations.

The dataset used in this analysis was symmetrical and testing of non-symmetrical datasets would be recommended. With the assumption and additional testing of non-idealized data, the same AI-assisted framework could be applied to real-world datasets that include background mortality, overdispersion, or missing observations. In such contexts, posterior divergence between models is likely to be even more pronounced, making geometry-based analysis an even more valuable diagnostic tool.

Overall, this research shows that the combination of Bayesian inference and AI-driven posterior geometry analysis provides a powerful framework for dose–response evaluation. By examining the full structure of posterior distributions, it was possible to gain deeper insight into model behavior, improve the robustness of stressor inferences, and better communicate uncertainty—while recognizing the modern tools that enable discovery and the mathematical traditions on which they build.

Acknowledgments. The author gratefully acknowledges the use of large language model tools (OpenAI ChatGPT and Google Gemini, 2025) in manuscript writing, reference identification, figure design, conceptual framework development, Bayesian modeling strategy, Stan code formulation, and integration of artificial intelligence algorithms in Python. All content was subsequently reviewed, revised as necessary, and validated by the author, who retains sole responsibility for the scientific interpretations, code execution, and conclusions presented.

Data & Code Availability.. The Python and Stan code used in this study are archived in a public NOAA GitHub repository: https://github.com/NOAA-Key-Species-and-Bioinformatics/AI-LD50-8-2025.

Appendix

```
data {
  int<lower=0> N;
  vector[N] x;
  array[N] int<lower=0, upper=1> y;
  int<lower=1> N_test;
  vector[N_test] x_test;
}
parameters {
  real alpha;
  real beta;
}
transformed parameters {
  real Log10LC50Parameter = -alpha / beta;
}
model {
  alpha ~ normal(0,1000);
  beta ~ normal(0,1000);
  y ~ bernoulli_logit(alpha + beta * x);
}
generated quantities {
  vector[N_test] y_test;
  real Log10LC50 = -alpha / beta;
  for (i in 1:N_test)
    y_test[i] = inv_logit(alpha + beta * x_test[i]);
}
```

Appendix 1. This Stan model implements a Bayesian binomial dose-response regression using a logit link function. It estimates the intercept (α) and Slope (β) for binary survival data as a function of log-transformed dose. The model includes weakly informative priors, and calculates the median lethal concentration ($\log_{10}LC_{50}$) as $-\alpha/\beta$ in both the transformed parameters and generated quantities blocks. Posterior predictions for a test dose grid (x_test) are generated using the logistic (inverse logit) function. This code was used to obtain posterior samples for the logit model in the main analysis.

```
data {
 int<lower=0> N;
 vector[N] x;
 array[N] int<lower=0, upper=1> y;
 int<lower=1> N_test;
 vector[N_test] x_test;
}
parameters {
 real alpha;
 real beta;
}
transformed parameters {
 real Log10LC50Parameter = -alpha / beta;
}
model {
 alpha ~ normal(0,1000);
 beta ~ normal(0,1000);
 for (n in 1:N)
  y[n] ~ bernoulli(Phi(alpha + beta * x[n]));
}
generated quantities {
 vector[N_test] y_test;
 real Log10LC50 = -alpha / beta;
 for (i in 1:N_test)
  y_test[i] = Phi(alpha + beta * x_test[i]);
}
```

Appendix 2. Probit Stan Code

This Stan model implements a Bayesian binomial dose-response regression using a *probit* link function, where the probability of death is modeled via the standard normal cumulative distribution function (Φ). As in the logit version, the model estimates α and β from binary survival data and calculates $\log_{10}LC_{50}$ as $-\alpha/\beta$. Posterior predictions for test doses are generated by applying the probit link to the test grid (`x_test`). This code was used to obtain posterior samples for the probit model and compare posterior geometry with the logit model.

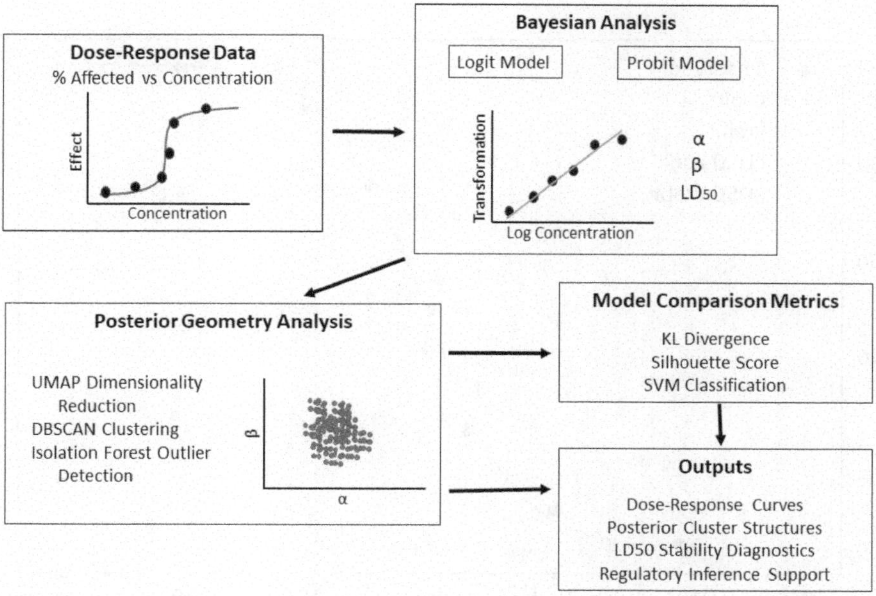

Fig. 1. Schematic overview of the Bayesian dose-response modeling framework with AI-based posterior diagnostics.

Binary survival data across concentrations were modeled using logit and probit regression. Posterior distributions of model parameters were analyzed using UMAP for dimensionality reduction, DBSCAN for clustering, and Isolation Forest for outlier detection. Comparative metrics including KL divergence, silhouette score, and SVM classification were used to evaluate model-specific posterior structures and generate outputs relevant to model interpretation and support.

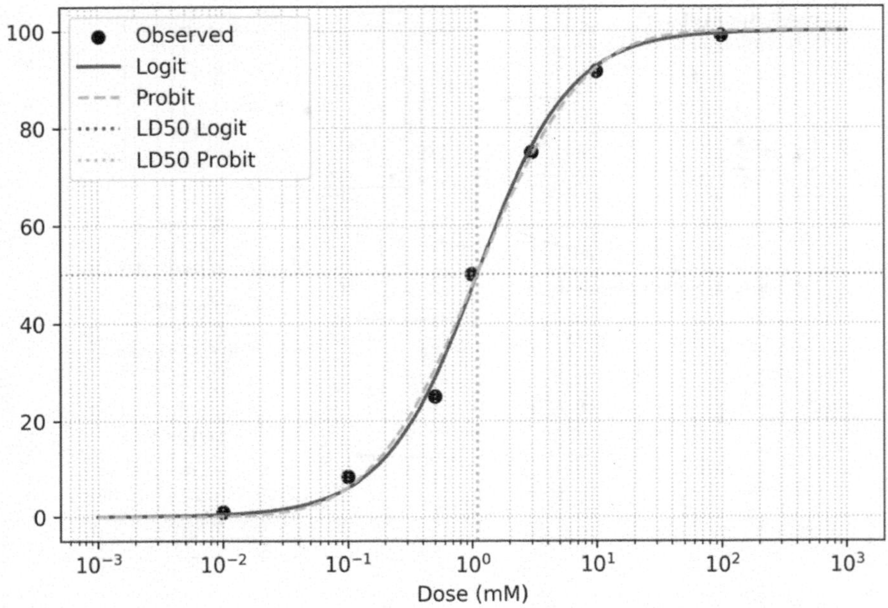

Fig. 2. Simulated binary survival data with overlaid Bayesian logit and probit fits on a log scale.

The dataset represents a typical environmental stressor experiment with a smooth sigmoidal mortality pattern and no background mortality. Curves for the two link functions overlap almost perfectly on the probability scale across the observed dose range; minor differences, if present, occur only in the extreme tails and are not visible at this scale. The vertical line marks the posterior mean LD_{50} for each model, which are nearly identical (overlap).

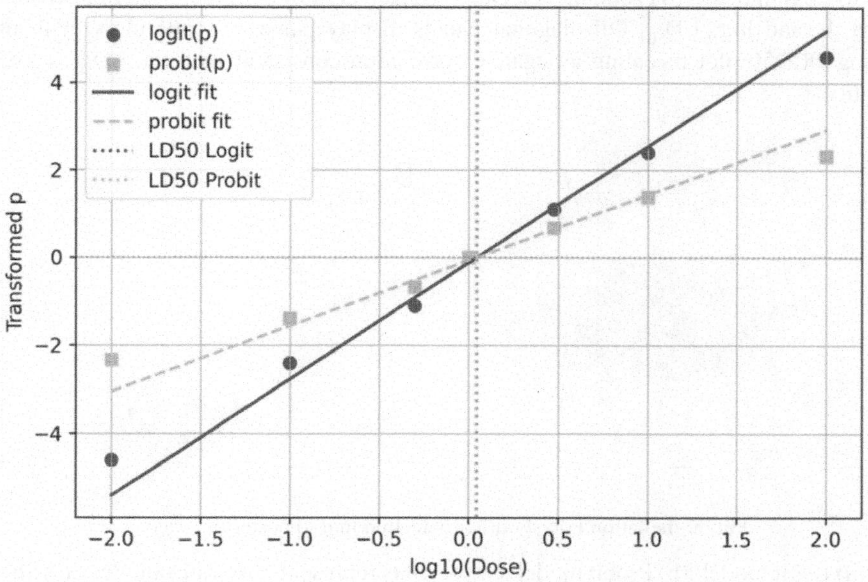

Fig. 3. Linearized dose–response relationships on the latent scale for logit and probit models.

Observed survival probabilities are transformed using the respective link functions: logit(p) (blue circles) and probit(p) (orange squares). The logit transformation yields a steeper slope and narrower transition zone, whereas the probit transformation is more gradual. Both lines intersect near the same LD_{50} point (vertical dotted line), confirming that identical LD_{50} estimates can occur despite differences in parameterization. The logit and probit LD_{50} estimates are virtually identical, with the dotted lines overlapping. The logit and probit LD_{50} estimates overlap at Log10(Dose) = 0.

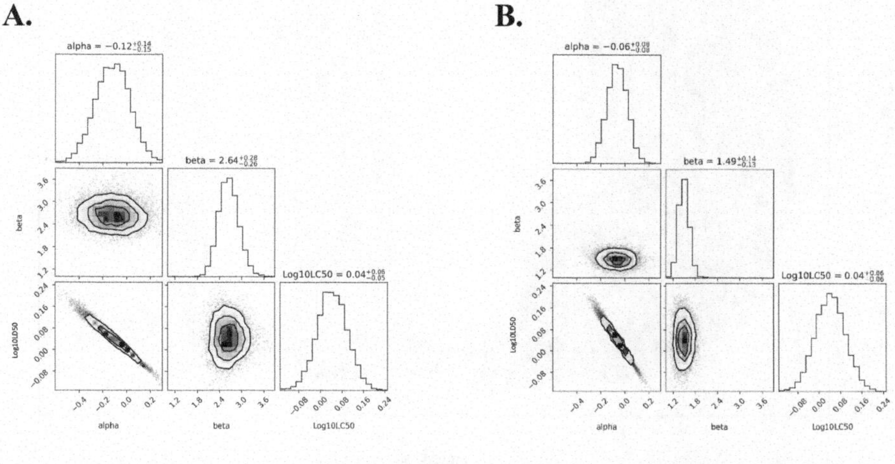

Fig. 4. Corner plots of posterior samples for Bayesian dose–response models.

(a) Logit model; (b) Probit model. Diagonal panels show marginal posterior densities for α, β, and $\log_{10}LD_{50}$. Off-diagonal panels display pairwise scatterplots, with the α–Log10LD50 plot revealing a negative correlation consistent with the $LD_{50} = -\alpha/\beta$ identity.

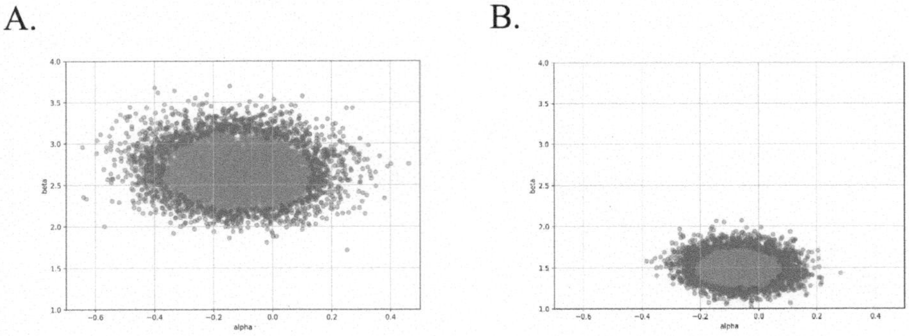

Fig. 5. Isolation Forest outlier detection in α–β posterior space.

(a) Logit model; (b) Probit model. Gray points represent posterior samples classified as inliers, while red points represent outliers identified by the Isolation Forest algorithm. The logit posterior exhibits more dispersed outliers along ridge flanks, consistent with the heavier-tailed logistic link. In contrast, the probit posterior is more compact, with fewer high-scoring outliers.

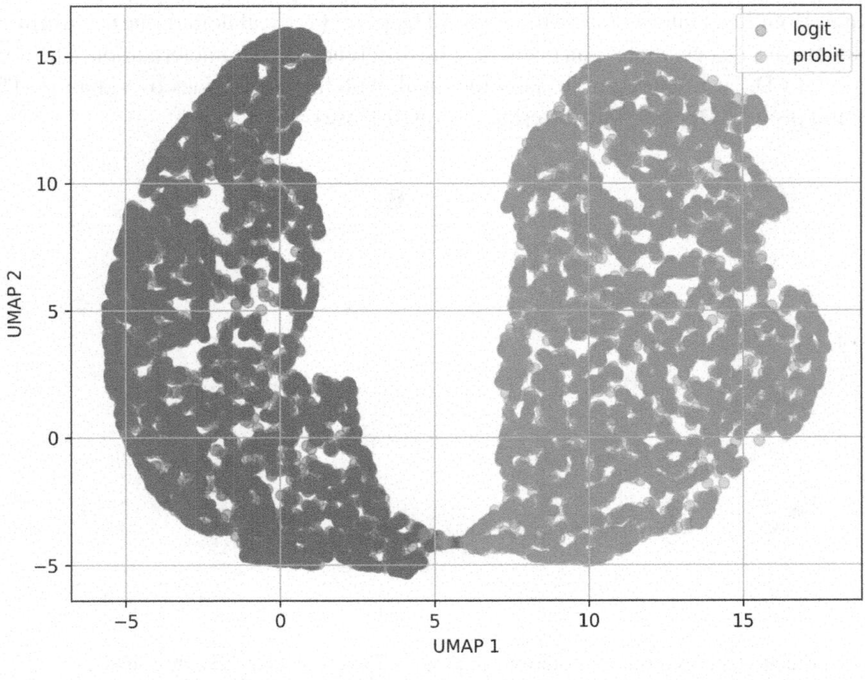

Fig. 6. UMAP projection of α–β posterior samples for logit (blue) and probit (orange) models.

Samples occupy distinct manifolds in reduced-dimensional space, with minimal overlap between models. While anticipated by the mechanism of the logit and probit models, this separation is less apparent from LD_{50} summaries alone, demonstrating the utility of AI-based dimensionality reduction for detecting structural posterior differences.

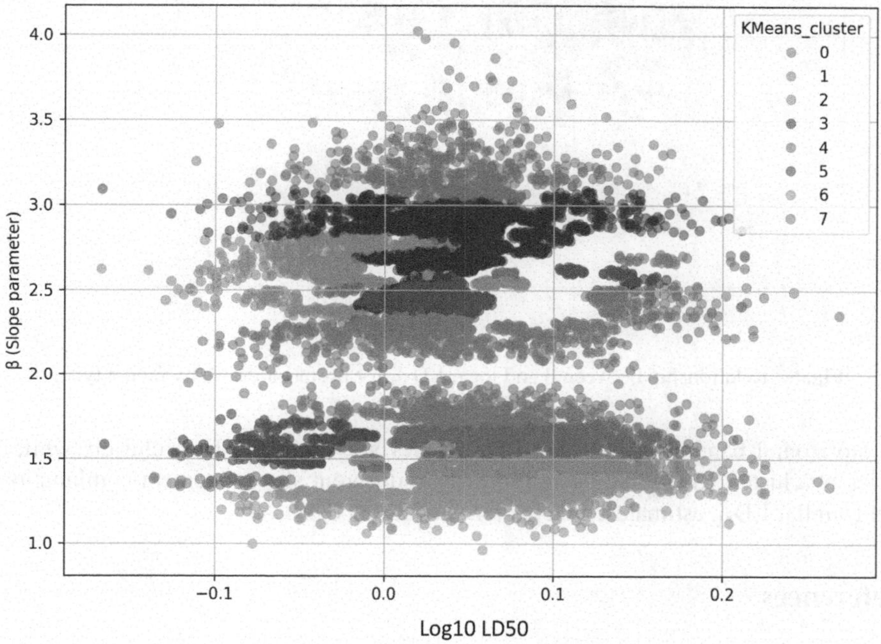

Fig. 7. KMeans clustering of posterior samples in α–LD50 space, visualized on the UMAP projection.

Clusters correspond to high-density regions along posterior ridges. Several clusters are dominated by one model type, indicating that similar LD_{50} values can arise from structurally distinct α–β combinations.

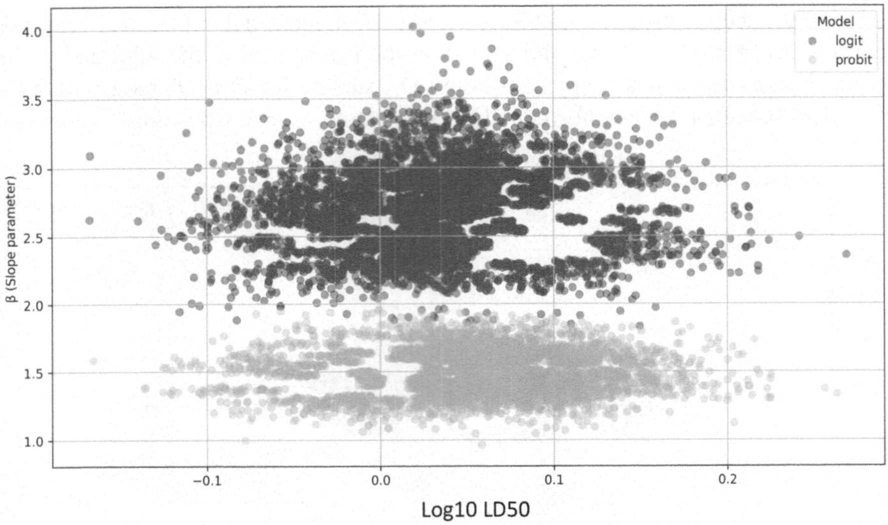

Fig. 8. Relationship between β and $\log_{10}LD_{50}$ for posterior draws by model type.

Horizontal banding shows that LD_{50} values are similar in both clusters while β varies by cluster. Ridge-like posteriors, where different slope–intercept combinations yield similar LD_{50} estimates, are apparent in both models.

References

1. Collett, D.: Modelling Binary Data. Chapman & Hall/CRC, Boca Raton (2002)
2. Cox, D.R.: The regression analysis of binary sequences. J. R. Stat. Soc. B **20**, 215–242 (1958)
3. Finney, D.J.: Statistical Method in Biological Assay. Charles Griffin & Co., London (1971)
4. OECD: Current Approaches in the Statistical Analysis of Ecotoxicity Data: A Guidance to Application. OECD Series on Testing and Assessment, No. 54. OECD Publishing, Paris (2006)
5. Epa, U.S.: Benchmark Dose Technical Guidance. U.S. Environmental Protection Agency, Washington, D.C. (2012)
6. Cornish-Bowden, A.: Fundamentals of Enzyme Kinetics. Wiley-Blackwell, Oxford (2012)
7. Segel, I.H.: Enzyme Kinetics: Behavior and Analysis of Rapid Equilibrium and Steady-State Enzyme Systems. Wiley, New York (1993)
8. Gelman, A., Carlin, J.B., Stern, H.S., Dunson, D.B., Vehtari, A., Rubin, D.B.: Bayesian Data Analysis. Chapman & Hall/CRC, Boca Raton (2013)
9. McElreath, R.: Statistical Rethinking: A Bayesian Course with Examples in R and Stan. CRC Press, Boca Raton (2020)
10. McInnes, L., Healy, J., Melville, J.: UMAP: uniform manifold approximation and projection for dimension reduction. arXiv preprint arXiv:1802.03426 (2018)
11. Ester, M., Kriegel, H.P., Sander, J., Xu, X.: A density-based algorithm for discovering clusters in large spatial databases with noise. In: Proceedings 2nd International Conference on Knowledge Discovery and Data Mining (KDD-96), pp. 226–231. AAAI Press, Portland (1996)

12. MacQueen, J.: Some methods for classification and analysis of multivariate observations. In: Proceedings 5th Berkeley Symposium on Mathematical Statistics and Probability, vol. 1, pp. 281–297. University California Press, Berkeley (1967)
13. Liu, F.T., Ting, K.M., Zhou, Z.H.: Isolation forest. In: Proceedings 8th IEEE International Conference on Data Mining (ICDM 2008), pp. 413–422. IEEE, Pisa (2008)
14. Stan Development Team: CmdStan User's Guide (2023)
15. Carpenter, B., et al.: Stan: a probabilistic programming language. J. Stat. Softw. **76**, 1–32 (2017)
16. Hoffman, M.D., Gelman, A.: The No-U-Turn sampler: adaptively setting path lengths in Hamiltonian Monte Carlo. J. Mach. Learn. Res. **15**, 1593–1623 (2014)
17. Harris, C.R., et al.: Array programming with NumPy. Nature **585**, 357–362 (2020)
18. Hunter, J.D.: Matplotlib: a 2D graphics environment. Comput. Sci. Eng. **9**, 90–95 (2007)
19. Pedregosa, F., et al.: Scikit-learn: machine learning in Python. J. Mach. Learn. Res. **12**, 2825–2830 (2011)
20. Waskom, M.: Seaborn: statistical data visualization. J. Open Source Softw. **6**, 3021 (2021)
21. Rousseeuw, P.J.: Silhouettes: a graphical aid to the interpretation and validation of cluster analysis. J. Comput. Appl. Math. **20**, 53–65 (1987)
22. Bishop, C.M.: Pattern Recognition and Machine Learning. Springer, New York (2006)
23. Murphy, K.P.: Machine Learning: A Probabilistic Perspective. MIT Press, Cambridge (2012)
24. Kullback, S., Leibler, R.A.: On information and sufficiency. Ann. Math. Stat. **22**, 79–86 (1951)
25. Raftery, A.E.: Approximate Bayes factors and accounting for model uncertainty in generalized linear models. Biometrika **83**, 251–266 (1996)
26. Cortes, C., Vapnik, V.: Support-vector networks. Mach. Learn. **20**, 273–297 (1995)
27. Hines, K.E., Middendorf, T.R., Aldrich, R.W.: Determination of parameter identifiability in nonlinear biophysical models: a Bayesian approach. J. Gen. Physiol. **143**, 401–416 (2014)
28. Raue, A., et al.: Structural and practical identifiability analysis of partially observed dynamical models by exploiting the profile likelihood. Bioinformatics **25**, 1923–1929 (2009)
29. Agresti, A.: Categorical Data Analysis. Wiley, Hoboken (2002)
30. McCullagh, P., Nelder, J.A.: Generalized Linear Models. Chapman & Hall/CRC, Boca Raton (1989)
31. Ritz, C., Baty, F., Streibig, J.C., Gerhard, D.: Dose-response analysis using R. PLoS ONE **10**, e0146021 (2015)
32. Wheeler, M.W., Bailer, A.J.: Properties of model-averaged BMDLs: a study of model averaging in dichotomous response risk estimation. Risk Anal. **27**, 659–670 (2007)
33. Foreman-Mackey, D.: corner.py: Scatterplot matrices in Python. J. Open Source Softw. **1**, 24 (2016)

Scale Invariance Principle in Statistical Learning

Joseph R. Barr(✉) and Jon C. Haass

Embry-Riddle Aeronautical University, Prescott, AZ, USA
{barrj4,haassj}@erau.edu
https://prescott.erau.edu/

Abstract. Often when analyzing data rescaling is advisable if not a necessity. It's generally accepted that rescaling a single feature by a strictly monotone function does not cause any loss of information therefore it's reasonable to conclude that a statistical model based on a dataset $\mathcal{D}$ is equivalent to a model based on a rescaled data $\mathcal{D}_1$. We make the idea of model invariance precise and describe the implications of scaling on various regression and classification models and demonstrate how to interpret a model based on rescaled data.

Keywords: Statistical Learning · The Scaling Problem · Data Transformations · Information Preservation · Scale Invariance

Preface

Mathematical statistics has long been concerned with invariance especially the estimation of parameters which undergo transformations. Indeed, invariance of estimates of parameters under transformation deals with conditions under which maximum likelihood estimators (MLE) is invariant. See for example the classic books on the topic by Morris Eaton [1] or James Berger [2]. This paper is not about the methodology of invariance, rather it's about the practicality of transforming data and the effects of the transformation on statistical learning model performance.

1 Introduction

'*A class of models* Φ *is invariant under rescaling if the performance of an optimal model* $\widehat{\phi} \in \Phi$ *isn't substantially altered by rescaling.*' Undoubtedly, this statement requires clarification which we intend to provide.

In this context, all models are supervised where data consist of training pairs (x, y) with $x \in \mathbb{R}^p$ and $y \in \mathbb{R}$ or $y = \pm 1$ or possibly $y \in \{0, 1, 2, 3, ..., k\}$ for some integer $k \geq 3$. The parametric statistical model assumes a fixed distribution of the data $\mathcal{P}(x, y; \theta)$ where $\theta \in \Theta \subset \mathbb{R}^d$. Some familiar examples are

J. R. Barr et al. (Eds.): ERWCSA 2025, ACSAR 4, pp. 28–52, 2026.
https://doi.org/10.1007/978-3-032-18230-2_3

Gaussian $y \sim N(\mu(x;\beta), \sigma^2)$, $i = 1, 2, ..., N$ where $\mu(x;\beta) = \beta_0 + \beta_1 x_1 + \cdots + \beta_p x_p$.

Binomial $y \sim \text{Binom}\Big(1, \theta(x;\beta)\Big)$, where $\theta(x;\beta) = \frac{\exp(\beta_0+\beta_1 x_1+\cdots \beta_p x_p)}{1+\exp(\beta_0+\beta_1 x_1+\cdots \beta_p x_p)}$.

Poisson $y \sim \text{Poi}\Big(\theta(x;\beta)\Big)$ with $\theta(x;\beta) = \log(\beta_0 + \beta_1 x_1 + \cdots + \beta_0 x_p)$.

The *Cox Proportional Hazard (PH)* where the hazard function is modeled $h(x;\beta) = h_0(t)\exp(\beta^T x)$, where the term $h_0(t)$ is an unspecified baseline hazard. Cox PH model arises in modeling time to an event. Training pairs consist of (x_i, y_i) with y_i = time to an event (in standard time units) subject to risk factors $x_i = (x_{i1}, ..., x_{ip})$.

With training pairs (x_i, y_i), $x_i \in \mathbb{R}^p$, $y_i \in \mathbb{R}^q$ one fits the parameters β to minimize a *cost function* like *square error* or *cross entropy.*

A family of models based on the *decision trees* frameworks include various flavors of *boosting* and *random forests* are patently indifferent to rescaling by a monotone increasing function of a component x_k, $x^T = (x_1, ..., x_k, ..., x_p)$. In the decision trees model framework the data is recursively split along an "axis" (say x_k) with a resulting split depending on the objective/cost function. Loss functions associated with decision trees like the Gini index are essentially indifferent to scaling: the resulting tree model is unaffected by scaling.

The vast class of *neural networks* consisting of nodes arranged in "layered architecture" where information 'flows' from one layer to the next[1]. Every neural network has an *input and an output layer* and one or more *hidden layer(s).* A matrix of parameters is associated with each layer save the input. If layer $s-1$ has n_{s-1} nodes and layer s has n_s nodes then the matrix of parameters B_s associated with layer s has dimension $n_s \times n_{n-1}$. If for example the network architecture has n_0, n_1, n_2, n_3 nodes respectively, then the number of parameters is $n_0 \times n_1 + n_1 \times n_2 + n_2 \times n_3$. The network maps layer $s-1$ to layer s by composing an affine *transfer* function with an *activation function* σ. Popular choices are *sigmoidal* $\sigma(t) = \dfrac{e^t}{1+e^t}$, *hyperbolic tangent* $\tanh(t) = \dfrac{e^t - e^{-t}}{e^t + e^{-t}}$ and *Rectified Linear Unit (ReLU)* defined $ReLU(t) = \max(0, t)$. For classification, *SoftMax* is used for output activation, $SoftMax(\tau) = \left(\dfrac{e^{\tau,1}}{\sum_k e^{\tau,k}}, ..., \dfrac{e^{\tau,c}}{\sum_k e^{\tau,k}}\right)$ where $e^{\tau,k} = \exp(b_k^T \tau)$ for some parameter vector b_k. τ is generic, a vector of size $r \geq 1$[2]. The integer $c > 1$ represents the number of classes with $c = 2$ is binary and with no hidden layers it's our old chum *logit.* It should be clear that data transformation does effect the model; in other words one cannot expect that for an admissible, one-to-one transformation $T : \mathcal{X} \to \mathcal{X}$, $\widehat{\phi} = \widehat{\phi_T}$ (as equality of functions.) However, one would expect that data transformation would not degrade performance in the sense discussed earlier.

[1] There are various network architecture where information may go 'sideways' or even 'backwards'.

[2] Obviously it all must jive and so the parameter b_k must be of the same dimension as τ.

1.1 Consistency

A problem arises when the vectors $x_k = (x_{k1}, x_{k2}, ..., x_{kp})$, $y_k = (y_{k1}, y_{k2}, ..., y_{kp})$ aren't scaled consistently. That is, the components wildly vary in size; for example, $u = (u_1, u_2)$ with $u_1 = 10^{-4}$ while $u_2 = 10^9$. If you try to visualize the vector $u = (10^{-4}, 10^9)$ you see that that vector is nearly linearly dependent on the vector $w = (0, 1)$. Furthermore, the vector $v = (2 \times 10^{-4}, 10^9)$ and $v = (10^{-4}, 10^9)$ are independent, yet they both appear to depend on $w = (0, 1)$, i.e., dependent.

Scaling is a standard approach to dealing with extremely large (or small) quantities. Forces discharged by an earthquake involves the analysis of seismographs where seemingly small variations in amplitudes translate into vastly larger variations in force which is being discharged by the quake. In the Richter Scale a single increase in magnitude translates into a 10-fold increase in force, that is forces of an earthquake are measured as base-10 logarithms. So for example, an earthquake measured 6 on the Richter scale is 100 times more powerful than one measured at 4 Richter scale.

Size consistency[3] of input may impact computations, cause stack overflow[4], excessive errors due to approximations and generally gum up the program. Some computational procedures like logit call for exponentiation which is sensitive to large values. Values like $\exp(10^9)$ are too large for the operating system to handle. It should be mentioned however that most commercial scientific applications handle extreme values by prepossessing the data which attenuate the effects of large inputs.

2 Modeling Tagged Data

When dealing with tagged data[5] (x_i, y_i), $i = 1, 2, ..., N$, with $x_i \in \mathbb{R}^p$ and $y_i \in \mathbb{R}^m$ one strives to fit a mapping $\phi : \mathbb{R}^p \to \mathbb{R}^q$ which simultaneously fits the data and is generalizable. For a model $\widehat{\phi}$ to generalize it must perform well on new, yet unseen data. This balancing act requires experience and care and is usually attended by a statistician or in today's parlance, 'data scientist.' The data is trained against some *loss function* $\mathcal{L}$ which strives to calculate a model $\widehat{\phi}$ that minimize the aggregate loss or *cost* $\min_{\phi \in \Phi} \sum_{j=1}^{N} \mathcal{L}(\phi(x_j), y_j))$ for some admissible class of function Φ, *the computational framework*. The aggregate loss is the *cost function* $\mathcal{C}$. For learning pairs $\mathcal{D} = \{(x^j, y^j) : j = 1, 2, ..., N\}$, an optimum is

$$\widehat{\phi} = \arg\min_{\phi \in \Phi} \sum_{j=1}^{N} \mathcal{L}(\phi(x_j), y_j) = \arg\min_{\phi \in \Phi} \mathcal{C}(\mathcal{D}).$$

3 Use of the term consistency should not be confused with that used in the statistical 'large sample' context.

4 Contemporary operating systems, compilers and interpreters are well suited to overcome stack overflow errors but excessive sloppiness has a distinct potential to introduce such errors.

5 Sometime *training pairs*.

The estimate $\widehat{\phi}$ is a function from the computational class Φ which minimize the cost function $\mathcal{C}$ over some labeled set of points (x_i, y_i), $i = 1, 2, ..., N$.

This however doesn't meet the second objective, that of *generalization.* The way it's set up here, an optimal model may, but usually doesn't generalize, i.e., performs well against new yet unseen labeled pairs (x, y). The phenomenon of model lacking generality is called *overfitting* and may be demonstrated by the high degree polynomial regression in Fig. 1.

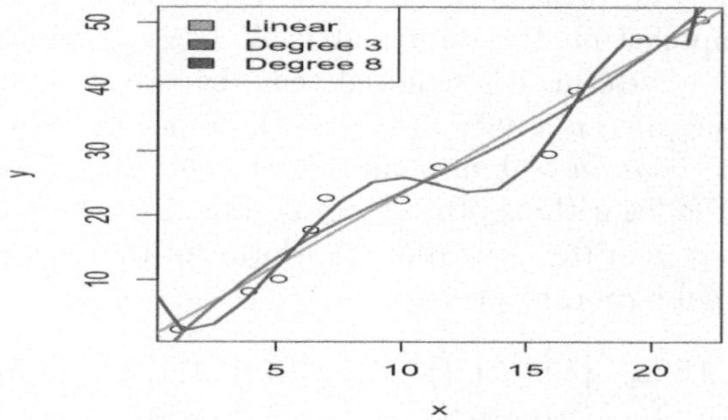

Fig. 1. Linear, cubic and degree 8 polynomial regression

Note that although the linear model doesn't pass through any of the points it appears to generalize better than a high degree polynomial. It just seems that a high degree polynomial is 'trying too hard.' However, it's not clear whether the polynomial of degree 3 is lacking in generalization and whether it generalizes better or worse than the linear model. To determine an optimal degree one must test the model against new yet unseen labeled pairs. In general, fitting a balanced model requires finding an optimal degrees of freedom; too many degrees of freedom and the model bias is low but the variance is high and on the other hand, too few degrees of freedom will result in high bias and neither are desirable. Model misspecification invariably leads to increase in variance. [3].

Although the model doesn't necessarily fits y for any x it fits a function which represents an aspect of the observed y. With binary data, (x, y), $x \in \mathbb{R}^p$, $y = \pm 1$ the model fits the conditional probability $\phi(x) = \mathbf{Pr}(y = +1 \| x)$[6] [4].

The art is to balance the bias and the variance consists of selecting degrees of freedom, a subset of the information at hand so that bias and variance appear to balance each other out. In a classification problem $y = \pm 1$ or perhaps $y \in \{1, 2, ..., c\}$. The class Φ consists of procedures which either strive to assign a class membership to an input x or, more commonly to estimate the probability that x corresponds to a class (either $+1$ or -1, etc.) [5].

6 Clearly there's no need to estimate the probability $\mathbf{Pr}(Y = -1 \| x)$ because it's simply $1 - \phi(x)$.

3 Data Transformation

3.1 Standardization

A list of numbers $x = (x_1, ..., x_n)$ is in *standard form* if the mean $\mu_x = 0$ and the variance $\sigma_x^2 = 1$. Most if not all of this classic material found in e.g., [6,7] however here we emphasize the column space and consider the alternatives concerning the column space $C(\mathcal{X})$ of $\mathcal{X}$: one is $\mathbf{1} = \left(1, 1, ..., 1\right)^T \in C(\mathcal{X})$ and the other $\mathbf{1} \notin C(\mathcal{X})$ where X is the design matrix[7].

The notion of *scale invariance* refers to certain types of common column transformations applied on the data matrix $\mathcal{X} = (x_{ij})$ which operate on an entire column term-by-term. It's required that the transformations $g : \mathbb{R} \to \mathbb{R}$ is strictly increasing, i.e., $u < v \Rightarrow g(u) < g(v)$. Some common transformations are the linear $g(u) = au$, $a > 0$, also the square root $g(u) = \sqrt{u}$, the cube root $g(u) = u^{1/3}$ and the logarithms $g(u) = \log(u)$ provided $u > 0$. For example the log, the square root, and the cube root transforms of the first column (log then square root then cube root, respectively)

$$\begin{bmatrix} 1000 & 1.4 \\ 6000 & 0.6 \end{bmatrix} \xrightarrow{log} \begin{bmatrix} 6.907 & 1.4 \\ 8.699 & 0.6 \end{bmatrix}; \xrightarrow{sqrt} \begin{bmatrix} 31.62 & 1.4 \\ 77.46 & 0.6 \end{bmatrix}; \rightarrow \begin{bmatrix} 10 & 1.4 \\ 18.17 & 0.6 \end{bmatrix}$$

Standardizing the k column x^k of a matrix $\mathcal{X}$ is the operation $x_{ik} \to \dfrac{x_{ik} - \mu_k}{\sigma_k}$ where μ_k is the mean of column k and σ_k is the standard deviation of column k. Below is a standardization of a 3-by-3 matrix

$$\begin{bmatrix} 12 & 3 & 5 \\ -3 & 0 & 2 \\ 0 & 3 & -1 \end{bmatrix} \rightarrow \begin{bmatrix} \frac{12-3}{7.93} & \frac{3-2}{1.73} & \frac{5-2}{3} \\ \frac{-3-3}{7.93} & \frac{0-2}{1.73} & \frac{2-2}{3} \\ \frac{0-3}{7.93} & \frac{2-2}{1.73} & \frac{-1-2}{3} \end{bmatrix} \approx \begin{bmatrix} 1.133 & 0.57 & 1 \\ -0.75 & -1.15 & 0 \\ -0.37 & 0 & -1 \end{bmatrix}$$

Note that the means $\mu_1 = \dfrac{12 - 3 + 0}{3} = 3$, $\mu_2 = \dfrac{3 + 0 + 3}{3} = 2$, $\mu_3 = \dfrac{5 + 2 - 1}{3} = 2$ and the standard deviations are $\sigma_1 = 7.937254$, $\sigma_2 = 1.732051$ and $\sigma_3 = 3$.

Standardizing a matrix is a common technique which is occasionally required to undertake for certain model frameworks to e.g., enhance computational stability. Note that since $\sigma > 0$ the mapping $x \to \dfrac{x - \mu}{\sigma}$ is one-to-one and (presumably) no information is lost when performing standardization.

Say $\mathcal{X} \in \mathbb{R}^{N \times p}$. The operation of standardization is the composite of two matrix operations. 1) subtract column average, and 2) divide by column's standard deviation.

[7] It seems that modeling issues pertinent to the column space of $\mathcal{X}$ are often overlooked.

Operation 1) is *centralization* and is a left multiplication by the $N \times N$ matrix $I - \frac{1}{N}\mathbf{1}\mathbf{1}^T$. Specifically, let $\mathbf{1}$ be the column 1-vector and define the $N \times N$ matrix

$$I_N - \frac{1}{N}\mathbf{1}\mathbf{1}^T = \begin{bmatrix} 1-\frac{1}{N} & -\frac{1}{N} & -\frac{1}{N} & \dots & -\frac{1}{N} \\ -\frac{1}{N} & 1-\frac{1}{N} & -\frac{1}{N} & \dots & -\frac{1}{N} \\ . & . & . & \dots & . \\ . & . & . & \dots & . \\ . & . & . & \dots & . \\ -\frac{1}{N} & -\frac{1}{N} & -\frac{1}{N} & \dots 1 - & \frac{1}{N} \end{bmatrix}$$

and

$$R = \begin{bmatrix} \frac{1}{s_1} & 0 & 0 \dots & 0 \\ 0 & \frac{1}{s_2} & 0 \dots & 0 \\ . & . & \dots\dots & . \\ . & . & \dots\dots & . \\ . & . & \dots\dots & . \\ 0 & 0 & \dots\dots & \frac{1}{s_p} \end{bmatrix}$$

where $s_k = \frac{\sum_{i=1}^{N}(x_{ik} - \mu_k)^2}{N}$ is the empirical standard deviation of the kth column and $\mu_k = \frac{1}{N}\sum_{j=1}^{N} x_{jk}$ the mean of the kth column. □

As an intermediate result we calculate the rank of $I_N - \frac{1}{N}\mathbf{1}\mathbf{1}^T$. This is done by successively reducing the matrix via elementary row and column operations.

$$I - \frac{1}{N}\mathbf{1}\mathbf{1}^T = \begin{bmatrix} 1-\frac{1}{N} & -\frac{1}{N} & -\frac{1}{N} & \dots & -\frac{1}{N} & -\frac{1}{N} \\ -\frac{1}{N} & 1-\frac{1}{N} & -\frac{1}{N} & \dots & -\frac{1}{N} & -\frac{1}{N} \\ -\frac{1}{N} & -\frac{1}{N} & 1-\frac{1}{N} & \dots & -\frac{1}{N} & -\frac{1}{N} \\ . & . & . & \dots & . & . \\ . & . & . & \dots & . & . \\ . & . & . & \dots & . & . \\ -\frac{1}{N} & -\frac{1}{N} & -\frac{1}{N} & \dots 1 - & \frac{1}{N} & -\frac{1}{N} \\ -\frac{1}{N} & -\frac{1}{N} & -\frac{1}{N} & \dots & -\frac{1}{N} & 1-\frac{1}{N} \end{bmatrix}$$

Add $(-1)\times$row N to rows $N-1$, $N-2$,..., 1 to get

$$(*) = \begin{bmatrix} 1 & 0 & 0 & 0 \,.\,. & . & -1 \\ 0 & 1 & 0 & 0 \,.\,. & . & -1 \\ 0 & 0 & 1 & \ldots & . & -1 \\ . & . & . & \ldots & . & . \\ . & . & . & \ldots & . & \\ . & . & . & \ldots & . & . \\ 0 & 0 & 0 & \ldots & 1 & -1 \\ -\frac{1}{N} & -\frac{1}{N} & -\frac{1}{N} & \ldots & -\frac{1}{N} & 1-\frac{1}{N} \end{bmatrix}$$

Next add columns 1,2,..., $N-1$ to column N to get

$$(**) = \begin{bmatrix} 1 & 0 & 0 & .. & . & 0 \\ 0 & 1 & 0 & .. & . & 0 \\ 0 & 0 & 1 & .. & . & 0 \\ . & . & . & .. & . & . \\ . & . & . & .. & . & . \\ . & . & . & .. & . & . \\ 0 & 0 & 0 & .. & 1 & 0 \\ -\frac{1}{N} & -\frac{1}{N} & -\frac{1}{N} & .. & -\frac{1}{N} & 0 \end{bmatrix} z$$

Adding $\frac{1}{N}\times$ rows $1, 2, ..., N-1$ to row N of $(*)$ yield

$$\begin{bmatrix} 1\,0\,0 \ldots 0 & -1 \\ 0\,1\,0 \ldots 0 & -1 \\ 0\,0\,1 \ldots 0 & -1 \\ . \ . \ . \ . \ . \ . \ . & . \\ . \ . \ . \ . \ . \ . \ . & . \\ . \ . \ . \ . \ . \ . \ . & . \\ 0\,0\,0 \,..\, 0\,1 & -1 \\ 0\,0\,0 \,..\, 0\,0 & 0 \end{bmatrix}$$

Let $M \in \mathbb{R}^{N\times N}$ be the matrix of elementary row operations so the last matrix equals $M(I_N - \frac{1}{N}\mathbf{1}\mathbf{1}^T)$ and since elementary row and column operations don't alter rank and the rank of the last matrix is visibly $p-1$ and so $\text{rank}(I - \frac{1}{N}\mathbf{1}\mathbf{1}^T) = p-1$.

Standardization of an $N \times p$ matrix $\mathcal{X}$ is the mapping $\mathcal{X} \to (I_N - \frac{1}{N}\mathbf{1}\mathbf{1}^T)\mathcal{X}R$; a few things are worth observing.

Theorem 1. *The $N \times N$ matrix $I - \frac{1}{N}\mathbf{1}\mathbf{1}^T$ is symmetric & idempotent.*

Proof. Clearly $(I-\dfrac{1}{N}\mathbf{1}\mathbf{1}^T)$ is symmetric. For the second part because $\mathbf{1}\mathbf{1}^T\mathbf{1}\mathbf{1}^T = N\mathbf{1}\mathbf{1}^T$ we have

$$(I-\frac{1}{N}\mathbf{1}\mathbf{1}^T)^T(I-\frac{1}{N}\mathbf{1}\mathbf{1}^T) = I-\frac{2}{N}\mathbf{1}\mathbf{1}^T+\frac{N}{N^2}\mathbf{1}\mathbf{1}^T = I-\frac{1}{N}\mathbf{1}\mathbf{1}^T.$$

Theorem 2. *Suppose $\mathcal{X}\in\mathbb{R}^{N\times p}$ where $1<p\le N$ and rank$(\mathcal{X})=p$.*

1) If $\mathbf{1}\in C(\mathcal{X})$, the column space of $\mathcal{X}$, then rank$\Big[(I-\dfrac{1}{N}\mathbf{1}\mathbf{1}^T)\mathcal{X}\Big]=p-1$

2) The converse is, if rank$(I-\dfrac{1}{N}\mathbf{1}\mathbf{1}^T)\mathcal{X}=p-1$, then $\mathbf{1}\in C(\mathcal{X})$.

Proof. 1) Suppose $\mathcal{X}$ is a $N\times p$ matrix and $p<N$. Assume that $\mathbf{1}$ is one of the columns of $\mathcal{X}$ and w.l.o.g that $\mathbf{1}$ is the last column of $\mathcal{X}$ and the first independent $p-1$ columns of $\mathcal{X}$ are $x^1,...,x^{p-1}$. (In fact, a constant multiple of the vector $\mathbf{1}$ but this requires a negligible alteration of the argument.) Then the centralized matrix $(I-\dfrac{1}{N}\mathbf{1}\mathbf{1}^T)\mathcal{X}$ has nonzero columns $x_j-\bar{x}_j\mathbf{1}$, $j=1,...,p-1$. Suppose on the contrary that there are scalars $c_1,...,c_{p-1}$ so that

$$0 = c_1(x_1-\bar{x}_1\mathbf{1})+c_2(x_2-\bar{x}_2\mathbf{1})+\cdots+c_{p-1}(x_{p-1}-\bar{x}_{p-1}\mathbf{1})$$
$$=\sum_1^{p-1}c_jx_j-\Big\{\sum_1^{p-1}c_j\bar{x}_j\Big\}\mathbf{1},$$

or,

$$\sum_1^{p-1}c_jx_j=\Big\{\sum_1^{p-1}c_j\bar{x}_j\Big\}\mathbf{1}.$$

and this says that $\mathbf{1}$ is in the column space the space spanned by the vectors $\Big(x_1,...,x_{p-1}\Big)$ and this contradicts the assumption that $\mathcal{X}$ is full rank. Now suppose $\mathbf{1}\in C(\mathcal{X})$. Then there is a $p\times p$ nonsingular matrix B so that $\mathcal{X}B$ has a constant column $\mathbf{1}$ and we may assume it's the last one. So $\mathcal{X}B=\Big[x^1,x^2,...,x^{p-1},\mathbf{1}\Big]$. Because the rank of $\mathcal{X}$ is p, the columns $x^1,...,x^{p-1}$ are independent. Centralizing we get

$$(I-\frac{1}{N}\mathbf{1}\mathbf{1}^T)\mathcal{X}B=\big[x^1-m_1\mathbf{1}\cdot x^2-m_2\mathbf{1}\cdot\cdots x^{p-1}-m_{p-1}\mathbf{1}\cdot\mathbf{0}\big]$$

where $m_k=\dfrac{\sum_{j=1}^N x_{jk}}{N}$ the mean of column k. Now the argument is nearly identical to the one before. Indeed, the columns $x^1-m_1\mathbf{1},...,x^{p-1}-m_{p-1}\mathbf{1}$ are independent. For that consider

$$d_1(x^1-m_1\mathbf{1})+d_2(x^2-m_2\mathbf{1})+\cdots+d_{p-1}(x^{p-1}-m_{p-1}\mathbf{1})=0$$

So

$$d_1x^1+d_2x^2+\cdots+d_{p-1}x^{p-1}=-(m_1+m_2+\cdots+c_{p-1})\mathbf{1}$$

and this means that $\mathbf{1}$ is in the column space spanned by $x^1, x^2, ..., x^{p-1}$ but this is contrary to the assumption that the rank of $\mathcal{X}$ is p. Therefore the rank of $(I - \frac{1}{N}\mathbf{1}\mathbf{1}^T)\mathcal{X}B$ is $p-1$ and since the rank of B is p and that of $I - \frac{1}{N}\mathbf{1}\mathbf{1}^T$ is $N - 1 \geq p$ it follows that the rank of $(I - \frac{1}{N}\mathbf{1}\mathbf{1}^T)\mathcal{X}$ is $p-1$.

2) Let $A = (I - \frac{1}{N}\mathbf{1}\mathbf{1}^T)\mathcal{X}$. If the rank of the $N \times p$ matrix A is $p-1$ then some column depends on the other, say it's the last column. So there exists a $p \times p$ nonsingular matrix D so that AD has a zero column, and w.l.o.g. we assume it's the last one. This means that the last column of D is $\mathbf{0}$ and this means that the constant vector $\mathbf{c} = \begin{bmatrix} c \\ c \\ . \\ c \end{bmatrix}$ is a column of $\mathcal{X}$, i.e., $\mathbf{1} \in C(\mathcal{X})$.

The case of the constant column[8]
Care must be taken when standardizing a matrix. If $\mathbf{1} \in \mathcal{X}$ then centralizing decrease the rank of $\mathcal{X}$ by 1. This is a common situation in linear model

$$y_k = \beta_0 + x_{1k}\beta_1 + x_{2k}\beta_2 + \cdots + x_{pk}\beta_p + \epsilon_k$$

where $k = 1, 2..., N$ and $\epsilon_k \sim N(0, \sigma^2)$ are iid and the *design matrix*

$$\mathcal{X} = \begin{bmatrix} 1 & x_{11} & x_{12} & \dots & x_{1p} \\ 1 & x_{21} & x_{22} & \dots & x_{2p} \\ 1 & x_{31} & x_{32} & \dots & x_{3p} \\ . & . & . & \dots & . \\ . & . & . & \dots & . \\ 1 & x_{N1} & x_{N2} & \dots & x_{Np} \end{bmatrix}$$

Centralizing that matrix results in $\mathbf{0}$ column which is fine. But the standard deviation s of a constant column $\mathbf{c}$ is 0 and the ratio $\frac{x - \bar{x}}{0} = \frac{0}{0}$ isn't defined.

To test whether $\mathbf{1} \in C(\mathcal{X})$ one employs part 2 of theorem 2.2 to check the rank of $(I - \frac{1}{N}\mathbf{1}\mathbf{1}^T)\mathcal{X}$. If it's $p-1$ then $\mathbf{1}$ is in the columns space of $\mathcal{X}$, else, it's not.

3.2 Singular Values and Principal Components

As always we start with an $N \times p$, $0 < p < N$ full rank design matrix[9]. The principal components of $\mathcal{X}$ are orthogonal vectors in the column space of $\mathcal{X}$. The principal components are arranged according to their variability. Specifically,

[8] Erle Stanley Gardner's Perry Mason tiles have the form "The Case of...", e.g., "The Case of the Absent Artist" and "The Case of the Reckless Romeo".

[9] In fact, often p is much smaller than N.

consider the $p \times p$ nonsingular symmetric matrix $\mathcal{X}^T\mathcal{X}$ and order eigenvectors of $\mathcal{X}^T\mathcal{X}$ according to the magnitude of their corresponding eigenvalues. (v_k, λ_k) $k = 1, 2, ..., p$ and $\lambda_1 \geq \lambda_2 \geq \cdots \geq \lambda_p > 0$. The vectors $\mathcal{X}v_1, \mathcal{X}v_2, ..., \mathcal{X}v_p$ are the principal components. Note that the principal components are in the column space of $\mathcal{X}$. The singular value decomposition of $\mathcal{X} \in \mathbb{R}^{N\times p}$ is

$$\mathcal{X} = U \begin{bmatrix} \sigma_1 & 0 & 0 & 0 \ldots & 0 \\ 0 & \sigma_1 & 0 & 0 \ldots & 0 \\ 0 & 0 & \sigma_3 & 0 \ldots & 0 \\ \cdot & \cdot & \cdot & \cdot\cdot\cdot\cdot & \cdot \\ \cdot & \cdot & \cdot & \cdot\cdot\cdot\cdot & \cdot \\ 0 & 0 & 0 & \ldots\ldots & \sigma_p \\ 0 & 0 & 0 & \ldots\ldots & 0 \\ \cdot & \cdot & \cdot & \cdot\cdot\cdot\cdot & \cdot \\ \cdot & \cdot & \cdot & \cdot\cdot\cdot\cdot & \cdot \\ 0 & 0 & 0 & \ldots\ldots & 0 \end{bmatrix} V^T = U\Sigma V^T$$

where U is $N \times N$ orthogonal matrix, V is $p \times p$ orthogonal matrix and $\sigma_1 \geq \sigma_2 \geq \cdots \geq \sigma_p > 0$. The latter implies $\mathcal{X}V = U\Sigma$ and because the columns of the matrix $\mathcal{X}V$ are linear combination of the columns of $\mathcal{X}$ it follows that $C(U) \subset C(\mathcal{X})$.

The *spectral decomposition* of $\mathcal{X}$ is $\sigma_1 u^1(v^1)^T + \sigma_2 u^2(v^2)^T + \cdots \sigma_p u^p(v^p)^T$.

Both principal components and singular values involve a linear transformation of the columns of $\mathcal{X}$ hence may be regarded as a special kind of scaling.

Principal components allow for reducing model complexity; to construct a, say classifier ϕ^* which predict class membership $\phi^*(x^*)$ for x^* in a subspace S of the column space of $\mathcal{X}$. Since the subspace S has fewer degrees of freedom a model ϕ^* has lower complexity than a classifier $\phi(x)$ with $x \in \mathcal{X}$. The problem of translating a model ϕ^* defined on a subspace of $C(\mathcal{X})$ to the corresponding model on the entire column space $C(\mathcal{X})$ isn't entirely straightforward. The problem is that the price of reducing complexity is a reduction of information content and so the problem becomes how much information lost is too much.

3.3 Nonlinear Scaling

Nonlinear scaling is needed to render consistency. An example for that is Newman's [10] study of mortality of mosquitofish subject to varying levels of toxicity. The levels studied are 0, 0.02, 0.23, 2.28, 22.8 and 228 parts per billion. Newman's mosquitofish mortality data in Table 1

Table 1. Mortality rate due to exposure

No	toxicity (x)	sample	dead	prop dead	$\log(x+1)$
1	0.00	40	0	0.000	0.0000
2	0.02	40	4	0.100	0.0198
3	0.23	40	15	0.375	0.2070
4	2.28	40	20	0.500	1.1878
5	22.80	40	23	0.575	3.1690
6	228.0	40	40	1.000	5.4330

Figure 2 is a dramatic illustration of the scale mismatch. The column toxicity (x) is measurement in parts per billion (PPB). In fact, ignoring the first record, successive toxicity grows by a factor of 10.

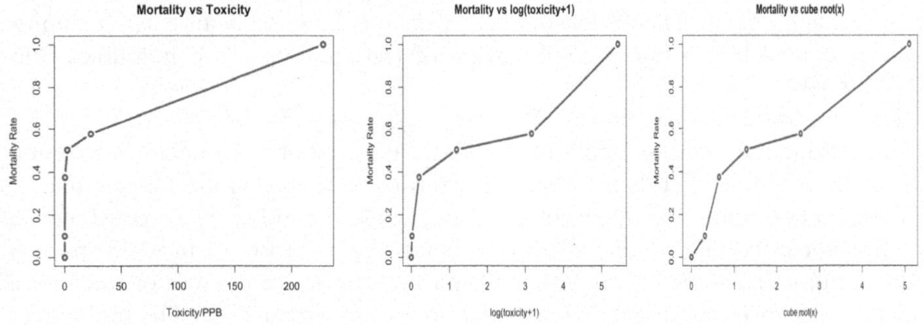

Fig. 2. Toxicity vs mortality (L), logarithm (C) and cube root (R)

Figure 2 exhibits effects of toxicity on mortality rate of mosquitofish. The left uses the data as-is, the center uses the mapping $x \to \log(x+1)$ while the right uses $x \to x^{1/3}$.

Clearly the left figure has little distinguishing power for low concentrations while the cube root seems to amplify distinctions in low concentrations[10].

4 Information

L. Boltzmann invented the notion of entropy to study & measure order or lack thereof. Later C. Shannon [8] studied the topic in the context of digital communication and S. Kullback and R. Leibler in the context of mathematical

[10] I used the mapping $x \to x^{0.3}$ as an approximate for $x \to x^{1/3}$ but that wouldn't have much impact on the results.

statistics [9]. Thus the concepts of entropy, mutual information and Kullback-Libler divergence play into statistical modeling and so one may may ask whether rescaling has an effect on those information-theoretical ideas. Entropy measures disorder in data via a probability distribution. The *entropy* of a probability vector $\mathbf{p} = (p_1, p_2, ..., p_n)$ is $\eta(\mathbf{p}) = -\sum_{k=1}^{n} p_k \log(p_k)$[11] [?], and the entropy of a discrete random variable X with probability mass function p_x is $\tau(X) = -\sum_x p_x \log p_x$, provided the series converges.

The entropy of a vector $\mathbf{x} = (x_1, x_2, ..., x_n) \in \mathbb{R}^n$ may be calculated in various ways. For example, if we aggregate and write $(y_1, m_1), ..., (y_r, m_r)$ where $y_1 = x_1$ and m_1 is the frequency of x_1. y_2 is x_2 unless $x_2 = x_1$ and if $x_2 = x_1$ the y_2 is the first $x_j \neq x_1$ and m_2 is the frequency of y_2, and so on. With that procedure, the entropy of $\mathbf{x}$ is $\rho(\mathbf{x}) = -\sum_{r=1}^{m} \dfrac{m_r}{n} \log(\dfrac{m_r}{n})$. In many practical cases binning is used to measure entropy of $\mathbf{x}$; say data is binned across bins $\mathbf{B} = (B_1, B_2, ..., B_s)$ with frequencies $f_1, f_2, ..., f_s$ and so the entropy with respect to $\mathbf{B}$ is therefore $\tau_{\mathbf{B}}(\mathbf{x}) - \sum_{j=1}^{s} f_s \log(f_s)$.

It's rather axiomatic that entropy is invariant under symmetries (rotations, translations and reflections.) Entropy however may not be invariant under any smooth bijection primarily because derivation of the probability vector $\mathbf{p}$ depends on the specifics in which entropy is measured. For example, if entropy is measured against binned data, then transformation may alter binning procedure, hence the entropy. We state the axiom as a theorem.

Theorem 3. *Isometry (distance-preserving transformation) preserves information.*

A linear mapping A on the vector space $\mathbb{R}^n$, i.e., a square matrix, is isometric if A is orthogonal. So is the affine transformation $\alpha + A$, $\alpha \in \mathbb{R}^n$. A non-singular symmetric matrix A has a singular value decomposition $A = UDV$ where U and V are orthogonal and D is diagonal matrix with non-zero reals $(\lambda_1, \lambda_2, ..., \lambda_n)$. λ_k represents a geometric contraction or dilation; $\lambda_k < 1$ means contraction, and dilation if $\lambda_k > 1$. If A is not symmetric then some eigenvalues may not be real and this will complicated the interpretation. However, if the condition number[12] of A isn't too large then it stands to reason that the entropy will be invariant under A and maintain the same distribution under any reasonable binning of $A\mathbf{x_1}, ..., A\mathbf{x_n}$. We can state a principle (and forgive for stretching it and calling it a theorem.)

Theorem 4. $A \in \mathbb{R}^{n \times n}$ *preserves information provided the condition number of the real symmetric matrix* A *is bounded by* βn, *with* n *the order of* A *and* $\beta \leq 1$.

[11] It's customary to take log base-2 but any base > 1 will alter entropy by a fixed scale.

[12] The condition number of A is the ratio of absolute largest eigenvalue and absolute smallest eigenvalue: $\left|\dfrac{\lambda_{max}(A)}{\lambda_{min}(A)}\right|$.

Mutual Information
Consider a discrete random vector (X, Y) on a state space $\mathcal{X} \times \mathcal{Y}$ having probability mass function $m(x, y)$ and marginal mass functions $p(x)$ and $q(x)$. We don't assume $m(x, y) = p(x)q(x)$. The *mutual information* of (X, Y) is

$$I(X, Y) = \sum_{(x,y) \in \mathcal{X} \times \mathcal{Y}} m(x, y) \log \frac{m(x, y)}{p(x)q(y)}.$$

If X and Y are independent then $m(x, y) = p(x)q(y)$ and so $I(X, Y) = 0$. The following is basic.

Theorem 5. *If X and Y are independent, then so are $f(X)$ and $g(Y)$ for any smooth one-one functions f and g.*

(In fact only measurability is necessary but that's too vague for the purpose of statistical models.) This means that rescaling of any kind does not disrupt independence and that if two measurements $\mathbf{x}$ and $\mathbf{y}$ are independent, then so is any rescaling of $\mathbf{x}$ and $\mathbf{y}$.

Kullback-Leibler Divergence (KL)
The *Kullback-Leibler Divergence* [?] $\kappa(\cdot, \cdot)$ of two probability vectors $\mathbf{p}$ and $\mathbf{q}$ is

$$\kappa(\mathbf{p}, \mathbf{q}) = \sum_k p_k \log \frac{p_k}{q_k}.$$

κ isn't a metric but it's a good measure of closeness of $\mathbf{p}$ and $\mathbf{q}$. Since we're on topic of rescaling the issue is that the probability vectors $\mathbf{p}$ and $\mathbf{q}$ often come about empirically where measurements $\mathbf{x} = (x_1, ..., x_n)$ and $\mathbf{y} = (y_1, ..., y_n)$ and the probability vectors $\mathbf{p}$ and $\mathbf{q}$ are derived from $\mathbf{x}$ and $\mathbf{y}$ (from first principles or empirically or via some procedure like binning.) In particular, meaningful binning must preserve relationship between $\mathbf{x}$ and $\mathbf{y}$ and we use a loose notation $\kappa(\mathbf{x}, \mathbf{y})$ for the Kullback-Leibler divergence of the two observations. Arguably under broad assumptions T will preserves κ and $\kappa(\mathbf{x}, \mathbf{y}) = \kappa(T\mathbf{x}, T\mathbf{y})$. Obviously isometry would preserve KL divergence. Similarly for a symmetric matrix A with bounded condition number would likely satisfy $\kappa(\mathbf{x}, \mathbf{y}) = \kappa(A\mathbf{x}, A\mathbf{y})$.

It's clear that this section is entirely general, perhaps a little vague, and intended to draw attention to invariance properties of topics from information theory related to statistical models.

5 Model Invariance

A model ϕ is invariant under column transformation T if transforming a column by T does not alters model performance. To elucidate, consider the training pairs[13] $\mathcal{D} = \{(x_i, y_i), x_i \in \mathbb{R}^p \text{ and } y_i \in \mathcal{R}, i = 1, 2, ..., N\}$. A standard procedure splits the data $\mathcal{D}$ into training set $\mathcal{T}$ and validation set $\mathcal{V}$, i.e., $\mathcal{D} = \mathcal{T} \cup \mathcal{V}$ and

[13] Also, *sample pairs*, or *learning pairs*.

$\mathcal{T} \cap \mathcal{V} = \emptyset$ where training data $\mathcal{T}$ is used used to train a model, where model is tested against $\mathcal{V}$. With a loss function $\mathcal{L}$[14], a model $\widehat{\phi}$ is trained on $\mathcal{T}$ by minimizing the *cost* (function)

$$\widehat{\phi} = \arg\min_{\phi \in \Phi} \frac{1}{|\mathcal{T}|} \sum_{(x,y) \in \mathcal{T}} \mathcal{L}(\phi(x), y)$$

where Φ is a class of estimators under consideration[15]. The aggregated cost $\mathcal{C}$ of $\widehat{\phi}$ over $\mathcal{V}$ is

$$\mathcal{C}(\mathcal{V})(\widehat{\phi}) = \frac{1}{|\mathcal{V}|} \sum_{(x,y) \in \mathcal{V}} \mathcal{L}(\widehat{\phi}(x), y).$$

Consider a transformation, an increasing function (T, k) applied on the kth component of x and let $x_{T,k} = (x_1, ..., T(x_k), ..., x_p)$ (T applied to the kth component.) Put $\mathcal{D}_{T,k} = \{(x_{T,k}, y) : (x, y) \in \mathcal{D}\}$ and the corresponding $\mathcal{T}_{T,k}$ and $\mathcal{V}_{T,k}$ and consider the optimal model ϕ_T in the class Φ trained on $\mathcal{T}_{T,k}$

$$\widehat{\phi_T} = \arg\min_{\phi \in \Phi} \frac{1}{|\mathcal{T}|} \sum_{(x_{T,k}, y) \in \mathcal{D}_{T,k}} \mathcal{L}(\phi(x_{T,k}), y)$$

with cost on validation set

$$\mathcal{C}(\mathcal{V})(\widehat{\phi_T}) = \frac{1}{|\mathcal{V}|} \sum_{(x_{T,k}, y) \in \mathcal{V}_{T,k}} \mathcal{L}(\widehat{\phi_T}(x_{T,k}, y).$$

Note that occasionally we suppress the coordinate k and write $\mathcal{D}_T$ to stand for $\mathcal{D}_{T,k}$ and similarly $\mathcal{T}_T$, etc.

DEFINITION: TRANSFORMATION-INVARIANT MODEL FRAMEWORK.
A model class Φ is *invariant under* (T, k) if for every $\epsilon > 0$ there exits $N > 0$ so that for all training set $\mathcal{D}$ with cardinality exceeding N and any training-validation split $(\mathcal{T}, \mathcal{V})$ it's imperative that

$$\left| \mathcal{C}(\mathcal{V}_T)(\widehat{\phi_T}) - \mathcal{C}(\mathcal{V})(\widehat{\phi}) \right| \leq \epsilon.$$

Consider a model framework $\Phi : \mathbb{R}^n \to \mathbb{R}$ and let $\tau \subset \{1, 2, ..., n\}$. Let $T_\tau =$ be a mapping which acts solely on the coordinates τ of $x \in \mathbb{R}^n$. If $\tau = \{1, 2\}$ then $T_\tau = \big(T_1(x_1), T_2(x_2), x_3, x_4\big)$. The model framework Φ is invariant under T_τ if for any $\epsilon > 0$ there is $N > 0$ so that any training set $\mathcal{D}$ of order $\geq N$ and for any train-test split $(\mathcal{T}, \mathcal{V})$ of $\mathcal{D}$

$$\left| \mathcal{C}(\mathcal{V}(\widehat{\phi}) - \mathcal{C}(\mathcal{V}_{T_\tau}(\widehat{\phi}_{T_\tau}) \right| \leq \epsilon.$$

---

[14] A loss function is the price for making a single prediction, the price is 0 if the prediction is spot on and is large is the prediction is way off and somewhere in between for a so-so prediction.

[15] Classes like liner models or feed-forward sigmoid networks.

An alternate definition of Φ is invariant under (increasing) transformation (T, k) utilizes measure goodness $\mathcal{C}$. In the examples below we use $\mathcal{C}$ =AUC, the area under the ROC curve, where the receiving operating characteristics (ROC) curve represents model's true positive rate vs false positive rate [16]. Admittedly the definition is a bit loose, perhaps rather aspirational. In practice there are strict constraints on sample size, the cardinality $|\mathcal{D}|$ of $\mathcal{D}$, and especially if the available supply of training pairs is limited, a rather smallish $|\mathcal{D}|$, the assessment whether a model is invariant under a transformation is rather subjective and occasionally inconclusive.

6 Empirics

It should be evident that model invariance isn't necessarily an equality, i.e., $\widehat{\phi_T} = \widehat{\phi}$. Indeed, a model $\widehat{\phi}$ is trained on data $\mathcal{D}$ while a model $\widehat{\phi_T}$ is trained on data $\mathcal{D}_{T,k}$. We demonstrate this with a simulated data[16] which is based on Newman's mosquitofish data (Table 1).

6.1 Newman's Exposure of Mosquitofish to Toxic Environment: LOGIT

From earlier note on Newman's mosquitofish mortality as measured against toxicity, concentration of toxins in the environment [10]. We construct two logistic regression models, $Y|z \sim \text{Binom}(p)$ where $p = p(z) = \dfrac{e^{b_0+b_1 z}}{1+e^{b_0+b_1 z}}$. One $\mathbb{P}(Y = 1\|x)$ where x = toxicity level measured in parts per billion (PPB) and the other is $\mathbb{P}(Y = 1\|z)$, with logarithmic dependence, $z = \log(x + 1)$[17].

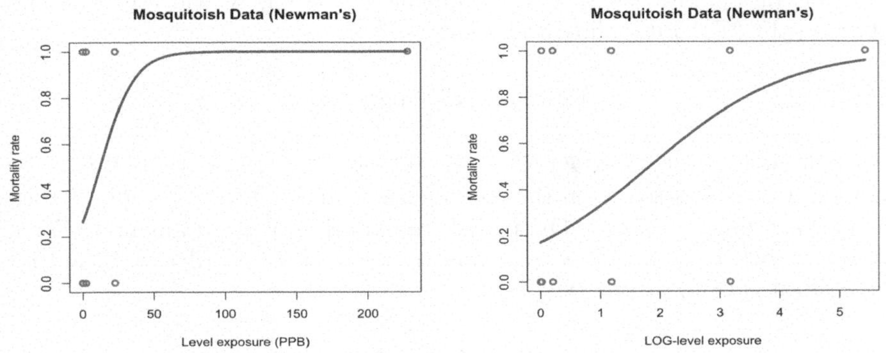

Fig. 3. Logit model of response y vs. toxicity (PPB) (L) and vs. the log (toxicity+1) (R).

[16] Newman's mosquitofish data is aggregated at each level of toxicity.
[17] $T(x) = \log(x + 1)$ is an increasing function and $T(x) \geq 0$ for any $x \geq 0$.

Figure 3 depicts logit models of death vs toxicity and logarithm of toxicity (+1 to ensure $T \geq 0$). The models appear quite different. The probability $\mathbb{P}(Y = 1\|0.0) > 0$ because there are a few observed deaths at low levels toxicity. At 0.02 parts per billion one observes mortality at a rate of 10 percent. To demonstrate consider a 50-50 split with 720 training pairs and an equal number of test pairs.

Logit of original data is $\mathbb{P}(Y = 1\|x) = \frac{\exp(-1.339774+0.071500\times x)}{1+\exp(-1.339774+0.071500\times x)}$ while logit of transformed model is $\mathbb{P}(Y = 1\|z) = \frac{\exp(-1.61407+0.85026\times z)}{1+\exp(-1.61407+0.85026\times z)}$.

Here $x =$ toxicity concentration measures in parts per billion (PPB) while z is the logarithmic transform $z = \log(x+1)$. Performances as measured with area under the ROC curve for both original Newman's data and the transformed are Observe that the AUC of the original is 0.875 while AUC of transformed is 0.849, lagging by mere 2% point. The lag of the transformed data isn't due to systemic degradation. Indeed we see below a case where a transformed data outperform the original albeit by a hair.

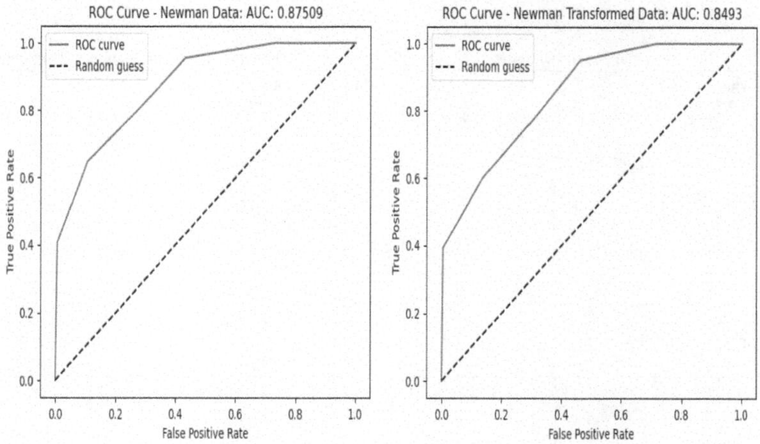

Fig. 4. Newman's mosquitofish mortality/exposure experiment. ROC of original data (L), and transformed data (R)

6.2 Consumer Credit Default: LOGIT

This demonstrates the effect of transformations on the credit card default data available at the UC Irvine Machine Learning Repository [11] The data consists of 30,000 examples, 22 features and a binary tag. All variables are numeric. We train on 20100 examples and test of the remaining 9,900 examples. We employ the ROC/AUC metric and compare the AUC of out of sample data from the original and transformed data.

The original data `DATA1` contains a field `LIMIT_BAL` which ranges between min$= 10,000$ and max$= 1,000,000$ with mean approximately $167,484$ and standard deviation approximately $129,745$.

The transformed data replaces `LIMIT_BAL` with the logarithm log (`LIMIT_BAL`). We test both models with the area under the curve (AUC) of the receiving operating characteristics (ROC) on the out of sample test data.[18]

`MODEL1` is the logistic regression (LOGIT) with l1 or LASSO penalty. `MODEL1 = linear_model.LogisticRegression(penalty='l1', solver='liblinear')` and implement it on the training set $(X1, y1)$ that contains the original fields. `MODEL1.fit(X1_train, y1_train)`.

The transformed data `DATAS2` contains a new field `LOGO` which is the logarithm log(`LIMIT_BAL`) and $X2$ is the input set where `LIMIT_BAL` is replaced with `LOGO`. `MODEL2` which is the same model (LOGIT with LASSO) applied to is deployed.

The receiving operator characteristic graphs (ROC) of `MODEL1` and `MODEL2` are depicted in Fig. 4 with corresponding AUC (`MODEL1`) is 0.7245191843821444 and (`MODEL2`) is 0.7254034718848767. You notice that the AUC of the two models are nearly identical with the first higher than the second by a difference less than 0.0012 (Fig. 5).

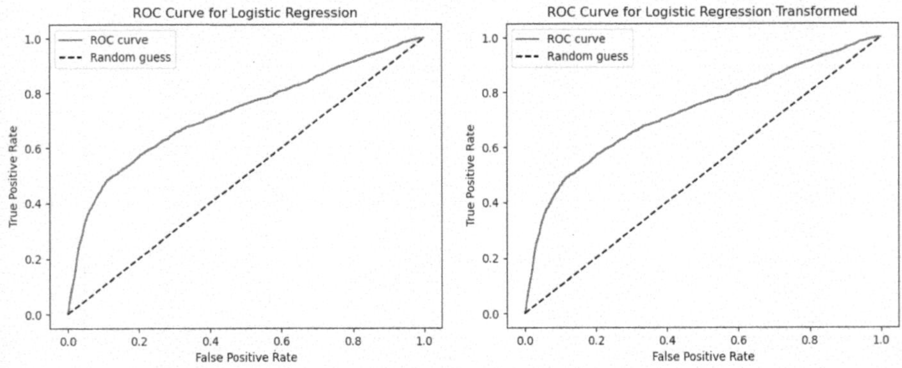

Fig. 5. ROC of logit on original consumer default and transformed data. The original (L) AUC$\approx$ 0.7245 while transformed (R) AUC$\approx$ 0.7254.

As you can see the performance as measured by AUC satisfies $\left|\texttt{AUC(MODEL1) - AUC(MODEL2)}\right| \leq 0.001$. The definition calls for $\epsilon > 0$, i.e., that the precision can be made as small as one wishes. However, we are constrained by the data; all we have to work with are 30,000 examples.

6.3 Consumer Credit Default: Gradient Boosting

Applying Gradient boost classifier (`GradientBoostingClassifier`) on the consumer credit data [11] we see an improved performance; boosting indeed boosts AUC performance by about 6% points, from AUC $\approx$ 0.72 to AUC $\approx$ 0.78. Figure 6 demonstrates that the performance of the original and the transformed

[18] AUC is not the only choice and it's possible to use other cost functions.

where a single column transformation LIMIT_BAL ← log(LIMIT_BAL+1) is applied (and of course, the column LIMIT_BAL is replaced by log(LIMIT_BAL + 1).

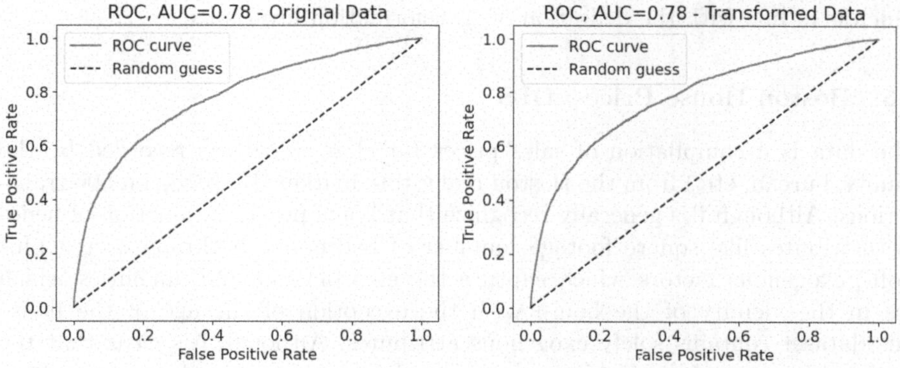

Fig. 6. ROC/AUC consumer credit: gradient boosting

6.4 Occupancy Detection: SVM

The data for the occupancy detection problem also found at the UCI Machine Learning Repository [12] is an experimental data used for binary classification (room occupancy) from Temperature, Humidity, Light and CO2. Ground-truth occupancy was obtained from time stamped pictures that were taken every minute. The classification data consists of 20,560 instances. We demonstrate a square root transformation on variables Light and CO2, i.e., replace Light and CO2 with their (positive) square roots and apply support vector machines

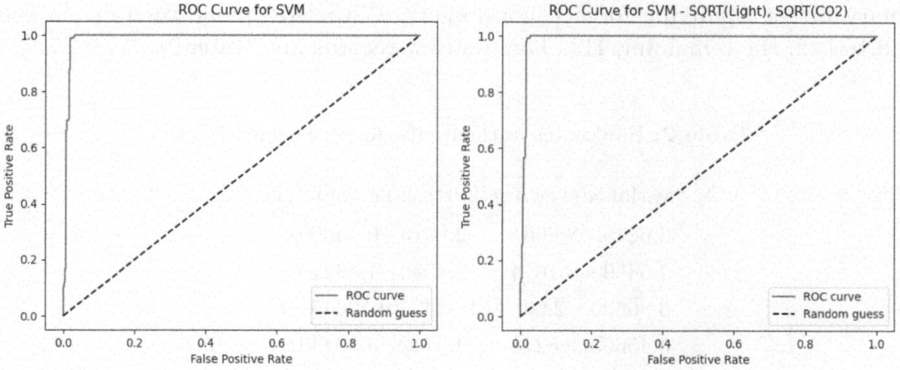

Fig. 7. ROC of the occupancy data SVM classifier, original (L), AUC≈0.9911, and transformed (R) AUC≈0.9904

(SVM) on both datasets. SVM classifier with Radial-Basis Function kernel is trained against 1332 examples and tested against and equal number of examples (a 50-50 split.) The metric of interest is area under the curve (AUC) and we exhibit the receiving operating characteristics (ROC) (Fig. 7).

The original data outperforms the transformed data by less than 0.1 percent which is in line with the definition of transformation invariance.

6.5 Boston House Prices: OLS

The data is a compilation of sales prices (at close of sale as recorded by the county, bureau, etc.) from the Boston real estate market [13] based on 506 transactions. Although it's generally recognize that home price is a function of hedonic attributes like square footage, number of bedrooms, bathrooms, etc., plus "soft" exogenous factors which capture the environment and amenities which are in the vicinity of the house with the exception of the age of the house this dataset contains solely exogenous attributes. Although it's clear that the model is fundamentally lacking, regression of price per square foot on the thirteen (mostly exogenous) attributes seems nevertheless reasonable to demonstrate the effects of transformation on model fitness. With the given design matrix, the coefficient of determination of a linear model (sans variable selection) $y_k = \beta_1 x_{k,1} + \beta_2 x_{k,2} + \cdots + \beta_{k,13} x_{k,13} + \epsilon_k$, with independent $\epsilon_k \sim N(0, \sigma^2)$, $k = 1, 2, ..., 506$ is approximately 0.684 while the coefficient of determination (R-squared) of the linear model $y_k = \beta_1 x^*_{k,1} + \beta_2 x^*_{k,2} + \cdots + \beta_{k,13} x^*_{k,13} + \epsilon_k$ with standardized $X^* = (I - \frac{1}{506}\mathbf{1}\mathbf{1}^T)X$ is also 0.684. In fact, R-squared of both equal 0.6842042799773889.

6.6 Banknotes: Random Forest Classifier

Data were extracted from images that were taken from genuine and forged banknote-like specimens [14]. The data consists of four continuous features and binary target signifying forgery/non-forgery. With 1372 pairs we train on 960 and test on the remaining 412. The first few records are (Table 2).

Table 2. Banknotes authenticity/forgery original data

variance	skewness	kurtosis	entropy	class
3.62160	8.6661	-2.8073	-0.44699	0
4.54590	8.1674	-2.4586	-1.46210	0
3.86600	-2.6383	1.9242	0.10645	0
3.45660	9.5228	-4.0112	-3.59440	0
0.32924	-4.4552	4.5718	-0.98880	0

The transformed data applies the $\tan^{-1}$ [arc tangent] function to variable **skewness** so skewness is replaced by $\tan^{-1}$(skewness). The performance of random forest constrained by min_samples_split=5 and max_depth=3, in terms of ROC/AUC, are identical Fig. 8.

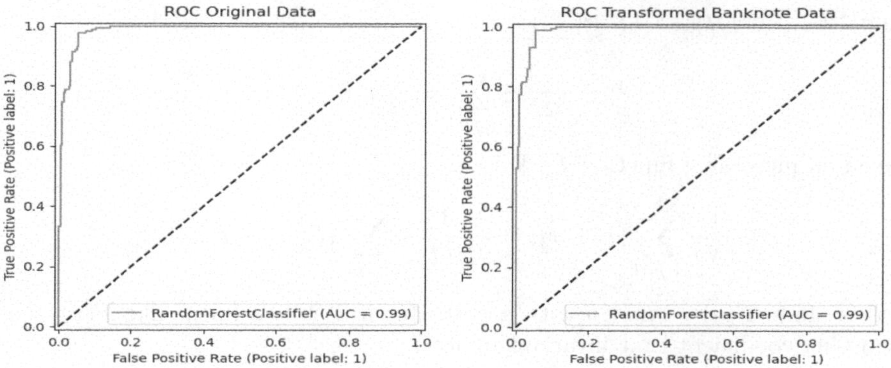

Fig. 8. ROC of original and transformed banknote data. Random forest classification model performed identically under either.

The effect of transformation is nil and in each case AUC = 0.99 when measured against 412 test data.

7 Theoretical Supplements

Let $\mathcal{M}_{N\times p}$ be the set of all real $N \times p$ matrices and refer to $\mathcal{X} \in \mathcal{M}_{N\times p}$ as the *data*, sometime the *design matrix. Data transformation* is a mapping $T : \mathcal{M}_{N,p} \to \mathcal{M}_{N\times p}$. A metric ν is *invariant under* T, if $\nu(T\mathcal{X}) = \nu(\mathcal{X})$.

SHANNON'S ENTROPY. For a probability vector $p = (p_1, p_2, ..., p_n)$, $p_i \geq 0$, $\sum_{i=1}^{n} p_i = 1$ *Shannon's entropy* of p is $\sum_{i=1}^{n} p_i \log_2(p_i)$. Notice that the definition of Shannon's Information does not involve an experiment, or outcomes, it only involves the probability distribution. The base-2 of the logarithm is a matter of tradition and it stems from C. Shannon's work on communications theory where information consists of strings of bits. If we regard data as stochastic where x_i is acquired with probability p_i then transforming x_i has no bearing on Shannon's information of the column.

SPEARMAN CORRELATION. The *Spearman correlation* of $\mathcal{D} = (x_i, y_i)$, $x_i \in \mathbb{R}, y_i \in \mathbb{R}, i = 1, 2, ..., N$ is the correlations of the ranks of x_i and of y_i. If T is an increasing real-valued function then the Spearman correlation of $\mathcal{D}$ is equal to the Spearman correlation of $\mathcal{D}_T = (T(x_1), y_1), ..., (T(x_N), y_N)$. For training pairs (x_i, y_i), with $x_i \in \mathbb{R}^p$, a transformation $T(x_{ik}$ of the kth component does not alter Spearman correlation.

RELATIVE DISTANCE (IS NOT INVARIANT UNDER INCREASING TRANSFORMATION.) For example $x_1 = (4, 6)$ and $x_2 = (1, 10)$. Then $52 = \|x_1\|^2 < \|x_2\|^2 = 101$. Under the quadratic transformation of the first component $T : x \to x^2$ we have $T(x_1) = (16, 6)$ and $T(x_2) = (1, 10)$ and $\|T(x_1)\|^2 = 292$ while $\|T(x_2)\|^2 = 101$ so $\|T(x_2)\| > \|T(x_1)\|$, i.e., the order is reversed.

GINI COEFFICIENT measured homogeneity of data. The Gini coefficient of a vector $x^T = (x_1, x_2, ..., x_N$ is

$$\frac{1}{2N\bar{x}} \sum_{i,j=1}^{N} |x_i - x_j|$$

Given an increasing function $T : \mathbb{R} \to \mathbb{R}$

$$\frac{1}{2N\bar{x}} \sum_{i,j=1}^{N} |x_i - x_j| = \frac{1}{2N(\bar{Tx})} \sum_{i,j=1}^{N} |T(x_i) - T(x_j)|$$

if T is affine $T(u) = au + b$ with $a > 0$. But if T is non-linear like $T(x) = x^2$ then Gini coefficient isn't invariant under T.

7.1 Shannon's Entropy

Consider any column x of the matrix $\mathcal{X} \in \mathcal{M}_{N,p}$, $x = (x_1, x_2, ..., x_N)^T$. There are several ways to measure the *entropy* of x. We present two approaches for entropy, discrete and binning.

DISCRETE ENTROPY. $H(x)$ of x is straightforward $-H(x) = \sum p_k \log(p_k)$ where p_k is the frequency of x_k. Since the components of x may not be unique, p_k is an aggregate value. For example the entropy of $x^T = (1, 2, 1, 5, 2, 2, 5, 1)$ is $-H(X) = \frac{3}{8}\log(3/8) + \frac{3}{8}\log(3/8) + \frac{2}{8}\log(2/8) = \frac{1}{8}(6\log(3) + 2\log(2)) = \frac{1}{8}(6\log(3) + 2 - 8\log 8) = \frac{1}{8}(6\log 3 - 16) \approx 0.8112781$.

If T is an increasing transformation of x then clearly $H(T(x)) = H(x)$ because the frequencies p does not change when applying T.

BINNED ENTROPY. There's a small problem with the definition of $H(x)$. The problem is that although the components of x may be distinct it's possible they are close in values.

Consider $x^T = (1.00001, 1.000015, 1.0002, 1.00025, 53, 68, 72, 115, 116)$.

Clearly the components of x are distinct but the first four differ by a 'round-off error'. Binning might be a better way to measure the entropy of x. With the five bins $[0, 25), [25, 50], [50, 75), [75, 100), [100, 125)$ the first contains 4, the second contains 0, the third 3, the fourth 0 and the fifth 2. The corresponding probabilities are $p_1 = 4/9$, $p_2 = 0$, $p_3 = 3/9$, $p_4 = 0$ and $p_5 = 2/9$ and the entropy with respect to the bins is $-H(x) = \frac{1}{9}(4\log(4/9) + 0 + 3\log(3/9) + 0 + 2\log(2/9)) = \frac{1}{9}(4\log 4 + 3\log 3 + 2\log 2 - 9\log 9) = \frac{1}{9}(10 - 15\log 3) \approx 1.530493.$[19].

[19] By L'Hopital rule $0 \times \log 0 = \lim_{h \to 0} h \log h = 0$.

Which of discrete or binned entropy is the better choice depends on the data and the objective. It's clear that discrete entropy is invariant under increasing transformation but may not be invariant under binned entropy because the latter depends on binning[20].

7.2 The Features Space

For $\mathcal{X} \in \mathbb{R}^{N \times p}$, the feature space is the column space of $\mathcal{X}$. If the rank, $\text{rank}(C(\mathcal{X})) = r < p$ then some optimal model $\widehat{\phi}$ depends on r features[21]. Equivalently, an optimal model depends on $[\mathcal{X}R]$ for some full rank $R \in \mathbb{R}^{p \times r}$, $r < p$. Because the rank of $\mathcal{X}$ is r and the rank of R is also r the rank of the $N \times r$ matrix $[\mathcal{X}R]$ is r. We have a meta-theorem: *If the rank of $\mathcal{X} \in \mathbb{R}^{N \times p}$, $p < N$, is r then the dimension of the feature space is effectively r in the sense that there exists an optimal model $\widehat{\phi} \in \Phi$ that depends on an r dimensional subspace of the column space of $\mathcal{X}$.*

It's possible to make mathematical statements. One of those cases is the class of linear model which is $Y = \mathcal{X}\beta + \epsilon$ with $\mathcal{X} \in \mathbb{R}^{N \times (p+1)}$, $p + 1 < N$, $\mathbf{1} \in C(\mathcal{X})$, $\beta \in \mathbb{R}^{p+1}$ unobservable parameters, $\epsilon \sim N(0, \sigma^2 I_N)$. If $\mathcal{X}$ is full rank and $A \in \mathbb{R}^{(p+1) \times (p+1)}$ non-singular then

Theorem 6. *The OLS solution of the model $Y = \mathcal{X}\beta + \epsilon$ is the same as the OLS solution of $Y = \mathcal{X}A\beta + \epsilon$.*

The OLS solution of the model $Y = \mathcal{X}\beta + \epsilon$ is $\widehat{\beta} = \arg\min \|Y - \mathcal{X}\beta\|^2$. Explicitly, in the first case, $\widehat{\beta} = (\mathcal{X}^T\mathcal{X})^{-1}\mathcal{X}^T Y$. The OLS solution of $Y = \mathcal{X}A\beta + \epsilon$ is $\widehat{\beta}_A = \arg\min \|Y - \mathcal{X}A\beta\|^2$ explicitly, $\widehat{\beta}_A = \left((\mathcal{X}A)^T(\mathcal{X}A)\right)^{-1} A^T\mathcal{X}^T Y = \left(A^T\mathcal{X}^T\mathcal{X}A\right)^{-1} A^T\mathcal{X}^T Y = A^{-1}(\mathcal{X}^T\mathcal{X})^{-1}(A^T)^{-1}A^T\mathcal{X}^T Y = A^{-1}(\mathcal{X}^T\mathcal{X})^{-1}\mathcal{X}^T Y$ and this is equivalent to $A\widehat{\beta}_A = (\mathcal{X}^T\mathcal{X})^{-1}\mathcal{X}^T Y$. In other words, linear model is "homogeneous" under the transformation $\mathcal{X} \to \mathcal{X}A$.

7.3 Robustness and Spectra

The following examples demonstrate that having a full rank does not translate into robustness. A square matrix A is "*nearly singular*" if $\det(A) \approx 0$ but not quite equal to 0. For example, consider the design matrix

$$\mathcal{X} = \begin{bmatrix} 1 & 1.1 & 0.900 \\ 1 & 1.2 & 0.920 \\ 1 & 1.3 & 0.930 \\ -1 & 1.01 & -0.902 \end{bmatrix} \text{ and } \mathcal{X}^T\mathcal{X} = \begin{bmatrix} 4 & 2.59 & 3.63 \\ 4.61 & 3.32 & 4.19 \\ 3.65 & 2.39 & 3.31 \end{bmatrix}.$$ The eigenvalues of $\mathcal{X}^T\mathcal{X}$ are $\lambda_1 = 10.00848$, $\lambda_2 = 2.686293$ and $\lambda_3 = 0.0002331551$[22]. Thus, for the linear model $Y = \mathcal{X}\beta + \epsilon$, the variance of the estimates $\widehat{\beta}$ are proportional

[20] The Akaike Information Criterion may be used to optimize binning.

[21] If the rank of $\mathcal{X}$ is deficient, then there exists an optimal model which depends on r features.

[22] The spectrum was computer using the R system.

to $(0.1, 0.3731343, 4288.99)$ (the reciprocal of the eigenvalues.) $\text{var}(\hat{\beta}_1) \propto 0.1$, $\text{var}(\hat{\beta}_2) \propto 0.3731343$, and $\text{var}(\hat{\beta}_3) \propto 4,288.99$. We see that the variance of $\hat{\beta}_3$ is five orders of magnitude bigger than that of $\hat{\beta}_1$. The determinant of $\mathcal{X}^T\mathcal{X}$, $\det(\mathcal{X}^T\mathcal{X}) \approx 0.00626854$, small compared to the entries of the matrix, reinforcing the fact that $\mathcal{X}$ is nearly deficient.

By way of analogy, one may compare the two 3-by-3 system of equations

$$\begin{aligned} \frac{1}{6}x + \frac{2}{6}y + \frac{3}{6}z\& = 1 \\ \frac{1}{3}x + \frac{1}{3}y + \frac{2}{3}z\& = \frac{4}{3} \\ 0.4999x + 0.4999y + z = 1.999 \end{aligned} \tag{1}$$

with solutions $x = 1, y = 1, z = 1$; and

$$\begin{aligned} \frac{1}{6}x + \frac{2}{6}y + \frac{3}{6}z\& = 1 \\ \frac{1}{3}x + \frac{1}{3}y + \frac{2}{3}z\& = \frac{4}{3} \\ 0.4999x + 0.4999y + z = 1.998 \end{aligned} \tag{2}$$

with solutions $x = 10, y = 10, z = -8$. The terms *ill conditioning* and *multicollinearity* are used interchangeably to describe a situation where small chances in inputs lead to dramatic changes in outputs. Notice that although the coefficient matrix B below is not quite singular, the determinant

$$\det \begin{bmatrix} 1/6 & 2/6 & 3/6 \\ 1/3 & 1/3 & 2/3 \\ 0.4999 & 0.4999 & 1 \end{bmatrix} = -0.00001$$

confirming that the matrix is nearly singular.

Transforming $\mathcal{X} = \begin{bmatrix} 1/6 & 2/6 & 3/6 \\ 1/3 & 1/3 & 2/3 \\ 0.4999 & 0.4999 & 1 \end{bmatrix}$, cube root of the third column $\mathcal{Z} = \begin{bmatrix} 1/6 & 2/6 & 0.7937005 \\ 1/3 & 1/3 & 0.8735806 \\ 0.4999 & 0.4999 & 1.000000 \end{bmatrix}$ results in the spectrum $\lambda_1 = 1.73055328, \lambda_2 = -0.05754146, \lambda_3 = -0.17301182$ and $\det(\mathcal{Z}) = 0.01722827 \approx 1.7 \times 10^{-2}$ which are three orders of magnitude larger than $\det(\mathcal{X}) = 10^{-5}$. The conclusion is that since variance is proportional to the spectra, done right, column transformation decreases variance and hence increases robustness of a model. The *condition number* $\rho(A)$ of a positive definite symmetric matrix A is the ratio $\rho(A) = \dfrac{\lambda_1}{\lambda_n}$ where λ_1, λ_n are the largest and smallest eigenvalues. For example, the condition number of $A = \begin{bmatrix} 1/6 & 1/3 & 1/2 \\ 1/3 & 1/3 & 2/3 \\ 0.4999 & 0.4999 & 1.00 \end{bmatrix}$ is $\rho(A) = 7,867.438$ because the spectrum of A is $\lambda_1 = 1.5706686072, \lambda_2 = -0.0708682489, \lambda_3 = 0.0001996417$. The condition number of the transformed matrix $B = \begin{bmatrix} 1/6 & 2/6 & 0.7937005 \\ 1/3 & 1/3 & 0.8735806 \\ 0.4999 & 0.4999 & 1.000000 \end{bmatrix}$ is $\rho(B) = \frac{\lambda_1}{\lambda_3} = \left|\frac{1.73055328}{-0.17301182}\right| = 10.00251$ and so by definition B is more robust than A.

8 Conclusion and Further Study

It's safe to say that the principle of invariance applies under rather broad conditions so one might ask when is it necessary to exercise due care to ensure that invariance is preserved and when it doesn't. Although it often requires an argument, it's intuitively clear that some favorite modeling frameworks like the generalized liner models, Cox proportional hazard regression, ARMA, feed-forward networks, etc. are invariant under monotone scaling so one might ask how to extend the notion of invariance that will apply to a larger family of model frameworks. It's worth investigating whether the class of stochastic dynamical system $x_t = f_t(x_{t-1}) + \epsilon_t$, $x_t \sim \mathcal{L}$ some class of distributions $\mathcal{L}$, is scale invariant with f_t in some class of functions, not necessarily linear. It seems reasonable that the condition applies provided that $f_t \in \mathcal{C}^k$, the class of k-times differential functions ($\mathcal{C}^0$ is the class of continuous functions.) Further we may ask whether the principle applies if ϵ_t aren't uncorrelated, that is $\mathbb{E}(\epsilon_s \epsilon_t) \neq 0$, $s \neq t$, or if variance Σ_t explodes. Similarly, invariance of a class of *state space* model, the "state" unobservable dynamic $x_t = f_t(x_{t-1}) + \epsilon_t$ observed via *observed dynamics* $Y_t = g_t(X_{t-1}) + \delta_t$ with ϵ_t, δ_s uncorrelated zero mean random vectors and f_t and g_t in class $\mathcal{C}^k$ or perhaps piecewise linear non-decreasing functions like ReLU. Our intuition suggests that essential properties of dynamical systems aren't altered by transforming features (a component of x_t). A more general problem is how popular logic workflow commonly used in AI like *Large Language Model (LLM) Transformers* [15] affects the performance of the model born out of complex workflow. This we believe will be harder to answer or even pose but it's a safe bet that scaling is applied throughout while entirely relying on performance and none on theoretical matters.

References

1. Eaton, M.: Group invariance applications in statistics. J. Inst. Math. Stat. (1989)
2. Berger, J.: Statistical Decision Theory and Bayesian Analysis, 2nd edn. Springer, Heidelberg (1985)
3. Barr, J.R., Shaw, P., Soble, M.: The Variability of Model Specification. ArXiv (2021)
4. Barr, J.R., Zacks, S.: GLiM: generalized linear models. In: Encyclopedia with Semantic Computing and Robotic Intelligence. World Scientific (2017)
5. Barr, J.R., Cavanaugh, J.: Goodness of machine learning models. In: Encyclopedia with Semantic Computing and Robotic Intelligence. World Scientific (2017)

6. Graybill, F.A.: Theory and Applications of Linear Models. Duxbury Press (1976)
7. Christensen, R.: Plane Answers to Complex Questions, 5th edn. Springer, Heidelberg (2020)
8. Shannon, C.: A mathematical theory of communication. Bell Syst. Techn. J. (1948)
9. Kullback, S., Leibler, R.: On information and sufficiency. Ann. Math. Stat. **22** (1951)
10. Newman, M.C.: Quantitative Methods in Aquatic Ecotoxicology. CRC Press, Boca Raton (1994)
11. Yeh, I.C.: Credit Card Default (Data) (2009). https://archive.ics.uci.edu/dataset/350/default+of+credit+card+clients
12. Candanedo, L.: Occupancy Detection (Data) (2016). https://archive.ics.uci.edu/dataset/357/occupancy+detection
13. Kaggle: Boston House Prices (Data). https://www.kaggle.com/datasets/vikrishnan/boston-house-prices
14. Banknote Authentication (Data) Lohweg Volker (2013). https://archive.ics.uci.edu/dataset/267/banknote+authentication
15. Vaswani, A., et al.: Attention is all you need. Adv. Neural Inf. Process. Syst. (2017)
16. Bradley, A.P.: The use of the area under the ROC curve in the evaluation of machine learning algorithms. Pattern Recogn. **30**(7), 1145–1159 (1997)

A Comparison of Artificial Intelligence and Statistical Models for Identifying Mixtures in Contaminant Data

Kimani Kimbrough[1(✉)], Faisal N. Abu-Khzam[2], Joseph R. Barr[3], Erik Davenport[1], and Lucas Isenmann[2]

[1] National Oceanographic and Atmospheric Administration, Silver Spring, MD, USA
{kimani.kimbrough,erik.davenport}@noaa.gov
[2] Department of Computer Science, Lebanese American University, Beirut, Lebanon
{faisal.abukhzam,lucas.isenmann}@lau.edu.lb
[3] Embry-Riddle Aeronautical University, Prescott, AZ, USA
barrj4@erau.edu

Abstract. The National Oceanic and Atmospheric Administration Mussel Watch Program (MWP) has assessed hundreds of contaminants using bivalves since the early 1980s. Polycyclic aromatic hydrocarbons (PAHs), the focus of this study, represent a ubiquitous suite of contaminants derived from sources such as forest fires, vehicle exhaust, oil, and roadway runoff that have been consistently measured by MWP since its inception. Many of the aforementioned sources of PAHs contain a suite of compounds that have a unique signature defined by their relative concentration. In the environment, multiple sources/signatures combine to make mixtures that can be used to distinguish between watersheds (i.e. developed, coastal, and reference). We used unsupervised artificial intelligence and combinatorial clustering to successfully identify different mixtures in PAH bivalve body burden results. Relationships between PAH mixtures, total PAH concentration, and developed land use were found. Mixtures are an integral part of the MWP contaminant framework, used to support prioritization, characterization, and forecasting of contaminants nationwide.

Keywords: Spatial classifications by chemical signatures · unsupervised random forests · encoder-decoder feature engineering · Bayesian regression · combinatorial-AI · correlation graphs · correlation clustering · bi-clustering

1 Introduction

The Mussel Watch Program (MWP) has monitored contaminants in United States waters since the early 1980s incorporating a temporal study design that is national in scope, in addition to regional and site-based assessments (Kimbrough et al., 2014; Hartell et al., 2018; Apeti et al., 2023). MWP works closely with state, local and private stakeholders to produce robust regional and site-based contaminant characterizations that support management and policy decisions (Rider et al., 2020). National characterizations are developed that allow managers to bring perspective to local contaminant results (Kimbrough et al., 2008). The development of national characterizations

J. R. Barr et al. (Eds.): ERWCSA 2025, ACSAR 4, pp. 53–65, 2026.
https://doi.org/10.1007/978-3-032-18230-2_4

involves the use of data derived from decades of studies, with different study designs, providing a great opportunity to identify new information (Freitag et al., 2021; Kimbrough et al., 2021).

The MWP contaminant framework uses United States Geological Survey Hydrologic Unit Codes (HUCs), a standardized hierarchical watershed classification system, to group PAH data from temporal and assessment studies. HUC watershed data is national in scope, and are readily available, making them suitable to group the PAH body burden results. As part of the MWP contaminant framework, hierarchical Bayesian analysis to compare HUC watershed contaminant concentrations with the overall goal of characterizing and forecasting contaminant concentration and toxicity using spatial data (Hartwell et al., 2018). The framework was developed using PAHs, a suite of compounds measured by MWP since the inception of the project, which represents one of the largest national contaminant datasets.

PAHs are a suite of compounds with pyrogenic and petrogenic sources. Pyrogenic sources are derived from the incomplete combustion of fossil fuels, and petrogenic sources are derived from oil sources. Pyrogenic sources include engine exhaust, forest fires, and petrogenic sources include oil and oil-derived products. Some of the pyrogenic sources are atmospheric, while others may stem from runoff. Source apportionment is possible with PAHs and can be used to distinguish between petrogenic and pyrogenic sources, and in-depth forensic studies can identify specific point sources (Mason et al., 2019; Kimbrough et al., 2019). However, on national and regional scales, we are interested in identifying mixtures that represent a combination of sources.

Random forest, autoencoding, and clustering methods are used to identify relevant mixture information in PAH bivalve body burden data. Random forest, an unsupervised methodology that has been used to find patterns in high-dimensional data (Kimbrough, et al., 2021) is an ensemble approach that is more robust to overfitting and provides feature importance information. Autoencoding is a deep learning methodology that includes dimension reduction and compression through the use of encoders and decoders. Clustering is one of the key methods for unsupervised learning, where the objective is to group data elements that represent common functionality.

The combination of these three methodologies in an ensemble approach that supports the identification of relevant PAH mixtures. Mixtures play an important role in the MWP contaminant characterization framework through supporting modeling. The relationship between PAH mixtures, elevated levels of PAH contamination, and developed land use is useful for characterizing and forecasting tasks and plays an important role in the MWP National Contaminant Framework.

2 Methods

2.1 Sampling

There were more than 2600 bivalve body burden PAH results included in this combined dataset. The samples were collected throughout the United States (Fig. 1) and included major bays, coastal zones, and estuaries. The bivalves were harvested using tongs, diving, and dredging. For a detailed sampling methodology, see Apeti et al., 2012. Once harvested, the bivalves were sent to a chemistry lab for PAH analysis. To ensure comparable results across laboratories, all samples underwent a thorough QA/QC process and were analyzed for PAHs using GC-MS (Lauenstein. and Cantillo, 1993; Kimbrough et al., 2006).

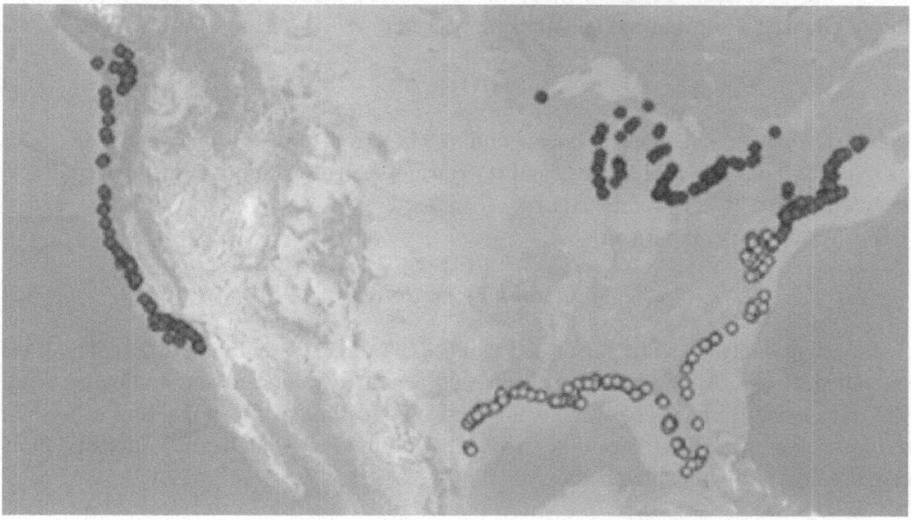

Fig. 1. This data included more than 2693 dreissendid (purple:128), oysters (pink:1444), and mussels (grey:1129) bivalve samples collected throughout the United States. Temporal samples that span several decades and samples from assessment projects are combined. (Color figure online)

2.2 Spatial Data

Geopandas.sjoin was used to select 241 HUC-12 watersheds that contained PAH study sites. Historic NOAA Coastal Change Analysis Program (C-CAP) land cover data (1996, 2001, 2010, 2016) raster images were used for land cover calculation using zonal stats python package and selected HUC-12 polygons (NOAA C-CAP, 2025). A temporally relevant C-CAP land use coverage was selected for each PAH result. The final land uses were open water, developed, forest, wetland, barren, pasture/hay, scrub/shrub, aquatic bed, and cultivated crops (NOAA C-CAP, 2025). Watershed land use was converted into percentages for visualization and use in models.

2.3 Bayesian Analysis

To summarize PAH results, a hierarchical Bayesian linear model was used (Stan Development Team, 2025). HUC-12 watersheds were readily available and national in scope, making them suitable to group the PAH body burden results. The Bayesian model took into account within and between watershed variation and was used to account for observation count differences in watersheds. Shrinkage (tau) allowed watersheds with limited data to be shrunk towards the global mean and included greater uncertainty in the estimate. Global/collective model knowledge benefits the watershed with limited observations. The use of HUCs, and the hierarchical Bayesian approach are both examples of how the Bioeffects Program methodologies were modified and applied to a large national dataset. Relevant model details appear below:

$$y_n \sim N(\alpha_n, \sigma^2) \tag{1}$$

where α_n = watershed group mean and σ^2 = error term within watershed. $\alpha = \mu + \tau + \alpha^*$ where μ = global mean and α^* = watershed deviation τ = shrinkage parameter/variation (between watersheds.)

For watershed comparison

$$hdi \leftarrow hdi(samples, credMass = 0.95). \tag{2}$$

Bayesian analyses were performed using `R STAN` (R Core Team, 2024). The PAH watershed means, Alphas (α)s were reported for each watershed and compared using HDI to assess differences between watersheds with estimates for global and watershed averages, and watershed variation (between/within). For visualization, density plots were used to compare watersheds.

2.4 Unsupervised Analysis

Unsupervised methods included random forest, autoencoding, and combinatorial cluster ((bicluster) analyses. To identify relevant PAH mixtures, a dataset that only included PAH relative concentration data was used. The first step in this analysis was to create a dimensionless dataset based on dividing the concentration of each PAH compound by the sum of all PAH compound concentrations in a sample. A second dataset combined PAH relative concentration data and land use to identify additional patterns based on the known relationship between PAH and land use.

1. Random forest analysis was used to find patterns in PAH mixture and combined PAH land use data sets using the R randomForest package. The analysis generates a proximity matrix where similar signatures/patterns were close and those that were different were farther away. Random forest generated a gini index to quantify feature importance. The random forest is a tree based ensemble approach that utilizes a subset of features for each tree. Multidimensional scaling was used for dimension reduction generating two axes used for visualization (Liaw and Mathew, 2002)
2. *Autoencoder* , a deep neural network, was used for dimension reduction of PAH mixture data and PAH mixture-land use datasets. A total of 5 layers were used with 5000 epochs, and a learning rate of 0.1. For comparison, the same number of clusters were used for autoencoder as for random forest analysis. The encoding dimension was set to 2 for visualization (Paszke et al., 2019).
3. *Combinatorial (graph) algorithm* formed a graph, applied (heuristic) clustering and translated the graph back to data. Recently, Abu-Khzam et al. (2025) introduced

an improved model, namely the Bicluster Editing with Vertex Splitting problem (BEVS). In addition to edge-editing operations, this model allowed vertices in the bipartite graph to be split, enabling overlaps between biclusters. This approach was used in our experiments and revealed interesting insights. In correlation clustering, elements of the same cluster are expected to be sufficiently close to each other, while elements belonging to different clusters are expected to be far apart, or dissimilar according to some similarity measure. When data is given in tabular form, a more effective clustering approach is to represent it as a bipartite graph and apply what is known as biclustering, where the goal is to transform a bipartite graph into a disjoint union of bicliques by performing a minimal number of edge additions or deletions, in addition to allowing observations to belong to more than one cluster.

3 Results and Discussion

PAH concentrations ranged from 2–88,079 ng/g dry weight and exhibited a log-normal distribution indicative of persistent organic pollutants (Kimbrough et al., 2021; Kimbrough et al., 2008) . Four PAH concentration clusters were identified, 69 percent of the samples were in the first two clusters and 90 percent of the samples had a concentration below 3,000 ng/g dry weight (Fig. 2). Most measurements fall within the two lower concentration clusters; however, the tail of the distribution, where the most variability exists, is the primary interest of this discussion.

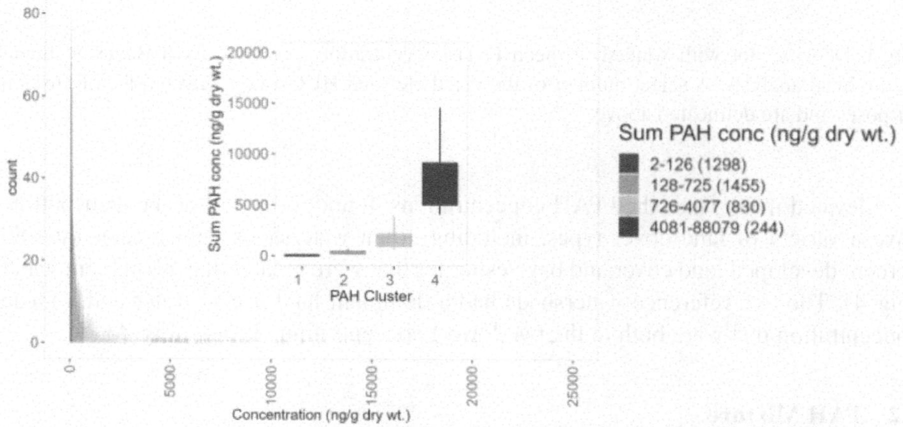

Fig. 2. Sum PAH concentrations for all 2,693 sites are displayed in a histogram and box plot. To aid visualization, samples greater than 28,000 were not included. Cluster analysis identified four concentration groups.

3.1 Bayesian

All PAH observations were grouped by watershed for comparison and characterization (Fig. 3). The means calculated for 241 watersheds, resulted in a PAH concentration range from 96–35,308 ng/g dry weight using a Bayesian hierarchical approach. Ninety percent of the Bayesian watersheds, similar to the original sample data (Fig. 2) that contained 2,693 samples, had a mean PAH concentration below 3100 ng/g dry weight.

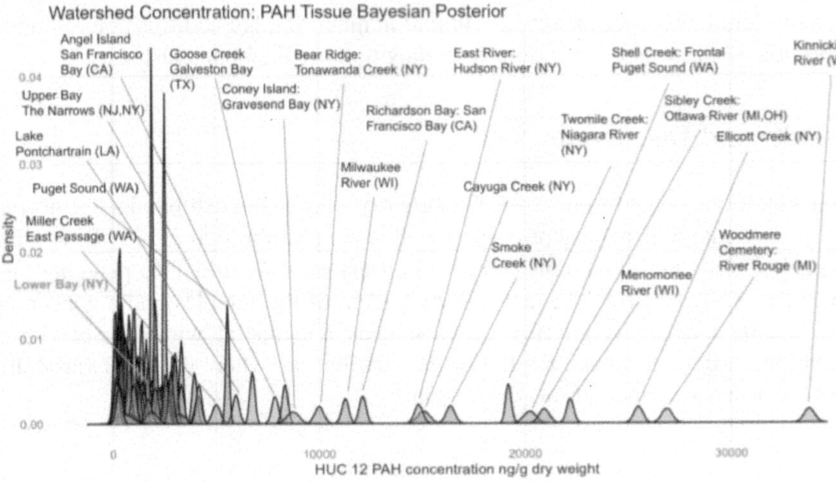

Fig. 3. Density plot with watershed mean PAH concentration generated by a Bayesian linear hierarchical analysis. A select number of the listed elevated HUCs were selected for discussion purposes and are delineated above.

Elevated mean watershed PAH concentrations, found in the tail of the distribution, have a variety of land cover types, including urban watersheds with greater than 80 percent developed land cover and bays/estuaries that were greater than 80 percent water (Fig. 4). The two reference watersheds had a dominant land use of water and a mean concentration that were both in the two lowest concentration clusters (Fig. 4).

3.2 PAH Mixture

Bar charts were used to compare PAH signatures from select watersheds with elevated concentrations and PAH signatures from reference sites (Fig. 5). Perylene, a naturally occurring PAH that is formed *in situ*, has a high relative concentration in offshore sites, with low anthropogenic sources of PAHs, such as those found at the Arroyo Sequuit, and Swan Lake reference watershed sites (Fig. 5). East River and Kinnickinnic watersheds had high relative concentrations of 4–6 ring compounds compared to the rest of the watersheds. Lake Pontchartrain had a high relative concentration of 3-ring compounds and also a high relative concentration of phenanthrene compared to other 3-ring

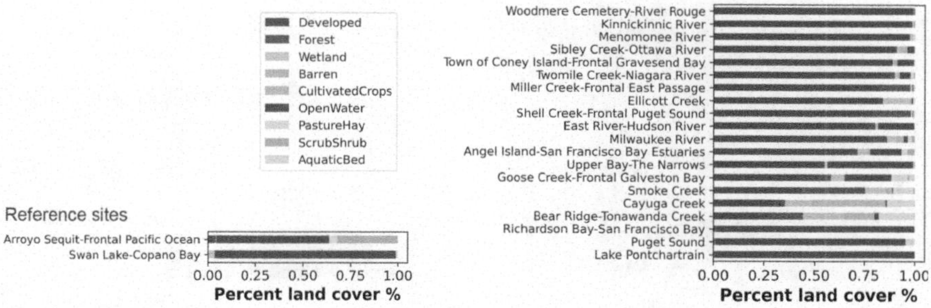

Fig. 4. Land cover percentages for reference watersheds (left) and land cover percentages for watersheds with elevated levels of PAHs (right).

compounds (Fig. 5). Distinct differences in watershed PAH signatures were identified between reference watersheds and watersheds with elevated PAH concentrations. Furthermore, three different signatures were identified for highly urbanized (Kinnickinnic River and East River), Lake Pontchartrain and two large estuaries (Puget Sound and San Francisco Bay).

The random forest and autoencoder results (Fig. 6) supported the signature results for each watershed (Fig. 5). Lake Pontchartrain had a unique PAH signature compared to the other highlighted watersheds. East River and Kinnickinnic River were among the most urban sites (Fig. 4) and had a signature with an elevated relative concentration of 5 ring PAHs, compared to the relative concentration of perylene (Fig. 6). Lake Pontchartrain had an elevated relative concentration for 3-ring PAHs compared to the other watersheds. Puget Sound and Richardson Bay had a similar signature with elevated phenanthrene relative concentration of PAHs when compared to the other 3 ring compounds, and a low relative concentration for 5 ring PAHs, similar to Lake Pontchartrain (Fig. 5). The watershed PAH signature comparison highlights distinct differences with the largest difference found between the reference sites and the East and Kinnickinnic Rivers, evidenced by a clear difference in 4–6 ring compounds (Fig. 5). Both Richardson Bay and Puget Sound had a similar signature.

Random forest and autoencoding had similar results with respect to the reference watersheds and developed watersheds. The two sites with the highest PAH concentrations had similar PAH signatures (Kinnickinnic and East Rivers) and were located near each other (Fig. 6). The reference watersheds were near each other in both random forest and autoencoder results, and were found on the opposite sides of axis 1 from the two developed watersheds. Lake Pontchartrain, with its unique PAH signature, was distant from other watersheds in both random forest and autoencoder analyses. Richardson Bay and Puget Sound had less distinct signatures and are found in the gradient between developed and reference watersheds. All of the watersheds were comprised of primarily pyrogenic sources as would be expected for reference and urban sites.

A clear relationship was seen between the PAH signature and the total PAH concentration. Elevated concentrations were found mainly on the left side of axis 1 (random forest), while the watersheds with the lowest concentrations were found in the lower

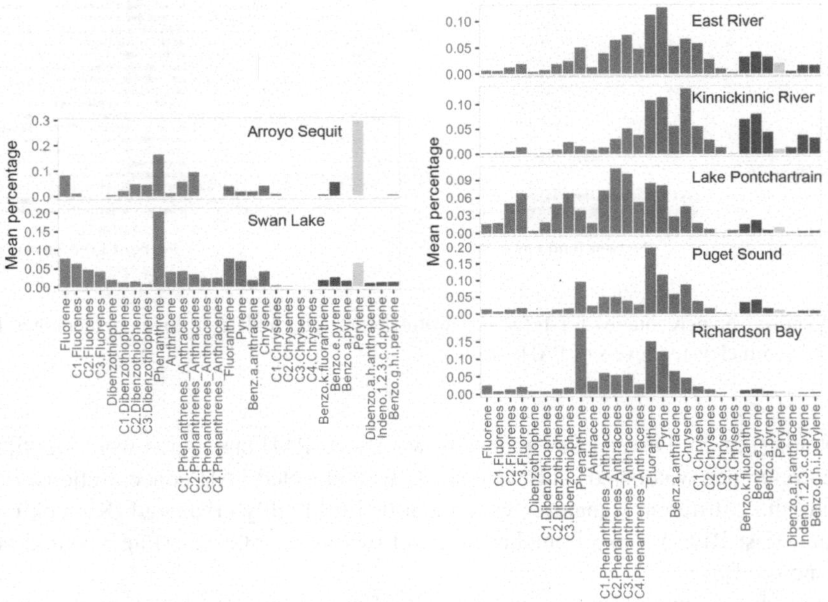

Fig. 5. Reference site PAH signature (left) and watershed PAH signature for sites with elevated concentrations (right).

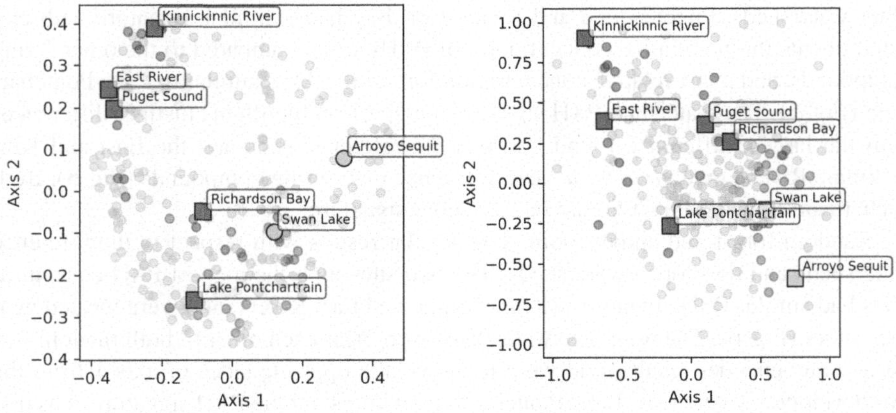

Fig. 6. Random forest (left) and autoencoder (right) PAH mixture visualizations with reference watersheds (gold) and watersheds with elevated PAH levels (purple). These figures represent the results for the PAH-only dataset. The background represents total PAH concentrations for clusters from Fig. 2. Developed watersheds (Kinnickinnic River and East River) are located near watersheds with similarly elevated concentrations, while reference watersheds (Arroyo Sequit and Swan Lake) are located near watersheds with low concentrations.

right quadrant of the random forest plot (Fig. 6). A similar distinction is found with the autoencoder results, except that the lowest concentrations were found in the upper right quadrant. Both the random forest and the autoencoder identified information regarding a relationship between the PAH signature and PAH concentration. From a modeling perspective, this showed that concentration and signature provided relevant information for prediction, which justifed their inclusion in the MWP characterization framework.

3.3 PAH and Land Use

Analysis of the combined PAH and land use dataset resulted in similar relationships between reference and developed watersheds found in the above PAH mixture only analysis. With respect to distance, location on opposite sides of the same axis, and proximity near similar types of watersheds, the two analyses generated similar results (Fig. 7). In addition, the gradient from reference watersheds to developed watersheds that included all sites but Lake Pontchartrain was similar. The PAH + land cover dataset was visualized with percent developed (Fig. 7). The developed and reference watersheds were located near watersheds with higher and lower percent developed land use respectively (Fig. 7). These clearly identified a relationship between land use and PAH watershed signatures.

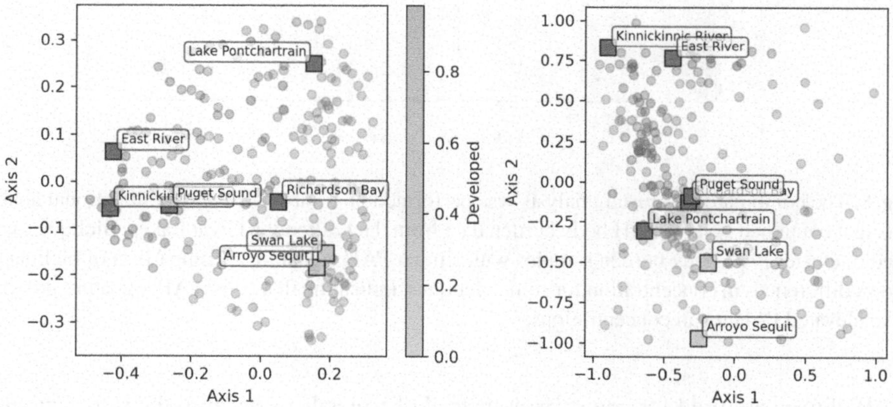

Fig. 7. Random forest (left) and autoencoder (right) plots for the combined PAH+land use dataset. Each plot includes reference watersheds (gold) and watersheds with elevated PAH sites (purple). The background represents percent developed.

3.4 Combinatorial Clusters

Due to the increased number of clusters identified, the combinatorial clusters analysis was performed on the Great Lakes PAH data, a subset of the national dataset. The same Bayesian analysis used to compare watersheds was also used to compare bicliques (clusters). Reference sites (Joseph Island-Lake Huron and Lake Superior) and developed sites (Ellicott Creek and Kinnickinnic River) with elevated PAH concentrations were used for discussion purposes. Four bicliques (2, 3, 5, 7) were grouped together that had low mean PAH concentrations compared to four bicliques (1, 4, 6, 8) with higher mean PAH concentrations (Fig. 8 and 9). The bicliques with the lowest concentrations contained sites with land use mainly below 50 percent and reference sites (Fig. 9). Two bicliques (4, 8) with elevated mean PAH concentrations contained observations with high and low PAH concentrations (Figs. 8 and 9).

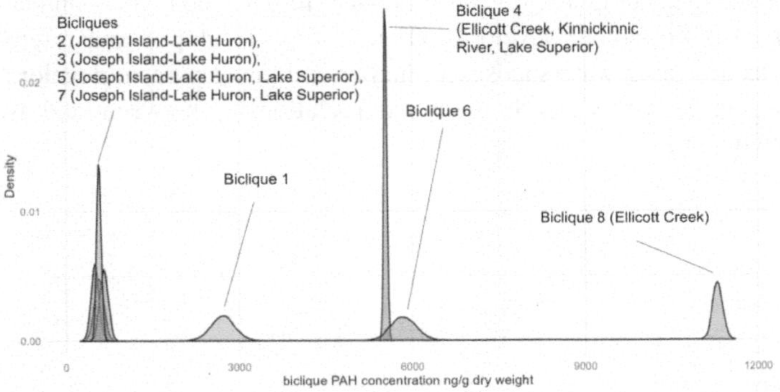

Fig. 8. The combinatorial cluster analysis was performed on a subset of the overall national analysis that contained bivalve PAH body burden data from the Laurentian Great Lakes. Bicliques are used to cluster PAH body burden samples with similar PAH signatures. Comparison of bicliques shows differences in concentration for some bicliques, indicating that some PAH signature groups have elevated PAH mean concentrations.

Bicliques are used for comparison instead of watersheds because the same sample can be found in multiple bicliques. Relative to the four bicliques with lower concentrations, the four bicliques with elevated concentrations had more measurements and included both high and low concentrations (Figs. 8 and 9). The combinatorial clustering results did not identify the same relationship with concentration and percent developed as the random forest and autoencoder methods. This methodology, as part of the MWP ensemble approach, provides a different perspective on grouping samples. This is a preliminary analysis used to access more detailed grouping information provided at the sample level. Additional work is needed to interpret the more complex combinatorial cluster results.

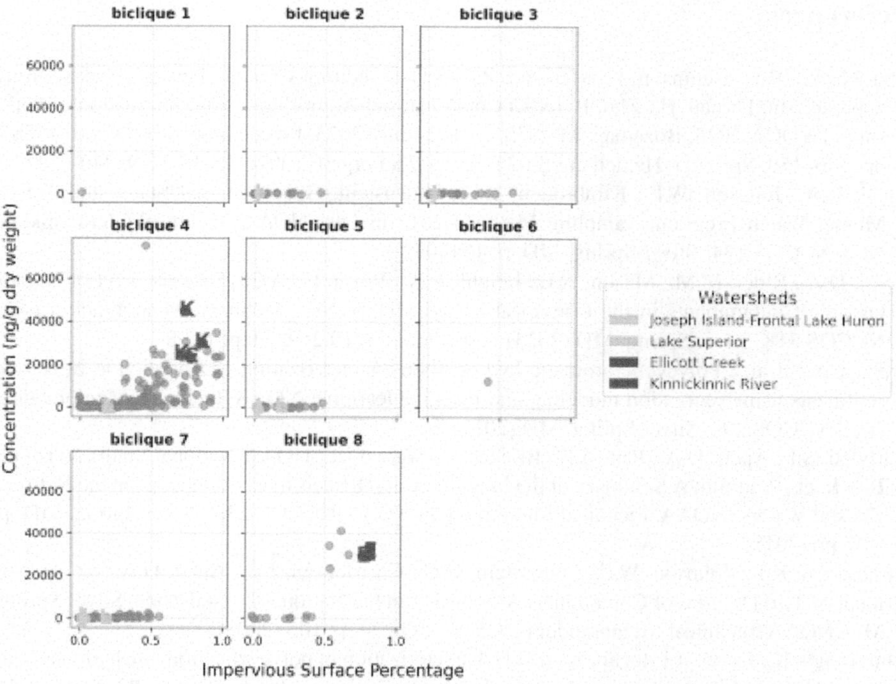

Fig. 9. Individual bicliques plotted separately. For visualization, reference sites are plotted in gold and watersheds with elevated concentrations are plotted in purple. These plots include all PAH bivalve body burden samples from the Laurentian Great Lakes.

4 Conclusion

In general, random forest and autoencoder techniques identified similar relationships. Specifically, a clear reference site and developed sited gradient was identified in addition to the uniqueness of the Lake Pontchartrain PAH signature. The PAH and PAH + land use datasets had similar results with respect to watershed gradients of developed and reference watersheds, the proximity of developed watersheds to each other and the proximity of watersheds with elevated PAH concentrations to each other. The combinatorial analysis provided a detailed sample-based analysis of PAH mixture results to support the random forest and autoencoder results. Autoencoder and combinatorial clustering techniques are more challenging to interpret, this is why they are included in an ensemble approach with supporting feature visualization. The production and analysis of this national dataset generated new information that increases our understanding of PAH distribution nationally and improves stakeholder ability to make management decisions.

References

Abu-Khzam, F.N., Isenmann, L., Merchad, Z.: Bicluster editing with overlaps: a vertex splitting approach. In: Fernau, H., Zhu, B. (eds.) Combinatorial Algorithms - 36th International Workshop, IWOCA 2025, Bozeman, MT, USA, 21–24 July 2025, Proceedings. LNCS, vol. 15885, pp. 146–159. Springer, Heidelberg (2025). https://doi.org/10.1007/978-3-031-98740-3_11

Apeti, D.A., Johnson, W.E., Kimbrough, K.L., Lauenstein, G.G.: National Status and Trends Mussel Watch Program: Sampling Methods 2012 update. NOAA Technical Memorandum NOS NCCOS 134. Silver Spring, MD, p. 46 (2012)

Apeti, D.A., Rider, M.M., Mason, A.L., Leight, A.K., Wirth, E.: A 2015 Assessment of Legacy Organic Contaminants in the Chesapeake Bay, MD. NOAA Technical Memorandum NOS NCCOS 318. Silver Spring, MD (2023). https://doi.org/10.25923/tept-6x98

Freitag, A., et al. : Polycyclic aromatic hydrocarbon characterization and prediction in coastal sediments using regression modeling and machine learning. NOAA Technical Memorandum NOS NCCOS 293. Silver Spring, MD (2021)

Hartwell, S.I., Apeti, D.A., Pait, A.S., Bricker, S., Warner, R.: NOAA National Status & Trends Bioeffects Program: A Summary of the Magnitude and Effects of Contaminants in the Nation's Coastal Waters. NOAA Technical Memorandum NOAA/NCCOS 236. Silver Spring, MD, p. 219. pp (2018)

Kimbrough, K.L., Johnson, W.E., Lauenstein, G.G., Christensen, J.D., Apeti, D.A.: An Assessment of Two Decades of Contaminant Monitoring in the Nation's Coastal Zone. Silver Spring, MD. NOAA Technical Memorandum NOS NCCOS 74, p. 105 (2008)

Kimbrough, K., Jacob, A., Regan, S., et al.: Characterization of polycyclic aromatic hydrocarbons in the Great Lakes Basin using dreissenid mussels. Environ. Monit. Assess. **193**, 833 (2021). https://doi.org/10.1007/s10661-021-09401-7

Kimbrough, K.L., Lauenstein, G.G., Johnson, W.E.:Organic Contaminant Analytical Methods of the National Status and Trends Program: Update. NOAA Technical Memorandum NOS NCCOS 30 (2000–2006) (2006)

Kimbrough, K.L., Johnson, W.E., Jacob, A., Edwards, M.A., Davenport, E.D.: Mussel watch Great Lakes contaminant monitoring and assessment: phase 1. NOAA Technical Memorandum NOS NCCOS 180 (2014)

Lauenstein, G.G., Cantillo, A.Y.:Sampling and analytical methods of the National Status and Trends Program National Benthic Surveillance and Mussel Watch Projects, 1984–1992. NOAA Technical Memorandum NOS ORCA 71. Silver Spring, MD. 157 (1993)

Liaw, A., Wiener, M.: Classification and Regression by randomForest. R News **2**(3), 18–22 (2002)

National Oceanic and Atmospheric Administration, Office for Coastal Management. Coastal Change Analysis Program (C-CAP) Regional Land Cover. Charleston, SC: NOAA Office for Coastal Management (2025). www.coast.noaa.gov/htdata/raster1/landcover/bulkdownload/30m_lc

Paszke, A., et al.: PyTorch: An imperative style, high-performance deep learning library. In: Advances in Neural Information Processing Systems, vol. 32, pp. 8024–8035. Curran Associates Inc (2019)

R Core Team (2024). R: A Language and Environment for Statistical Computing. R Foundation for Statistical Computing, Vienna, Austria. https://www.R-project.org/

Rider, M., et al.: A synthesis of ten years of chemical contaminants monitoring in national park service - Southeast and Southwest Alaska Networks. A collaboration with the NOAA National Mussel Watch Program. NOAA Technical Memorandum NOS NCCOS 277. Silver Spring, MD, p. 110 (2020). https://doi.org/10.25923/dbyq-7z17
Stan Development Team. RStan: the R interface to Stan. R package version 2.32.7 (2025). https://mc-stan.org/

Multi-level Graph Fusion for Intelligent Document Merging: Integrating FPT Algorithms with Large Language Models: Merge2Docs

Peter Shaw[1,2](✉)

[1] Prescott AI, Prescott, USA
peter.shaw.cs@gmail.com
[2] Oujiang Lab, Wenzhou, Zhejiang, China

Abstract. Merge2Docs is a multilevel graph fusion framework that leverages the computational power of Fixed-Parameter Tractable (FPT) algorithms to enable the synergistic combination of ideas from disparate documents - a capability traditionally limited by the NP-hard nature of optimal document merging problems.

The underlying rationale for this approach is that FPT algorithms can solve many NP-hard problems efficiently when parameterized appropriately. In particular, we utilize novel parameters from the Machine Learning (ML) domain, like Vapnik-Chervonenkis (VC) dimension, Kolmogorov complexity, and treewidth. We prove theoretically and demonstrate experimentally that by setting the threshold to ensure the discrete graphs produced have bounded treewidth, significant improvements in model accuracy and results are obtained. Where traditional approaches either concatenate documents or rely purely on statistical methods, Merge2Docs employs biologically inspired algorithms to identify optimal merge points, enabling our novel SAT solver to generate genuinely new insights by uncovering beneficial logical relationships.

The framework implements a toolkit of semi-exact parameterized heuristics, including: Cluster Editing with Vertex-Splitting (CE-VS), Bipartite Cluster Editing with Vertex-Splitting (BCE-VS), Vertex Cover (VC), Red-Black Domination (RB-domination), and treewidth-bounded graph analysis to transform document merging from an intractable combinatorial explosion into a parameterized problem solvable in practice. These algorithms were combined with category-theoretic knowledge representation, multigranularity semantic graphs, monadic second-order logic (MSOL) queries, and agentic LLM orchestration.

Category-Theoretic Foundation: Documents are modeled using both syntactic-semantic networks with connecting edges that work like functors and show how, utilizing a genetic read-repair mechanism very similar to BCE-CS, we can preserve well-quasi-ordering (w.q.o) properties.

The significance of the identified w.q.o is that they enable principled reasoning about document relationships through Monadic Second-Order Logic (MSOL) queries. We then utilize Courcelle's Theorem to extract insights from bounded-treewidth knowledge graphs efficiently.

Using a multi-granularity semantic architecture, the system integrates word-level precision through Word2Vec/GloVe. This provides category-like relationships for the semantic embeddings of words that form a word-based bridge

J. R. Barr et al. (Eds.): ERWCSA 2025, ACSAR 4, pp. 66–110, 2026.
https://doi.org/10.1007/978-3-032-18230-2_5

between the syntactic and semantic graphs. And embeddings that allow for semantic matching of the topic. This structure provides a basis for discussions on the fundamental limitations and advantages of our approach and guidance on how to build a GNN to model other lncRNA-inspired relationships. An LLM-based conceptual understanding via Pydantic-AI orchestrated knowledge graphs, Agentic processing pipelines with type-safe graph operations, and sophisticated error handling.

Rather than concatenating documents, the system identifies structural patterns in which ideas from different sources can be mathematically combined to generate novel hypotheses. The FPT parameterization makes previously intractable optimal solutions computationally feasible, enabling genuine intellectual synthesis.

Keywords: Document Merging · Large Language Models · Graph Neural Networks · Semantic Graph Fusion · FPT Algorithms · Cluster Editing · Knowledge Graph Integration · Multi-Level Graph Architecture

1 Introduction

In this paper, we present a thought experiment that considers the question: how can we merge two documents so that the output is not just a trivial concatenation of the documents?

This project is an amalgam of two thought experiments that complement each other with synergistic effects. The first was from a recent reflection on the connection between biological and spoken knowledge, referred to in this paper as 'yada' after the Hebrew word for knowledge. In biological transcription, mechanisms translate information encoded in genes into knowledge, and finally proteins via various read and repair mechanisms stored within the non-coding RNA (ncRNA). The Second is a thought experiment on how FPT concepts and algorithms could be utilized to provide a synergistic way to merge two documents (ideas).

1.1 Traditional Diff – Concatenation

Perhaps the simplest approach to combine the documents is to concatenate them or find the union of the documents by finding the longest common sequence (LCS) and, for example, using the UNIX command *diff*.

When considering this question, there are a few obvious cases, when the documents contain interleaved matching sections (the traditional diff well handles this case). When there are no apparent similarities between these documents and a mixture of the two (see Fig. 1). This concept can be generalized to the fuzzing matching of these sections using techniques such as embeddings of words, sentences, or paragraphs in documents.

The idea was that if we could find some 'trivial' corollaries or lemmas that could be obtained from the merger that were more than just the logic in the original papers(idea). This problem appears closely related to the Boolean SATISFIABILITY (SAT) problem, which defines the NP-hard problem class (Beware! dragons lie here). However, LLMs cannot handle the combinatorial explosion needed to uncover or solve these underlying

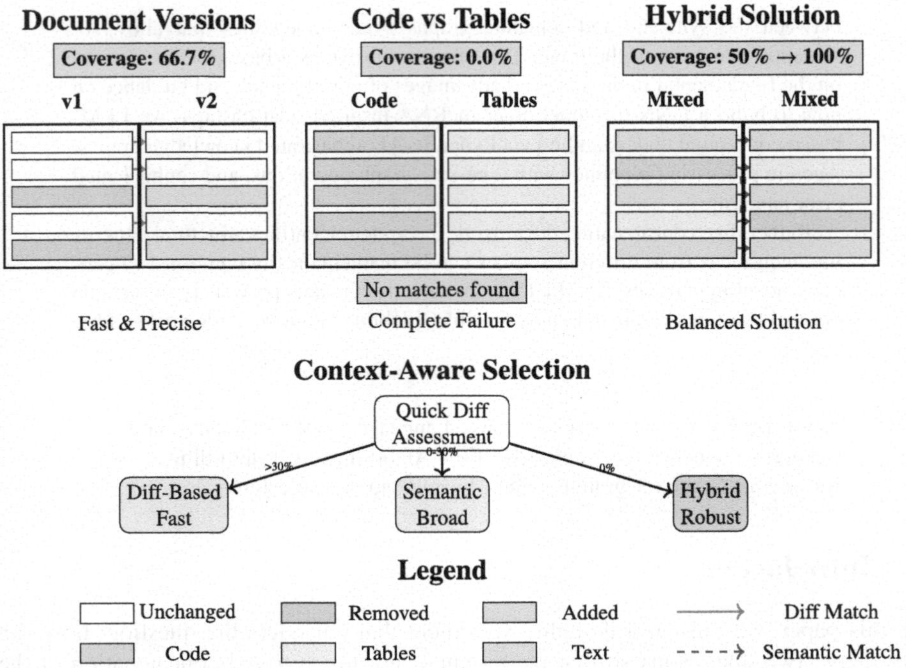

Fig. 1. Three simple diff scenarios.

ideas. An LLM trained on 1 T tokens is limited in its ability to solve NP-hard problems beyond 13 steps ($13! \gg 1T$).

We can extend this analogy from the perspective of VC dimension as well. The VC dimension d_{VC} of a hypothesis class, for example, a GNN on G_θ, is the size of the largest set of points it can shatter. For a GNN with L layers and local degree $d(v_i)$, a local estimate is:

$$d_{\mathrm{VC}}^{\mathrm{local}}(v_i) \approx L \cdot d(v_i)^L \cdot \log d(v_i). \quad (1)$$

The NP-hard combinatorial explosion mirrors the high d_{VC}, as both require exploring exponentially many configurations. For LID prediction, high p and small n exacerbate this, as k-NN searches scale as $\mathcal{O}(n \cdot 2^p)$, resembling SAT's intractability.

An LLM trained on 1T tokens can't handle problems beyond 13. $\approx 6.2 \times 10^9$. This reflects the exponential growth of NP-hard problems, such as SAT, where the search space outstrips the training data.

Parameterized complexity offers a valuable toolkit for addressing tractability issues, including NP-hard problems. A related class is the FPT class of problems. A decision problem (π, κ) is said to be in the complexity class FPT (Fixed Parameter Tractable) if given an instance (I, κ) (Note k could be a set of parameters) [3,20] there is an algorithm where $k\kappa(I)$ is the (concrete) parameter that answers YES or NO in time $\mathcal{O}(f(k) \cdot p(\sigma(I)))$, where f is some arbitrary (computable) function, σ measures the size of an instance I, and p is some polynomial. In our case, I may be genetic, documents, or a graph, and the parameters can include a limit on the size of the solution k, or some topological properties such as the size of the VERTEX COVER or the treewidth (tw).

Parameterized complexity provides a more nuanced framework for understanding complexity [26].

$$P \subseteq FPT \subseteq M[1] \subseteq W[1] \cdots \subseteq XP$$

Here, the complexity classes of P and FPT describe what is solvable. We will utilize this to design a framework that guides our identification of potential synergies in computationally feasible areas, and we hope to avoid these dragons.

The primary objective of this study was to examine how the FPT toolkit, with both theoretical and implemented algorithms, could be used to help achieve this goal. We then extend the idea by looking for a bridge(s) between the two documents using a knowledge base and some fundamental connecting bridges.

2 Mathematical-Philosophical Framework

A key part of this approach was to base the investigation on fundamental concepts and theorems. One of the non-trivial aspects of such an idea is the need for a mechanism to create bridges between quite different fields, such as literature and mathematics [9]. One approach to this dilemma is to consider some fundamental texts, also known as wisdom literature. These would include Job, The Epic of Gilgamesh [29], Psalms, and Proverbs [37].

2.1 Avoiding Dragons!

Beyond just a simple concatenation, several fundamental challenges present themselves:

- **The Curse of Dimensionality**: As document complexity grows, the semantic space expands exponentially. [31,44]

$$\text{Semantic Dimensions} \propto 2^{\text{Concepts}} \tag{2}$$

- **The Demon of Complexity** refers to the combinatorial explosion, such as NP-hard problems, that renders computational solutions impossible for large problem instances. lurk in document synthesis [20]. Current LLMs are not efficient at dealing with computational explosions and are essentially limited by the size of their training set. Thus, LLMs trained on 1 T tokens falter beyond 13 steps.

$$13! \gg 1\,T \text{ (training tokens)} \tag{3}$$

- **The Pit of Folly**: Raw information without wisdom leads to "ever learning, and never able to come to the knowledge of the truth" (2 Timothy 3:7) [37]. For example, LLMs that accumulate tokens without bounding complexity (i.e., with d_{VC}) are "ever learning" syntactic patterns, but fail to generalize to semantic truth, mirroring the biblical warning. Thus, unbounded models chase raw information without converging to wisdom.

2.2 Parameter Ecology

Fellows and Rosamond introduce the paradigm of 'parameter ecology' as the idea that the inputs of the computational problem are not just random; they originate from natural processes constrained by complexity [24]. Consequently, input distributions for abstract computational problems exhibit inherent structural patterns or 'relevant parameters,' derived from the limitations of the generative process.

2.3 Physics Minimal Energy

After utilizing these thresholds, we have a reasonable density but a low treewidth.

We implemented an FPT-Guided AI System that automatically adapts its processing strategies based on a mathematical analysis of problem complexity. We observed a significant reduction in computational time and energy requirements. See Table 1. More related results are presented below in Sect. 13.

Table 1. Memory and CPU Reduction for Different Services

Problem	Memory Reduction	CPU
VertexCoverService	68%	92%
FVS Service	57%	88%
RAG Hierarchy Service	42%	79%
Graph Comparison Service	61%	91%

3 Background

3.1 From Shannon Information to VC-Bounded Knowledge

Shannon entropy can be interpreted as the average amount of information supplied by the source, or the average (a priori) uncertainty associated with the source output [40].

Shannon: Quantitative complexity (entropy, bits). Given a discrete random variable X, where X is a member of $p : \mathscr{X} \to [0,1]$, the Shannon entropy is defined [18,40],

$$H(X) = -\sum_{i=1}^{K} p(x_i) \log p(x_i) \tag{4}$$

Joint Entropy: The joint Shannon entropy (in bits) of two discrete random variables x and y with images $\mathscr{X}$ and $\mathscr{Y}$ is defined as[18,40]:

$$H(Y,X) = -\sum_{x\in\mathscr{X},y\in\mathscr{Y}} p(x,y) \log[p(y,x)] \tag{5}$$

Theorem 1 (Shannon source code theorem) [18,40]. *Given X is an independent and identically distributed (i.i.d.) source, such that its time series $X_1, \ldots, X_n$ is i.i.d. with entropy $H(X)$ in the discrete-valued case and differential entropy in the continuous-valued case. For any $\varepsilon > 0$, there is an n and an encoder that takes n i.i.d. repetition of the source, $X_{1:n}$, and maps it to $n(H(X) + \varepsilon)$ binary bits such that the source symbols $X_{1:n}$ are recoverable from the binary bits with probability of at least $1 - \varepsilon$.*

Proof (Proof of Theorem 1). The proof follows from the asymptotic equipartition property (AEP) and typical set encoding. For the detailed proof, see [18] Chap. 3.

For example, DNA, viewed as a sequence over A, C, G, T, Shannon entropy $H(X) \approx 1.8$ bits per base pair (due to nonuniform nucleotide frequencies) suggests that long genomes can be compressed to approximately $nH(X)$ bits. This ensemble-based metric assumes a passive data source, ignoring the biological reality where DNA actively participates in its own interpretation and maintenance.

3.2 Kolmogorov Complexity

Kolmogorov complexity is defined based on the ideal compression of a string using an algorithm. [21]. i.e., the compressibility of a sequence s as $K(s)$, which is the length of the shortest program that outputs s on a universal Turing machine (for the above DNA example, s represents an individual DNA sequence).

Chaitin's more formal definitions of Kolmogorov complexity, Ω, as the probability that a universal prefix-free Turing machine U halts on a given input [23].

$$\Omega = \sum_{U(\sigma)\text{ halts}} 2^{-|\sigma|}$$

For typical sequences from an i.i.d. source, $K(s_{1:n}) \approx nH(X)$ asymptotically aligns with Shannon's bound. As these are incomputable (equivalent to the Halting problem), we approximate $K(s)$ using compressors like gzip: [19,45]

$$K_{\text{approx}}(G_{v_i}) = |\text{gzip}(E_{v_i})|,$$

normalized:

$$K_{\text{norm}} = \frac{K_{\text{approx}}(G_{v_i})}{\log \binom{d(v_i)+1}{2}}.$$

3.3 The Vapnik-Chervonenkis Foundation

Vapnik-Chervonenkis (VC) dimension provides a mathematical framework for how much genuine information a system can encode. Here, we consider the novel approach of using VC as a parameter for FPT problems.

Formally, for a hypothesis class $\mathscr{H}$ on domain $\mathscr{X}$, the VC dimension $VC(\mathscr{H})$ is defined as the size of the largest set $S \subseteq \mathscr{X}$ that can be shattered by $\mathscr{H}$. A set is shattered when $\mathscr{H}$ can realize all possible binary labels [10]:

$$\exists S \subseteq \mathscr{X} : |S| = d \text{ s.t. } \forall y \in \{0,1\}^d, \exists h \in \mathscr{H} : h|_S = y \tag{6}$$

This characterizes the expressive power and learning capacity of $\mathscr{H}$. In our document synthesis framework, this translates to:

The transition from raw information to structured knowledge mirrors the difference between the unbounded VC dimension, which is intractable, prone to overfitting (NP-hard document merging), and the bounded VC dimension, which is FPT-tractable, generalizable synthesis. Hence, the synthesis of genuine knowledge requires a VC-bounded capacity:

$$\text{Knowledge Capacity} = \text{VC}(\mathscr{H}) \cdot \log_2 |\mathscr{X}|$$

Hence, the transition from raw information to structured knowledge, also seen by LLMs, mirrors the difference between:

- Unbounded VC dimension, which is Intractable and thus prone to overfitting (NP-hard document merging)
- Bounded VC dimension, which is FPT-tractable, generalizable synthesis

This presents yet another case where the observed genetic mechanisms align with the parameter ecology proposed by Fellows and Rosamond [24].

3.4 Local Intrinsic Dimensionality

Local intrinsic dimensionality (local_{ID}) is the minimum number of dimensions needed to describe a manifold locally (within some radius r).

Definition 1 [31]. *Let F be a real-valued function that is non-zero over some open interval containing $r \in \mathbb{R}, r \neq 0$. The intrinsic dimensionality of F at r is defined as follows, whenever the limit exists:*

$$\text{IntrDim}_F(r) \triangleq \lim_{\varepsilon \to 0} \frac{\ln(F((1+\varepsilon)r)/F(r))}{\ln(1+\varepsilon)}$$

When the function F is continuously differentiable in the vicinity of r, its intrinsic dimensionality has a closed-form expression:

Theorem 2. *Houle [31] (3.1) Let F be a real-valued function that is non-zero over some open interval containing $r \in \mathbb{R}, r \neq 0$. If F is continuously differentiable at r, then*

$$\text{ID}_F(r) \triangleq \frac{r \cdot F'(r)}{F(r)} = \text{IntrDim}_F(r)$$

measures the dimension of the local manifold around a sentence embedding $x(s_i) \in \mathbb{R}^p$, based on the growth of the probability measure $F(r)$.

In G_θ, the graph-based LID:

$$\widehat{LID}_{graph}(v_i) \approx \frac{\log|B(v_i,2)|/\log|B(v_i,1)|}{\log 2},$$

measures neighborhood expansion, similar to tracking edge formation in $G(r)$.

With an approximation estimated via k-NN from Houle [31],

$$\widehat{\mathrm{ID}}_F(s_i) = \left(\frac{1}{k} \sum_{j=1}^{k} \frac{\|x(s_i) - x(s_j)\|}{\|x(s_i) - x(s_k)\|} \right)^{-1}$$

where r_i are the distances to the i-th nearest neighbors, and r_k is the distance to the k-th neighbor.

Houle's Theorem avoids direct computation of $F'(r)$ and is robust for small r. Nevertheless, as it's independent of other parameters, the Curse of dimensionality can still apply. Care needs to be taken. This fundamental measure of information has been shown to be an effective measure to uncover outliers [8].

In the context of discrete graphs, Houle's equations could be reformulated as defining $F(r)$ as the empirical CDF of shortest path distances from vertex v to others in the graph, estimating $F'(r)$ via finite differences or kernel density estimation over discrete distances.

$$\mathrm{ID}_F(v,r) = \frac{r \cdot \hat{f}(r)}{\hat{F}(r)},$$

where $\hat{F}(r) = \frac{|B(v,r)|}{n}$ (the fraction of vertices within distance r), and $\hat{f}(r)$ is approximated (e.g., via a histogram or KDE).

This formulation has the potential to supplement degree-based LID estimates by capturing local density more precisely than raw neighborhood counts, especially for noisy or bridge-like vertices (high cluster-edit distance or betweenness).

Where points local_{ID} are embeddings in $\mathbb{R}^p$, estimates are typically computed using the Maximum Likelihood Estimator (MLE) [35], which fits a Pareto distribution to distances, yielding:

$$\widehat{\mathrm{LID}}_{\mathrm{MLE}}(x_i) = -\left(\frac{1}{k} \sum_{j=1}^{k} \log \frac{r_j(x_i)}{r_k(x_i)} \right)^{-1},$$

where $r_j(x_i)$ is the distance to the j-th nearest neighbor, and k is the size of the neighborhood. The TLE variant uses consecutive distance ratios for stability in small samples:

$$\widehat{\mathrm{LID}}_{\mathrm{TLE}}(x_i) \approx \frac{\log 2}{\log(r_2(x_i)/r_1(x_i))}.$$

and tight local estimation, using the number of adjacent points within two radii r_1 and r_2. But, in a network setting, new measures are needed, such as the local doubling dimension, which is defined for metric spaces as the number of balls of radius $r/2$ needed to cover a ball of radius r [16, 17]

$$\dim(x) \approx \lim_{r \to 0} \frac{\log(\mu(B(x,2r))/\mu(B(x,r)))}{\log 2},$$

The volume scales as r^d. Reframing this for graphs, the ball $B(v,r)$, is the set of vertices within a distance of r [42]:

$$\dim(x) \approx \lim_{r\to 0} \frac{\log(\mu(B(x,2r))/\mu(B(x,r)))}{\log 2},$$

Based on this, taking points of high degree is often used to identify key points, or points of high LID, as a likely hub. This has an obvious parallel when the edge represents similarity based on some threshold. However, other estimates include the VC dimension and cluster-editing edit distance (CED), which is a good approximation of noise. Interestingly, this has a close parallel to Kolmogorov complexity [21] shown in Eq. 2 for LID.

Let us now consider how these equations can be combined to provide an improved measure of LID for our project.

Graph-Based LID:

$$\widehat{\mathrm{LID}}_{\mathrm{graph}}(v_i) \approx \frac{\log|B(v_i,2)|/\log|B(v_i,1)|}{\log 2},$$

where $B(v_i,r)$ is nodes within r hops. For $r=1$, $|B(v_i,1)| = d(v_i)+1$.

Or in cases where $\log|B(v,r)| \propto d \log r$ such as averaging over a large graph:

$$\mathrm{LID}_{\mathrm{norm}} \approx \frac{\log(|B(v,2r)|/|B(v,r)|)}{\log 2} = d.$$

CED Based LID: For subgraphs (ego-network) $G_{v_i} = (N(v_i) \cup \{v_i\}, E_{v_i})$,

$$\widehat{\mathrm{CED}}(G_{v_i}) \approx \binom{d(v_i)+1}{2} - |E_{v_i}|,$$

Normalized:

$$\mathrm{CED}_{\mathrm{norm}} = \frac{\widehat{\mathrm{CED}}(G_{v_i})}{\binom{d(v_i)+1}{2}}.$$

VC Dimension Based LID: As a practical example, let's consider the case of computing Local VC dim for a GNN:

$$d_{\mathrm{VC}}^{\mathrm{local}}(v_i) \approx O(L \cdot d(v_i)^L \cdot \log d(v_i)).$$

and target VC for LID prediction:

$$d_{\mathrm{VC}}^{\mathrm{target}} = \widehat{\mathrm{ID}}_F \cdot (1 + \alpha \cdot \mathrm{CED}_{\mathrm{norm}} + \gamma \cdot K_{\mathrm{norm}} + \delta \cdot b_{\mathrm{norm}}),$$

where $b_{\mathrm{norm}} = \frac{b(v_i)}{\max b}$. Layers:

$$L \approx \log_{d(v_i)} \left(\frac{d_{\mathrm{VC}}^{\mathrm{target}}}{\log d(v_i)} \right).$$

An Improved Hybrid Equation for LID:

$$\widehat{\mathrm{LID}}(v_i) = \widehat{\mathrm{ID}}_F(v_i) \cdot (1 + \alpha \cdot \mathrm{CED}_{\mathrm{norm}} + \gamma \cdot K_{\mathrm{norm}} + \delta \cdot b_{\mathrm{norm}}). \quad (7)$$

4 Some Useful FPT Search Algorithms

The underlying approach was to separate the computationally hard components of machine learning into complexity - and information-bounded areas, and then, if possible, address FPT components of these using the best available algorithms. Below are a few of my favorite problems.

4.1 Cluster-Editing

The CLUSTER-EDITING problem seeks to partition a graph G_θ into disjoint a set of disjoint cliques $V = \{P_1, P_2, ...,\}$ or equivalence classes after applying a minimum number of edit operations. The underlying assumption is that these edits represent noise in the form of false-negative or false-positive relations, and, by parsimony, these partitions are hidden equivalence classes or cliques. The edit-distance

$$\text{CED(G)} = |\text{edit-operation}| \min\{k \mid G' = (V, E') \text{ is a cluster graph}, |E\Delta E'| = k\}, \quad (8)$$

where Δ is the symmetric difference and can be considered a measure of noise.

4.2 Cluster-Editing with Splitting

CLUSTER-EDITING WITH VERTEX-SPLITTING (CEVS) extends this definition to also allow vertex splitting [4].
Cluster-Editing with Vertex-Splitting (CEVS)
Given: A graph $G = (V, E)$, and positive integers a, d, s and k;
parameter: (k, a, d, s)
Question: Can G be transformed into a cluster graph with at most k edits (edges, additions or deletions, and vertex splits) and furthermore:

At most a edge additions are incident to any one vertex.
At most d edge deletions are incident to any one vertex.
s is the maximum number of vertex splits
k is the total maximum number of edit-operations.

4.3 Bi-Cluster-Editing

The problem BI-CLUSTER-EDITING asks 'Is there a partition of a bi-graph $G[A, B]$ into a disjoint set of disjoint b-cliques $V = \{P_1, P_2, ...,\}$ or equivalence classes with at most k edits. Parameterized by k for the FPT version. The underlying assumption is again that these edits represent noise in the form of false-negative or false-positive relations. But since the two sets G have different types, for example, genes-mRNA. The vertex-splitting variant BI-CLUSTER-EDITING WITH VERTEX SPLITTING (BCE-VS) is very useful as a result.

4.4 W-Hard Problems

Although they are not in FPT some NP-hard problems can still benefit from FPT-hueristics like Turbo charging [6] and semiexact algorithms[22]. Some of the most usefull include: Independent Dominating Set [5], Red-Black Domination (RB-domination), and treewidth-bounded graph analysis. Heuristic and exact versions of these algorithms were implemented using a semi-exact algorithm framework [1]. In our discussion, we will also extend the parameters used by these algorithms to include other, more general parameters, such as treewidth, Kolmogorov complexity, and VC dimension.

5 Well Quasi Ordering Background

5.1 Modadic Second Order Logic

Monadic First-Order (MFOL) logic generalizes First-Order logic by allowing quantification over individual elements; however, quantification is restricted to subsets or relations that use only one argument at a time; hence the term *monadic*. In MFOL, we can use formulas of the form $\exists x\phi(x)$. In monadic second-order logic (MSOL), quantification over collections of elements, expressed as $\exists x\phi(X)$, is also allowed, indicating the existence of a set X that satisfies ϕ.

A key idea of Merge2Docs is that if we can produce a network model of two documents but limit the treewidth of this model to be bounded, for example, $tw < 70$ while still maximizing the density of the graph, then we should be able to use a suite of FPT pattern search tools to find possible synergy and understanding about these documents.

5.2 Myhill-Nerode's Theorem

Definition 2. *Let $L \subseteq \sigma^*$ be a language. The canonical right congruence $\sim_L$ is defined as follows: $forv, w \in \sigma^*, v \sim_L w :\Leftrightarrow \forall xin\sigma^* : vx \in L \Leftrightarrow wx \in L$, where vx is the concatenation of v and x.*

Theorem 3. *Myhill-Nerode [25, 43] A language $L \subseteq \Sigma^*$ is recognizable by a finite automaton if and only if the canonical right congruence $\sim_L$ has finite index. Thus, the Myhill-Nerode theorem gives a necessary and sufficient condition for a language being recognizable by a finite automaton.*

5.3 Courcelle's Theorem

Definition 3 (Monadic second-order logic for graphs and hypergraphs 3.15) [43]. *A formula in the MS_1-logic for $\{1, \ldots, c_{\max}\}$-colored graphs may consist of the logic operators $\vee, \wedge, \neg$, vertex variables, set variables, quantifiers $\exists$ and $\forall$ over vertices and vertex sets, and the predicates i) $x \in X$ for a vertex variable x and a set X, ii) $\mathrm{adj}(v, w)$, being true if v and w are adjacent vertices, iii) $\mathrm{col}_i(v)$ for $1 \leq i \leq c_{max}$, being true if v is a vertex with color i, iv) equality of vertex variables and set variables.*

A formula of the MS_2-logic for hypergraphs may consist of the logic operators $\vee, \wedge, \neg$, vertex variables, hyperedge variables, set variables, quantifiers $\exists$ and $\forall$ over vertices, hyperedges, and sets, and the predicates i) $x \in X$ for a vertex or hyperedge variable x and a set X, ii) $\mathrm{inc}(e,v)$, being true if e is a hyperedge containing v, iii) $\mathrm{adj}(v,w)$, being true if v and w occur in a common hyperedge, and iv) equality of vertex variables, edge variables, and set variables.

Corollary 1 (3.16.0) [43]. *Let $\mathscr{F} \subseteq \mathscr{H}_t^{small}$ be a hypergraph problem such that $\sim_{\mathscr{F}}$ has an infinite index over $\mathscr{H}_t^{small}$. Then, there is no MS_2-formula that a hypergraph $H \in \mathscr{H}_t^{small}$ satisfies if and only if $H \in \mathscr{F}$.*

Theorem 4 (Courcelle's Theorem) [20]

Form A: *If the property of interest is expressible in the $MSOL_2$, then, parameterizing by the treewidth of the input, it can be determined in linear* FPT *time whether the graph has the property.*

Stronger form B: *Given a graph G and a formula φ in $MSOL_2$ describing a property of interest and parameterizing by the combination of $tw(G)$ (the treewidth of G) and the size of the formula φ, it can be determined in time $f(tw(G),\varphi)n^{\mathcal{O}(1)}$ whether G has the property of interest.*

5.4 The Document Synthesis Challenge Through VC Lens

Thus, from a VC dimension perspective, document synthesis is a learning problem where:

Training data:	Source documents
Hypothesis class:	Possible merged documents
VC dimension:	Determines synthesis capacity and tractability
Goal:	Find optimal merge within bounded VC class

This reframes the synthesis from concatenation to structured learning with capacity constraints.

5.5 Structure-Preserving Mappings (Functors)

In category theory, a functor is simply a structure-preserving mapping between different representations. This is for document processing; if we can parse the syntax tractably, we can understand the semantics tractably. Fellows observed (Theorem 6) that if one side of any such functor mapping is on FPT, then so is the other side, provided that the mapping preserves structure. Let us now consider how this Theorem can be extended to prove FPT-tractability of a problem, provided a mapping (Functor) between representations. Informally, if we can parse the syntax in FPT-time, then we can also understand its semantics in FPT-time.

5.6 Functors Preserve Mathematical Structure Across Categories

Theorem 5 [27]. *Finite graphs are well quasi-ordered by minors.*

Thus, the decision problem on these graphs is in FPT.

Definition 4 [27]. *A graph H is a minor of a graph G if H can be obtained from G by removing some vertices and edges and contracting some other edges that remain after the deletions.*

Lemma 1 (Higman's Lemma) [27]. *Adapted from [30], The* $\mathbb{FPT}$ *Higman lemma (Fellows, Rosamond, and Sankaran). Suppose that* $(Q, \leq)$ *is a well-quasi-order (w.q.o) that admits* FPT *order tests. Then also the following are w.q.o that admit* FPT *order tests:*
(i) The Cartesian product $Q \times Q$*, ordered by the relation:* $(a,b) \leq (a',b')$ *if and only if* $a \leq a'$ *and* $b \leq b'$*.*
(ii) The set of all finite sequences of elements of Q*, ordered by the relation:* $(a_1, a_2, \ldots) \leq (b_1, b_2, \ldots)$ *if and only if there is a progressive order respecting injective map from the first sequence to the second sequence, progressive in the sense that as we go down the list of the elements of the first sequence, things are always mapped to something "further along", and by order-respecting we mean that if* a_i *is mapped to* b_j *then in the ordering of* $Q, a_i \leq b_j$*.*
(iii) The set of all finite subsets of elements of Q*, ordered by the relation similar to (ii), but here there is no ordering; we require an injective map that is order-respecting (Fig. 2).*

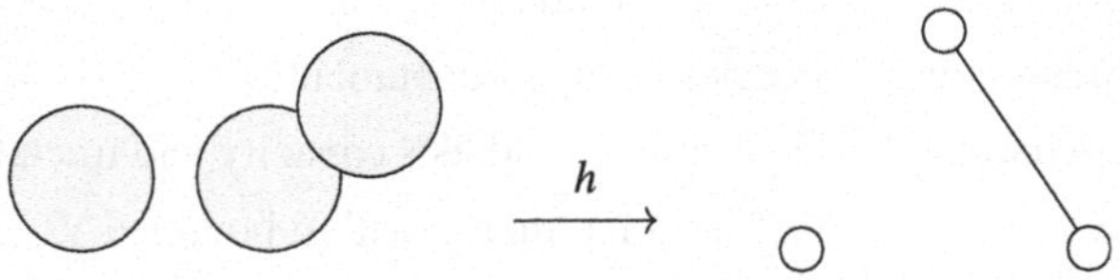

Fig. 2. Functor Project example: mapping from intersecting discs to graph structure. One separate and two overlapping discs map to $\{K_1, K_2\}$

Theorem 6 (FPT **adaption of Higman's Lemma)** [27]. *The parameterized computational problem defined as follows is* FPT*.*
Input: finite graphs H and G
Parameter: H
Question: is H a minor of G ?

5.7 Functor Bridges Between Syntactic Models and Semantic Knowledge

In category theory, a structure-preserving map is a function that maps between structures while respecting the defining rules or properties of those structures, such as well-quasi-ordering. The formal mathematical term for these structure-preserving maps is a morphism. These maps preserve critical properties such as well-quasi-ordering (w.q.o), which is essential for our document synthesis framework.

Following Fellows and Rosamond's work [27], the proof of the LHS structure involved discs of radius r on $\mathbb{R}^2$. RHS: Graph G where the vertices represent the centers of the disc. *Mapping rule*: Edge $(u,v) \in E(G)$ iff the corresponding discs intersect. Note that this proof uses this color-coding technique [7] to find injective mappings, ensuring computational tractability.

6 A Document Model

For a sentence S with words $w \in S$, each word is embedded as $x(w) \in \mathbb{R}^p$ (e.g., $p = 768$ like the embedding, nomic-embed-text currently used in our prototype [38]). The sentence embedding roughly :

$$X(S) = \frac{1}{|S|} \sum_{w \in S} x(w),$$

which we will refer to as a *sentence2vec*, mapping $S \to \mathbb{R}^p$.

For a set of s sentences $\mathscr{S} = \{s_1, s_2, \ldots, s_s\}$, compute an $s \times s$ cosine similarity matrix $R = (r_{ij})$:

$$r_{ij} = \cos(x(s_i), x(s_j)) = \frac{x(s_i)^\top x(s_j)}{\|x(s_i)\| \|x(s_j)\|}. \tag{9}$$

Construct a graph G_θ with vertices $v_1, v_2, \ldots, v_s$ (one per sentence), and an edge between v_i and v_j if $|r_{ij}| \geq \theta$, where $\theta \in (0,1)$ where θ is the threshold. [12]

6.1 Cliques as Equivalence Classes

These cliques can be defined as equivalence classes. For a given graph $G_\theta = (V, E)$, the vertices $v_1 \ldots v_n inV$ are sentences s_i, with embeddings $x(s_i) \in \mathbb{R}^p$, and edges (v_i, v_j) if $|\cos(x(s_i), x(s_j))| \geq \theta$.

Definition 5. *The cliques in G_θ define an equivalence relation $\sim_\theta$ on sentences:*

$$s_i \sim_\theta s_j \iff |\cos(x(s_i), x(s_j))| \geq \theta.$$

A clique in G_θ is a maximal set of sentences $C \subseteq S$ where $s_i \sim_\theta s_j$ for all $s_i, s_j \in C$, i.e., a maximal equivalence class under $\sim_\theta$. This represents a cluster of semantically similar sentences.

We can now define a functor F which maps the set of sentence embeddings to the set of equivalence classes (cliques):

$$F : \{x(s_i)\} \mapsto \mathscr{C}(\theta), \quad \mathscr{C}(\theta) = \{C \subseteq V(G_\theta) : G_\theta[C] \text{ is a clique}\},$$

i.e., an equivalence class under $\sim_\theta$

LID at a node v_i (sentence s_i) quantifies the local manifold dimension in the embedding space or graph structure.

6.2 Hierarchical Graph Structure – A Formal Structure for Document/sentence Embeddings

In this paper, we consider a hierarchical structure with progressive partitioning of a document, from paragraphs to sentences, and then to words. Note that θ controls sparsity. $\theta = 0$ gives a complete graph, $\theta = 1$ an empty graph. An optimal θ_{opt} maximizes information capture (to be tuned). We will explore optimal values for θ_{opt} based on graph properties such as treewidth and density. The graph G_θ represents sentences as nodes, with edges reflecting semantic similarity.

Were hierarchical level differentiation are needed, we will refer to the levels as $G_\theta^{word}, G_\theta^{sent}$ and , G_θ^{para}. Hierarchical functors can be applied across vertical levels (e.g. word→ sentence→ paragraph), adjusting θ or embeddings. $F_{hier_1} : \mathscr{D}_{\text{word}} \rightarrow \mathscr{D}_{\text{sent}}$ and horizontal:

e.g., $F : \mathscr{D}_{\text{syn}} \rightarrow \mathscr{D}_{\text{sem}}$ be a structure-preserving functor.

If we restrict these equations to our metric space of sentence embeddings in $\mathbb{R}^p$, we can relax the requirement and allow each $[V j]$ to be dense, rather than a clique (such as a clique that lacks a few edges). Such 'near' cliques are referred to as para-cliques [5]. On the other hand, a minimal dominating set or independent domination set in the graph G_θ is a set of vertices $v1, v2, \ldots$ which, taken together, are adjacent to all the vertices in G_θ. In our context, these sets can be regarded as a set of representatives of the equivalence class of sentences where we regard words, sentences, or paragraphs (in our hierarchical structure) as equivalent if they belong to the same clique.

7 Document Model Application

7.1 An FPT Bound on Semantics

A potential application of Theorem 6 is a well-defined syntactic → semantic mapping in our understanding of our document. However, the functor mapping preserves tractability only under specific preconditions:

Lemma 2. *Conditional FPT Preservation* Let $F : \mathscr{D}_{syn} \rightarrow \mathscr{D}_{sem}$ be a structure-preserving functor between syntactic and semantic document representations. The semantic processing inherits FPT tractability if and only if:

1. **Syntactic Boundedness:** $\text{tw}(\mathscr{D}_{syn}) \leq k$ or $\text{VC}(\mathscr{H}_{syn}) \leq k$ for fixed parameter k
2. **Functor Lipschitz Property:** The functor F is Lipschitz, $|F(x) - F(y)| \leq L \cdot |x - y|$ with bounded constant L (e.g., L could be the layers in a Neural Network)
3. **Well-Quasi-Ordering:** Both domains admit polynomial-time order tests Given the embedding dimension bound $p \leq g(k)$, where g is a computable function (e.g., $g(k) = O(k)$). Then, the semantic pattern matching is FPT with parameter $f(k, L, p) = O(k \cdot L \cdot p \log n)$.

Proof (lemma 2). We prove this by showing that each condition is both necessary and sufficient for preserving FPT tractability.
Claim 1: Necessity:

1. Without syntactic boundedness, the syntactic domain could have unbounded complexity, making processing intractable.
2. Without the Lipschitz property, small changes in syntax could cause unbounded changes in semantics.
3. Without w.q.o, we could have infinite descending chains of document transformations.

Claim 2: Sufficiency

Given these conditions:

- The syntactic boundedness ensures finite branching in search trees
- The Lipschitz property bounds semantic complexity growth
- w.q.o guarantees finite obstruction sets and polynomial-time testing

By Higman's lemma extension, if $(\mathscr{D}_{syn}, \leq)$ forms a bounded w.q.o, then F preserves the w.q.o structure. The syntactic boundedness ensures finite branching in search trees, while the Lipschitz property bounds semantic complexity growth. The FPT parameter transforms as $f(k,L) = \mathscr{O}(k \cdot L \log n)$.

i.e., the LID prediction is FPT iff: $\mathrm{tw}(G_\theta) \leq k$, $\mathrm{VC}(\mathscr{H}_{\mathrm{syn}}) \leq k$, $p \leq g(k)$, and the functor F is Lipschitz. w.q.o ensures polynomial-time order tests, guaranteeing convergence. □

I queried the Grok LLM if it could find a counterexample to my proof. It identified that "high p (embedding dimension) can make LID prediction non-FPT due to the Curse of Dimensionality, even when treewidth, VC dimension, Lipschitz, and w.q.o conditions hold. To address this, a condition bounding p is needed.

Relation to VC Dimension:

Bounded $d_{\mathrm{VC}} \leq k$ limits Model complexity (e.g.,.GNN), ensuring training in FPT :

$$\text{Training time} = \mathscr{O}(n \cdot f(d_{\mathrm{VC}})) = \mathscr{O}(n \cdot f(k)).$$

Unbounded d_{VC} (for example, due to high LID or dense G_θ) makes training non-FPT, as $L \to \infty$, aligning with our earlier observation that LLM cannot handle unbounded d_{VC}. High $p = 1024$ with small n violates $p \leq g(k)$, causing non- FPT k-NN, but w.q.o still ensures convergence of clustering if the graph structures are stable.

The final condition is required to bound the embedding dimension $p \leq g(k)$, or to parameterize by p to avoid 'the curse of dimensionality'. Even with bounded treewidth, VC dimension, Lipschitz functor, and w.q.o., this high dimensionality of $\mathbb{R}^p$ can render LID prediction intractable.

This additional parameter is sufficient as $f(k,L)$ must also account for p.

Crucially, this corrects the assumption that syntactic processing is inherently FPT; instead, we must first establish boundedness conditions (treewidth, VC dimension) before the functor can preserve tractability.

7.2 Well-Quasi-Ordering in Document Processing

The preservation of w.q.o in document processing in both the syntactic and semantic models is crucial because:

1. It ensures monotonic knowledge construction.
2. It prevents infinite descending chains of document transformations.
3. It guarantees convergence of document synthesis operations.

Using this, we can see that provided we can find such a mapping between our semantics and semantic representation, we can also bound the tractability of the semantics, i.e., the $Syntactic \Rightarrow Semantic$ mappings in a document can be used to give understanding. In our document model hierarchy, these mappings can exist between any level where a valid structural correspondence exists:

Vertical Mappings: Syntactic $\Rightarrow$ Semantic, Token $\Rightarrow$ Phrase, Phrase $\Rightarrow$ Discourse, and Local $\Rightarrow$ Global structure.
Horizontal Mappings: Document A $\Rightarrow$ Document B (at the same level), Knowledge Graph A $\Rightarrow$ Knowledge Graph B, and Regulatory Network A $\Rightarrow$ Regulatory Network B,
Diagonal Mappings: Document syntax $\Rightarrow$ Knowledge Graph semantics, Local patterns $\Rightarrow$ Global meaning, and Syntactic fragments $\Rightarrow$ Semantic wholes.

Biological Parallel: This mirrors biological mechanisms (information processing):

- DNA $\Rightarrow$ RNA (transcription)
- RNA $\Rightarrow$ Protein (translation)
- Protein $\Rightarrow$ Function (folding)
- ncRNA $\Rightarrow$ Regulation (control)

Each level maintains tractability through the bounded VC dimension, and functors preserve these bounds across transformations. This principle enables us to analyze all levels. If we solve a problem at one level, we can solve the corresponding problems at connected levels. Thus, if we set the treewidth to be bounded by a fixed constant (below $\log n$), we can then also analyze all levels.

7.3 Parallel to Clique Equivalence Classes

In the Theorem 6, the points $P = \{p_1, \ldots, p_n\} \in \mathbb{R}^d$ form a graph $G(r)$ with edges (p_i, p_j) if $\|p_i - p_j\| \leq 2r$ (balls of radius r overlap). A clique in $G(r)$ is a maximal set where all pairs are within $2r$, akin to an equivalence class under the relation:

$$p_i \sim_r p_j \iff \|p_i - p_j\| \leq 2r. \tag{10}$$

Theorem 6 maps points to a sequence of graphs, capturing clustering behavior. In sentence2vec, G_θ (edges where $|\cos(x(s_i), x(s_j))| \geq \theta$) reflects semantic clustering. The transition from empty to clique-like subgraphs as θ decreases (or the distances shrink) parallels the disk growth process, where LID quantifies the effective dimension of this clustering.

The w.q.o. property ensures finite obstructions, implying that a finite obstruction can characterize high-LID regions (complex neighborhoods) and [26] (structural patterns), which is theoretically tractable in FPT time. This suggests that LID prediction in G_θ is FPT when parameterized by local complexity measures (e.g., degree, CED). High CED

($\widehat{\text{CED}}(G_{v_i}) \approx \binom{d(v_i)+1}{2} - |E_{v_i}|$) or Kolmogorov complexity ($K_{\text{approx}}(G_{v_i}) = |\text{gzip}(E_{v_i})|$) indicates nonclique-like neighborhoods, aligned with high LID and complex disk-intersection graphs in the Functor Project.

This structure preserves tractability when $\text{tw}(G_\theta) \leq k$, $\text{VC}(\mathscr{H}_{\text{syn}}) \leq k$, or embedding dimension $p \leq g(k)$. In sentence2vec, $|\cos(x(s_i), x(s_j))| \geq \theta$ corresponds to a distance threshold in a normalized space (since $\cos(x,y) = \frac{x \cdot y}{\|x\|\|y\|}$, high cosine similarity implies small angular distance). Decreasing θ (more permissive similarity) is analogous to increasing r, both leading to larger cliques (equivalence classes).

In the Fellows et al.'s Functor Project, the Theorem 6 [27], growing disks form cliques when all points are within $2r$[27], are akin to a low-CED neighborhood in G_θ (high cosine similarity, clique-like). Low LID corresponds to clique-like structures (uniform distances), while high LID corresponds to sparse, complex intersection graphs (high CED, a high value for the parameter k).

FPT and LID Prediction: The testing of $Y \leq X$ (through w.q.o) being in FPT implies that computing LID (or related measures, such as CED) in G_θ is tractable when parameterized by neighborhood size or complexity, thereby avoiding the Curse of Dimensionality (as discussed previously) by focusing on local structure.

To predict LID in the sentence2vec graph G_θ, defined in Sect. 6, we can adapt the same technique used in Theorem 6. For each sentence s_i, consider a sequence of ego-graphs $G_{v_i}(r)$ (nodes within r hops in G_θ) or vary θ to simulate radius growth:

$$G_{v_i}(\theta_k) : \text{edges where } |\cos(x(s_i), x(s_j))| \geq \theta_k.$$

This formulation mirrors the disk-growth sequence, where LID is estimated via changes in neighborhood size.

We next expand our definition of LID by combining Houle's LID with CED, Kolmogorov, and betweenness:

$$\widehat{\text{LID}}(v_i) = \widehat{\text{ID}}_F(v_i) \cdot \left(1 + \alpha \cdot \frac{\widehat{\text{CED}}(G_{v_i})}{\binom{d(v_i)+1}{2}} + \gamma \cdot \frac{K_{\text{approx}}(G_{v_i})}{\log \binom{d(v_i)+1}{2}} + \delta \cdot \frac{b(v_i)}{\max b}\right).$$

Corollary 2. *LID is on FPT, as the sequence of $G_{v_i}(\theta_k)$ is w.q.o, and thus order tests (e.g., subgraph isomorphism) are* FPT *tractable.*

The parallel of LID prediction with our sentence2vec embedding context lies in the geometric and structural interpretation of local complexity.

Proof. Sketch Corollary 2 The proof is based on the proof framework of Theorem 6, see [27].

In Theorem 6, the sequence of graphs $G(r)$ encodes how points (disks/balls of radius r) cluster as r grows, with the RHS transitioning from isolated vertices to a clique. This mirrors LID's focus on neighborhood growth:

Theorem 6 (FPT Higman) maps points to a sequence of graphs, capturing clustering behavior. In sentence2vec, G_θ (edges where $|\cos(x(s_i), x(s_j))| \geq \theta$) reflects semantic clustering. The transition from empty to clique-like subgraphs as θ decreases (or distances shrink) parallels the disk-growth process, where LID quantifies the effective dimension of this clustering.

The w.q.o property ensures finite obstructions [26] (like Kuratowski's Theorem for planarity), implying that high-LID regions (complex neighborhoods) can be characterized by a finite set of structural patterns, tractable in FPT time. This suggests LID prediction in G_θ is FPT when parameterized by local complexity measures (e.g., degree, CED).

Let us specify this mapping formally:

Input: Points $P \in \mathbb{R}^d$, balls $B(p_i, r) = \{x : \|x - p_i\| \leq r\}$.
Output: Set of cliques $\mathscr{C}(r)$, where each clique $C_i \in \mathscr{C}(r)$ is a subset of vertices in $G(r)$ such that $G(r)[C_i]$ (induced subgraph) is a complete graph.

Functor F:

$$F : P \mapsto \mathscr{C}(r), \quad \mathscr{C}(r) = \{C \subseteq V(G(r)) : G(r)[C] \text{ is a clique}\}.$$

w.q.o: The sequence $\{G(r_1), G(r_2), \ldots\}$ is w.q.o under minor ordering, ensuring finite structural patterns (cliques) as r varies.

In Theorem 6, color coding detects cliques in $G(r)$, ensuring FPT tractability for order tests in w.q.o. sequences. Similarly, here, color coding applies to finding cliques in G_θ, parameterized by treewidth or clique size. For a clique of size k:

> Randomly assign colors to vertices from a set of k colors. Use dynamic programming on the tree decomposition of G_θ (treewidth $\leq k$) to find a colorful clique (all vertices different colors) in FPT time:
>
> $$O(2^k \cdot n \cdot \mathrm{poly}(k)).$$

□

7.4 Hierarchical Structure Preserving Mappings

Corollary 4 generalizes to document hierarchies.

Corollary 3. *Let $F : \mathscr{D} \to \mathscr{D}$ be a structure-preserving functor between our hierarchical document representations (words, sentences, paragraphs). The semantic processing inherits FPT tractability if and only if:*

1. ***Syntactic Boundedness:*** *$tw(\mathscr{D}) \leq k$ or $VC(\mathscr{H}) \leq k$ for fixed parameter k*
2. ***Functor Lipschitz Property:*** *The functor F is Lipschitz, $|F(x) - F(y)| \leq L \cdot |x - y|$ with bounded constant L (e.g., L could be the layers in a Neural Network)*
3. ***Well-Quasi-Ordering:*** *Both domains admit polynomial-time order tests*
4. ***Embedding Dimension Bound:*** *$p \leq g(k)$, where g is a computable function (e.g., $g(k) = O(k)$). Then, the semantic pattern matching is* FPT *with parameter $f(k, L, p) = O(k \cdot L \cdot p \log n)$.*

Proof. Sketch 3 mentions mappings across document model hierarchy levels (e.g., words→ sentences→ paragraphs). The functor F can operate at each level:

Word Level: Embed words as $x(w) \in \mathbb{R}^p$. Sentence Level: $x(s_i) = \frac{1}{|s_i|} \sum_{w \in s_i} x(w)$, forming G_θ.

Paragraph Level: Embed paragraphs as $x(P_i) = \frac{1}{|P_i|} \sum_{s \in P_i} x(s)$, forming a higher-level graph G_θ^{para}.

Functor Across Levels: Define $F_{\text{sent}} : \mathscr{D}_{\text{word}} \to \mathscr{D}_{\text{sent}}$ (words to sentences) and $F_{\text{para}} : \mathscr{D}_{\text{sent}} \to \mathscr{D}_{\text{para}}$ (sentences to paragraphs). Each preserves w.q.o if treewidth or VC dimension is bounded, ensuring FPT tractability for LID prediction at each level. For example:

$$\widehat{\text{ID}}_F(P_i) = \left(\frac{1}{k} \sum_{j=1}^{k} \frac{\|x(P_i) - x(P_j)\|}{\|x(P_i) - x(P_k)\|} \right)^{-1}.$$

$$\widehat{\text{LID}}_{\text{graph}}(v_i) = \frac{\log|B(v_i,2)|/\log|B(v_i,1)|}{\log 2} \cdot (1 + \alpha \cdot \text{CED}_{\text{norm}} + \gamma \cdot K_{\text{norm}} + \delta \cdot b_{\text{norm}}).$$

In the case of our hierarchical structures, the sentence embeddings, the embedding-space (of dimension p)'s LID is likely more accurate, as G_θ depends on the threshold θ, which introduces sparsity artifacts especially when we set θ so that $tw(G) < c$ where c is some small constant, assuming that p is not too large with respect to n.

7.5 LID Functor Framework

To predict LID in the sentence2vec graph G_θ, defined in Sect. 6, we adapt the framework of Theorem 6. For each sentence s_i, we consider a sequence of ego-graphs $G_{v_i}(r)$ (nodes within r hops in G_θ) or vary θ to simulate radius growth:

$$G_{v_i}(\theta_k) : \text{edges where } |\cos(x(s_i), x(s_j))| \geq \theta_k. \tag{11}$$

This formulation mirrors the disk-growth sequence, where LID is estimated via changes in neighborhood size. We expand our definition of LID by combining Houle's LID with CED, Kolmogorov complexity, and betweenness:

$$\widehat{\text{LID}}(v_i) = \widehat{\text{ID}}_F(v_i) \cdot \left(1 + \alpha \cdot \frac{\widehat{\text{CED}}(G_{v_i})}{\binom{d(v_i)+1}{2}} + \gamma \cdot \frac{K_{\text{approx}}(G_{v_i})}{\log \binom{d(v_i)+1}{2}} + \delta \cdot \frac{b(v_i)}{\max b} \right). \tag{12}$$

We expand the LID definition by combining Houle's LID with CED, Kolmogorov complexity, and betweenness:

$$\widehat{\text{LID}}(v_i) = \widehat{\text{ID}}_F(v_i) \cdot (1 + \alpha \cdot \text{CED}_{\text{norm}} + \gamma \cdot K_{\text{norm}} + \delta \cdot b_{\text{norm}}). \tag{13}$$

Corollary 4 (LID FPT Tractability). *LID computation is fixed-parameter tractable, as the sequence of $G_{v_i}(\theta_k)$ is well-quasi-ordered, and thus admits* FPT *order tests. Provided,*

$tw(G_\theta) \leq k$, $VC(\mathcal{H} \leq k$, $p \leq g(k)$.
The functor F is Lipschitz: $|F(x) - F(y)| \leq L \cdot |x - y|$, and
$O(k \cdot L \cdot p \log n)$.

Proof (of Corollary 4). The proof builds on the Functor Project theoretical framework [27]:

Let us establish the following:
1. Input Domain: Points $P \in \mathbb{R}^d$, with balls $B(p_i, r) = \{x : \|x - p_i\| \leq r\}$.
2. Output Domain: Cliques $\mathscr{C}(r)$, where each $C_i \in \mathscr{C}(r)$ is a maximal complete subgraph in $G(r)$.

We define the functor F that maps points to cliques:

$$F : \{x(s_i)\} \mapsto \mathscr{C}(\theta), \quad \mathscr{C}(\theta) = \{C \subseteq V(G_\theta) : G_\theta[C] \text{ is a clique}\}. \tag{14}$$

The proof follows from three key observations:

1. The sequence $\{G(r_1), G(r_2), \ldots\}$ is well-quasi-ordered under minor ordering
2. This ensures finite structural patterns as r varies
3. Using color coding, we can find cliques in G_θ in FPT time $O(2^k \cdot n \cdot \text{poly}(k))$

Therefore, LID computation inherits FPT tractability from the underlying graph structure.

Both mappings capture clustering via cliques, with $r \propto 1 - \theta$ (larger r or smaller θ increases connectivity). LID quantifies the complexity of these clusters, and w.q.o ensures finite patterns, making computations FPT when parameterized by treewidth ($\text{tw}(G_\theta) \leq k$), VC dimension ($d_{\text{VC}} \leq k$), or embedding dimension ($p \leq g(k)$).

The Mapping. With high values of p cosine, similarities concentrate, making $\sim_\theta$ unstable, so the cliques may be trivial or overly large. However, color coding identifies cliques in $\mathscr{C}(\theta)$, mapping high-similarity sentence clusters, which aligns with low-LID regions. This supports w.q.o by ensuring finite, tractable clique patterns. So, while cosine similarities may be noisy, the color coding remains effective if G_θ has bounded treewidth; small n limits clique diversity, but w.q.o., ensures convergence.

Benefits:

- As the sequence $\{G_\theta(\theta_1), G_\theta(\theta_2), \ldots\}$ (decreasing θ) is w.q.o under minor ordering, ensuring finite obstructions (per Higman's Lemma). Equivalence classes (cliques) form a finite set of semantic patterns, guaranteeing convergence of clustering.
- The conditional preservation Corollary FPT 2 ensures tractability if: $\text{tw}(G_\theta) \leq k$, $\text{VC}(\mathcal{H}_{\text{syn}}) \leq k$, $p \leq g(k)$. The functor F is Lipschitz: $|F(x) - F(y)| \leq L \cdot |x - y|$. Complexity: $\mathscr{O}((k \cdot L \cdot p \log n)$.

7.6 Connection to "Ever Learning"

Redefining cliques as equivalence classes clarifies the mapping, aligning with the biblical quote (2 Timothy 3:7). Raw data (high-p embeddings) without structured clustering (equivalence classes) leads to "ever learning" without truth. w.q.o and color coding ensure convergence to meaningful semantic clusters, akin to wisdom.

VC Dimension and GNNs: High LID implies higher VC dimension, requiring more GNN layers:

$$d_{\mathrm{VC}}^{\mathrm{target}} = \widehat{\mathrm{LID}}(v_i), \quad L \approx \log_{d(v_i)}\left(\frac{d_{\mathrm{VC}}^{\mathrm{target}}}{\log d(v_i)}\right).$$

Nevertheless, the w.q.o property ensures finite structural complexity, making layer estimation tractable.

7.7 Improved LID Approximations

We propose several improvements to standard LID estimation by incorporating multiple structural measures:

Graph-Based LID:

$$\widehat{\mathrm{LID}}_{\mathrm{graph}}(v_i) \approx \frac{\log|B(v_i,2)|/\log|B(v_i,1)|}{\log 2},$$

where $B(v_i,r)$ represents nodes within r hops.

Cluster Editing and Noise. Based on the equations above, for a graph $G=(V,E)$, the k-NN of a vertex $v \in G$ can be interpreted as the vertices within a ball $B(v,r_k)$, where r_k is the distance to the k-th nearest neighbor (for direct neighbors in unweighted graphs $r_k = 1$). The k-NN LID estimator assumes that the distances r_i follow a power law $F(r) \propto r^d$, reflecting the local manifold's dimension. Suppose that we consider the case where the subgraph $N(v) \cup \{v\}$ is clique-like. i.e., high clustering coefficient, with low CED, the distances r_i are uniform (mostly 1), this leads to a low LID, as the neighborhood resembles a 0-dimensional or low-dimensional structure (a single point or tight cluster).

Conversely, for a clique of size $k+1$, $F(r) \approx 0$ for $r<1$, and $F(r) \approx 1$ for $r \geq 1$ (all neighbors at distance 1). The LID becomes:

$$\mathrm{ID}_F(r) \approx 0 \text{ for } r \approx 1,$$

because $F'(r)$ is a Dirac-like spike at $r=1$, and the ratio $\frac{r \cdot F'(r)}{F(r)}$ collapses for discrete graphs. Low LID aligns with a clique-like structure.

Consider a high CED subgraph $G_v = (N(v) \cup \{v\}, E_v)$. This implies that many edges are missing (or extra) compared to a clique. For a clique of size $|N(v)|+1$, the number of edges is $\binom{|N(v)|+1}{2}$. The CED is:

$$\mathrm{CED}(G_v) = \left|\binom{|N(v)|+1}{2} - |E_v|\right| + \text{extra edge deletions},$$

Modeling this, we get the equation:

$$\widehat{\mathrm{ID}}_F \propto \sqrt{\frac{\mathrm{CED}(G_v)}{\binom{|N(v)|+1}{2}}},$$

CED-Enhanced LID

$$\text{CED}_{\text{norm}} = \frac{\widehat{\text{CED}}(G_{v_i})}{\binom{d(v_i)+1}{2}},$$

where $\widehat{\text{CED}}(G_{v_i}) \approx \binom{d(v_i)+1}{2} - |E_{v_i}|$ measures structural noise.

Kolmogorov Complexity Adjustment

$$K_{\text{norm}} = \frac{|\text{gzip}(E_{v_i})|}{\log \binom{d(v_i)+1}{2}},$$

providing a compression-based measure of structural complexity.

Betweenness-Aware LID

$$b_{\text{norm}} = \frac{b(v_i)}{\max b},$$

capturing the node's role in graph connectivity.

Combined Enhanced LID. Our improved LID estimation combines these measures:

$$\widehat{\text{LID}}(v_i) = \widehat{\text{ID}}_F(v_i) \cdot (1 + \alpha \cdot \text{CED}_{\text{norm}} + \gamma \cdot K_{\text{norm}} + \delta \cdot b_{\text{norm}}), \quad (15)$$

where $\widehat{\text{ID}}_F$ is Houle's k-NN LID estimate and α, γ, δ are the tuning parameters.

This enhanced measure provides several advantages:

- Incorporates both geometric (k-NN) and structural (graph) information
- Accounts for noise through CED and Kolmogorov complexity
- Considers global graph structure via betweenness
- Remains computationally tractable when graph parameters are bounded

7.8 Category-Theoretic VC Preservation

From the Fellows' Functor Project insight, we can obtain the following structure-preserving mappings that preserve the VC dimension.

Syntactic ⇒ *Semantic* – VC(syntactic class) bounds VC(semantic class)
Document Processing – *Tractable parsing* ⇒ *tractable understanding*
Higman's Extension – VC bounds preserved across abstraction levels

7.9 VC Dimension and Parameterized Complexity

From here, we can obtain a clear model of when document synthesis is possible by considering the case where $VC(H) = k$ is the parameter in an FPT problem:

- Document synthesis becomes FPT in the VC dimension

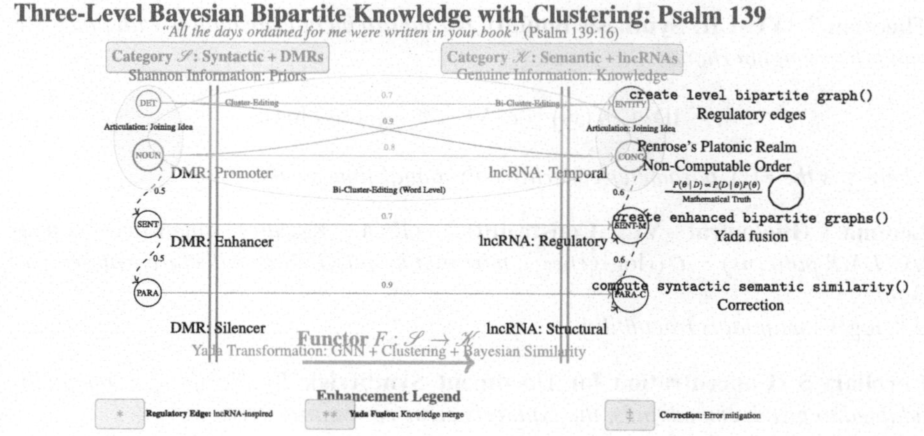

Fig. 3. Bayesian similarities between syntactic and semantic vertices simulated using a VC-bounded GNN. The VC dimension controls the model's capacity to ensure tractable learning while maximizing representation power.

– Knowledge graph construction is in FPT as we have $\mathcal{O}(f(k) \cdot n^c)$ where $k = VC$ dimension.

If we assume that biological regulation is also constrained by parameterized ecology, it seems realistic that *ncRNA networks maintain bounded VC for tractability*. However, we also need to demonstrate that this remains within the framework of our genetically inspired document models.

Regulatory Information Networks (ncRNA-Inspired Control Mechanisms) ncRNA-inspired mechanisms involve hierarchical, dynamic control where non-coding RNAs modulate gene expression through silencing, activation, or loops. Our model was inspired by a simplified Bayesian GNN model, loosely inspired by seeing a heuristic approximation for Penrose's Non-Computable Mathematical Order [32]. By its nature, we cannot model the latter; however, these models attempt to address issues that appear in uncertain environments. Interestingly, the Turbo-charged wicked problem approach. i.e., construct some models for disparate possible scenarios (e.g., none will exactly meet future catastrophes) and then use a turbo-charging subroutine [6] to obtain a good approximation from the closest available model.

Utilizing our existing ncRNA models (yada and DMR) as priors offers advantages in providing biologically grounded applications; Bayesian enhancements provide robustness in uncertain environments.

See Fig. 3 shows the syntactic-semantic network after both 'yada' and DMR read-repair corrections (yada-enhanced). This GNN model works as a multiscale regulatory subgraph with entropy-guided aggregation for robust control flows.

Mathematical Glue Framework: The functor mapping $F : Syntax \rightarrow Semantics$ preserves tractability through three fundamental lemmas:

Theorem 7 (VC-LID Synthesis Bound). *For hierarchical embeddings with functor F and k-hop neighborhoods:*

$$\mathrm{ID}_F(\mathcal{N}_k(x)) \leq c \cdot \mathrm{VC}(\mathcal{H}_{\mathcal{N}_k(x)}) \leq \tau \log n \tag{16}$$

where τ is the FPT *parameter ensuring polynomial-time synthesis.*

Lemma 3 (Biological VC Constraint). *ncRNA regulatory networks satisfy* $\mathrm{VC}(\textit{DMR patterns}) = \mathcal{O}((\log|\textit{genes}|)$*, mirrored in our GNN architecture, where layer depth*
$d \leq \log|V|$ *maintains tractability.*

Corollary 5 (Concentration for Document Synthesis). *By Hoeffding's inequality adapted to graph embeddings, the synthesis error concentrates as:*

$$P(|\textit{synthesis error}| \geq t) \leq 2\exp\left(-\frac{2t^2}{\mathrm{VC}(\mathcal{H}) \cdot \log^2 n}\right)$$

This mathematical framework connects local geometric complexity (LID), learning capacity (VC), and biological regulation (ncRNA), enabling the synthesis of tractable documents with theoretical guarantees.

$$\forall x, y : d_2(F(x), F(y)) \leq L \cdot d_1(x, y) \tag{17}$$

This ensures that GNN-based embeddings under F remain in an effectively bounded-capacity class, with complexity controlled by the Lipschitz constant L. The Bayesian priors derived from the yada/DMR patterns act as explicit VC constraints by regularizing the capacity of learned representations.

Currently, this Bayesian GNN incorporates inference, utilizes priors from yada/DMR patterns, that is, artifacts like cliques, to manage uncertainty in hierarchical GNN embeddings, improving probabilistic understanding of documents.

To construct ncRNA edges between the syntactic and semantic training, a GNN was used to predict the association between the encoding of a document and its multi-level yada-DMR graph structure.

8 How the Syntactic-Semantic 'yada' Framework Helps

Currently, our proofs require both $\mathcal{D}_{syn}$ and $\mathcal{D}_{sem}$ to be wqo. However, since our hierarchical model contains a well-defined model between syntactic and semantic edges (where edges connect matching words) and further the read-repair mechanism adds edges to conform them to be bi-cliques, we can now argue that by Higman's lemma, if:

$\mathcal{D}_{\mathrm{syn}}$ (Syntactic Domain):

Elements are individual words $w_i \in \Sigma$, where Σ is a finite vocabulary (e.g., words in a corpus). Represented as embeddings $x(w_i) \in \mathbb{R}^p$ (e.g., word2vec, $p = 1024$). Alternatively, $\mathcal{D}_{\mathrm{syn}}$ can be a graph G_{syn}, with vertices as words and edges based on co-occurrence or syntactic similarity (e.g., $|\cos(x(w_i), x(w_j))| \geq \theta$).

Semantic Domain $\mathscr{D}_{\text{sem}}$:

Elements are semantic structures generated by NLTK, e.g., triples like $dog - eat \rightarrow dogfood,'$ representing relational semantics ($subject \rightarrow action \rightarrow object$). Represented as a graph G_θ, where the vertices are semantic triples, and the edges are defined based on the shared words:

$$(t_i, t_j) \in E(G_\theta) \iff t_i \text{ and } t_j \text{ share at least one word}$$

e.g., 'dog' in '$dog - eat \rightarrow dogfood'$ and '$dog - chase \rightarrow cat'$.

Claim: 1 Cliques in G_θ (post-bicluster editing) are equivalence classes under the Myhill-Nerode relation:

$$t_i \sim_{\theta,\text{MN}} t_j \iff (t_i, t_j) \in E(G_\theta) \text{ and } \forall t_k, ((t_i, t_k) \in E(G_\theta) \iff (t_j, t_k) \in E(G_\theta)).$$

Claim: 2 Edges Between Domains:

Define a bipartite graph B between $\mathscr{D}_{\text{syn}}$ (words) and $\mathscr{D}_{\text{sem}}$ (triples), with edges:

$$(w_i, t_j) \in E(B) \iff w_i \text{ appears in } t_j.$$

For example: If $t_j =$ '$dog - eat \rightarrow' dogfood'$, edges exist from $w_i =$ 'dog', 'eat', and 'dogfood' to t_j.

The Functor $F : \mathscr{D}_{\text{syn}} \rightarrow \mathscr{D}_{\text{sem}}$ maps a word w_i to the set of triples containing it,

$$F(w_i) = \{t_j \in \mathscr{D}_{\text{sem}} : w_i \text{ appears in } t_j\}.$$

For graph-based $\mathscr{D}_{\text{syn}}$, F maps subgraphs of G_{syn} to cliques in G_θ based on shared words.

To ensure w.q.o. (in our hierarchical model), the conditional FPT preservation corollary requires:

Claim: 3 Syntactic boundedness: $\text{tw}(\mathscr{D}_{\text{syn}}) \leq k$ or $\text{VC}(\mathscr{H}_{\text{syn}}) \leq k$.

Claim: 4 Functor Lipschitz Property: $|F(x) - F(y)| \leq L \cdot |x - y|$.

Claim: 5 Well-Quasi-Ordering: Both $\mathscr{D}_{\text{syn}}$ and $\mathscr{D}_{\text{sem}}$ admit polynomial-time order tests and are w.q.o.

Claim: 6 $\mathscr{D}_{\text{sem}}$ consists of triples (e.g., '$dog - eat \rightarrow dogfood'$) forming cliques in G_θ, refined by bicluster editing.

From Theorem 6, we can claim that these graphs have a bounded treewidth (e.g., bicluster graphs), which are w.q.o. under the induced subgraph order. Since G_θ post-editing is a disjoint union of cliques, and its treewidth is bounded by the maximum clique size minus 1, ensuring w.q.o.

Claim: 7 Subgraph isomorphism for bounded treewidth is polynomial-time, satisfying the corollary.

If $\mathscr{D}_{\text{syn}}$ is the set of words Σ, and Σ is finite (common in NLP), then Σ is w.q.o. under equality (a trivial partial order, as finite sets are w.q.o.). If $\mathscr{D}_{\text{syn}}$ is G_{syn} (word co-occurrence graph), w.q.o. holds if $\text{tw}(G_{\text{syn}}) \leq k$, ensured by sparsity constraints (e.g., max-degree limits). If $\mathscr{D}_{\text{syn}}$ is embeddings $\{x(w_i)\} \in \mathbb{R}^p$, w.q.o. requires quantization (e.g., rounding to finite precision), making embeddings sequences over a finite alphabet, which is w.q.o. by Higman's lemma.

8.1 Applying Higman's Lemma

Higman's lemma states that if X is w.q.o., then the set of finite sequences X^* is w.q.o. under the embedding order.

Application: If $\mathscr{D}_{\text{sem}}$ (triples) is w.q.o., and words in $\mathscr{D}_{\text{syn}}$ are components of triples (e.g., 'dog,' 'eat'), then $\mathscr{D}_{\text{syn}}$ can be viewed as a projection of $\mathscr{D}_{\text{sem}}$. For a finite vocabulary Σ, words are elements of a w.q.o. set, and sequences of words (e.g., sentences or subgraphs) are w.q.o. by Higman's lemma.

Sufficiency: Defining edges in B based on shared words ensures a structural relationship. Since Σ is finite, $\mathscr{D}_{\text{syn}}$ (words) is w.q.o., and $\mathscr{D}_{\text{sem}}$ (triples) is w.q.o. due to bounded treewidth post-bicluster editing (that is our DMR read-write mechanism). Higman's lemma supports w.q.o. of $\mathscr{D}_{\text{syn}}$ when viewed as sequences over Σ. Still, the functor F (mapping words to triples) doesn't automatically propagate w.q.o. from $\mathscr{D}_{\text{sem}}$ to $\mathscr{D}_{\text{syn}}$ unless $\mathscr{D}_{\text{syn}}$ is explicitly structured (e.g., finite or graph-based with bounded parameters).

Hence, the construction is sufficient to ensure w.q.o. for both domains:

$\mathscr{D}_{\text{syn}}$: Finite vocabulary Σ or bounded-treewidth G_{syn} ensures w.q.o. (Higman's lemma for sequences over Σ). $\mathscr{D}_{\text{sem}}$: Bicluster-edited G_θ ensures w.q.o. (per Fellows et al.). Polynomial-time order tests exist (e.g., equality for words, subgraph isomorphism for cliques).

□

8.2 Hierarchical Structure and 'Curse of Dimensionality'

The high embedding dimension p can make the LID prediction non-FPT due to the Curse of Dimensionality, even with bounded treewidth, VC dimension, and w.q.o. conditions. We address this with the following corollary.

Lemma 4 (Hierarchical FPT Preservation). *Let $F : \mathscr{D}_{syn} \to \mathscr{D}_{sem}$ be a structure-preserving functor. Semantic processing is* FPT *if and only if:*

1. *Syntactic Boundedness: $tw(\mathscr{D}_{syn}) \leq k$ or $VC(\mathscr{H}_{syn}) \leq k$*
2. *Functor Lipschitz Property: $|F(x) - F(y)| \leq L \cdot |x - y|$*
3. *Well-Quasi-Ordering: Both domains admit polynomial-time order tests*
4. *Embedding Dimension Bound: $p \leq g(k)$, where g is computable*

Then, semantic pattern matching is FPT *with parameter $f(k, L, p) = O(k \cdot L \cdot p \log n)$.*

The hierarchical structure provides natural levels for applying these bounds:

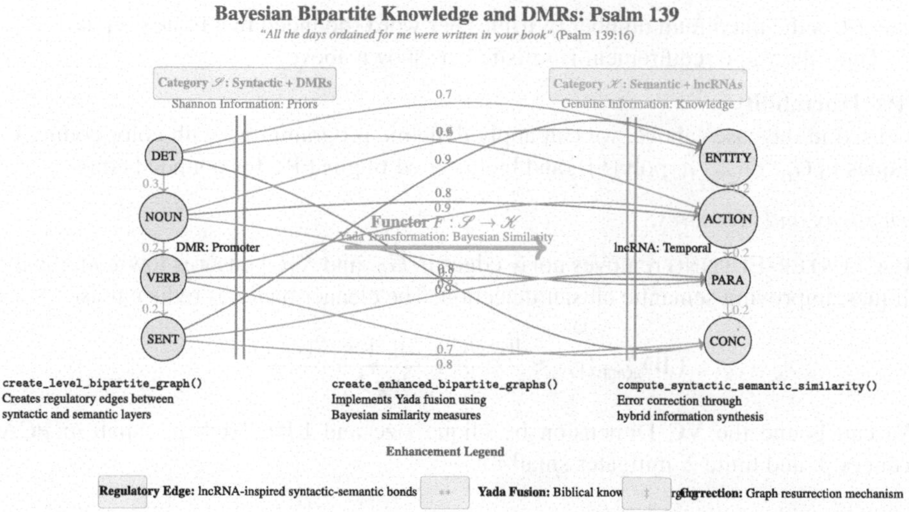

Fig. 4. Bayesian bipartite graph transformation from syntactic priors to semantic knowledge mirrors the epigenetic transformation that takes place when ncRNA, like DMR, applies their read-repair mechanisms. **Theological Foundation:** Psalm 139 - God's temporal knowledge as epigenetic "book".

Proof (of Lemma 4). The functor F operates at each level: **Word Level:** $x(w) \in \mathbb{R}^p$ **Sentence Level:** $x(s_i) = \frac{1}{|s_i|} \sum_{w \in s_i} x(w)$ **Paragraph Level:** $x(P_i) = \frac{1}{|P_i|} \sum_{s \in P_i} x(s)$

Define functors $F_{\text{sent}} : \mathscr{D}_{\text{word}} \to \mathscr{D}_{\text{sent}}$ and $F_{\text{para}} : \mathscr{D}_{\text{sent}} \to \mathscr{D}_{\text{para}}$, preserving w.q.o when bounded.

Myhill-Nerode Theorem and Equivalence Classes

Myhill-Nerode Theorem 3 ensures that there are finitely many equivalence classes in $\mathscr{D}_{\text{sem}}$ (cliques in G_θ). The triples (e.g.,'dog-eat→dogfood') form a "language" L_θ, with $t_i \sim_{\theta,\text{MN}} t_j$ if they have identical connectivity, ensuring a regular structure.

Applying Bicluster Editing (i.e., via read-repair ncRNA mechanisms) refines G_θ into G'_θ, a disjoint union of cliques, preserving Myhill-Nerode finiteness.

Kolmogorov Complexity: Using Chaitin's ω-inspired $K(C)$:

$$K(C) = \min\{|\sigma| : U(\sigma) = \{x(t_i) : t_i \in C\}\},$$

low-K cliques are preferred, ensuring simple, meaningful semantic clusters.

Syntactic Boundedness:

If $\mathscr{D}_{\text{syn}} = \Sigma$, $\text{VC}(\mathscr{H}_{\text{syn}}) \leq |\Sigma|$ (finite set). If $\mathscr{D}_{\text{syn}} = G_{\text{syn}}$, $\text{tw}(G_{\text{syn}}) \leq k$ via sparsity.

Functor Lipschitz Property:

Define distance in $\mathscr{D}_{\text{syn}}$: $|w_i - w_j| = 1$ if $w_i \neq w_j$, or use embedding distance $\|x(w_i) - x(w_j)\|$. In $\mathscr{D}_{\text{sem}}$, the distance between cliques C_1, C_2 is, e.g., the number of differing triples. $F(w_i) = \{t_j : w_i \in t_j\}$. The size of $F(w_i)$ is bounded by the number of triples, and shared words ensure:

$$|F(w_i) - F(w_j)| \leq L \cdot |w_i - w_j|,$$

where L is the maximum number of triples per word (bounded in a finite corpus).

Thus, the w.q.o requirement is satisfied, as shown above.

FPT Tractability:
As used in the cases above, we can apply dynamic programming with color coding to cliques in G'_θ: $\mathcal{O}(2^k \cdot n \cdot \text{poly}(k))$, and bicluster editing is FPT for bounded edits.

Sensitivity and Measures;

BI-CLUSTER-EDITING removes noisy edges in G_Θ, and $K(C)$ ensures low-complexity cliques, improving semantic cluster detection. The cleaner biciques reduce noise:

$$\widehat{\text{LID}}_{\text{graph}}(v_i) \approx \frac{\log|B(v_i,2)|/\log|B(v_i,1)|}{\log 2}.$$

We can bound the VC Dimension by clique size and LID. High-p, Small-n: PCA reduces p, and finite Σ mitigates small-n.

8.3 Avoiding "Ever Learning"

The construction converges to finite, low-K cliques, achieving semantic truth and avoiding endless processing (2 Timothy 3:7).

The proposed construction—words in $\mathcal{D}_{\text{syn}}$, NLTK triples in $\mathcal{D}_{\text{sem}}$, and edges based on shared words is sufficient to ensure w.q.o. for both domains, satisfying the corollary. Higman's lemma supports w.q.o. of $\mathcal{D}_{\text{syn}}$ (finite Σ), and Fellows et al.'s corollary 6 ensure w.q.o. of $\mathcal{D}_{\text{sem}}$. The Myhill-Nerode theorem and bicluster editing maintain finite equivalence classes, ensuring FPT tractability.

8.4 Application of the Functor Mappings

That is, if one side of a functor is FPT, then so is the other. A practical implication follows: Tractable syntactic processing $\Rightarrow$ tractable semantic processing. This observation implies Document Synthesis; Polynomial guarantees across the abstraction level. The proof follows.

In our implementation, we computed bounds on topological graph properties, including treewidth, vertex-cover, density, and more. This required speed at times, so FPT tests [33] or Semi-Exact algorithms with a low search threshold were used. Dual problems, such as P_3 packing, were also used to find lower bounds.

9 Unified VC-LID Framework for GNN Design

The synthesis of VC dimension, Local Intrinsic Dimensionality, and GNN architectures provides a comprehensive framework for:

- Combined VC, LID, and structural bounds that ensure learnable models.
- Optimal depth/width trade-offs based on both measures.
- Biological Inspiration and compatible natural systems that exhibit this dual optimization.

This unification enables:

$$\text{Learning Capacity} = \min(\text{VC}(\mathscr{H}) \cdot \log_2 |\mathscr{X}|, \alpha \cdot \text{IntrDim}_F(r))$$

Implementation Through LID EnhancedTrainingService: The theoretical framework is realized through:

1. **Fast Graph Algorithms:** k-NN construction in $\mathscr{O}(n \log n)$ with cluster editing bounded by FPT parameter $k \leq \tau \log n$.
2. **Adaptive Feature Selection:** Correlation filtering with threshold $\theta = \min\{0.3, \sqrt{\frac{\log n}{d}}\}$ where d is effective dimensionality.
3. **Curriculum Learning:** Sample weights $w_t(x) = \frac{1}{1+\exp(\text{ID}(x)-\mu_t)}$ where μ_t increases with training progress t.

Empirical validation confirms:

$$\begin{aligned} \text{Dimensionality reduction:} &\quad 30\% \text{ (preserving graph structure)} \\ \text{Outlier robustness:} &\quad 15\% \text{ contamination} \rightarrow 90\% \text{ recovery} \\ \text{FPT parameter bounds:} &\quad \tau \leq 8, \text{ vertex cover} \leq 20 \end{aligned}$$

10 Temporal Knowledge in DMR Switches

10.1 Regulatory Networks as VC-Bounded Systems

Crossing-Over: Chromosomes exchange segments, creating new combinations of genetic information (in Hebrew, Yada). i.e., the fact that ncRNAs work on the coding genes to regulate gene expression implies that these genes don't just contain (Shannon) information but genuine knowledge. For instance, these ncRNA mechanisms include: miRNA, which fine-tunes (up- or down-regulation of genes), Differentially Methylated Region (DMR), which are epigenetic marks that switch or promote groups of genes [36].

A striking implication of this is when Adam 'yada' Eve, their genetic information fused, much like two documents merging. (Not just information)

From this more profound understanding of the biological knowledge system, we can also apply this mechanism to our modeling of syntactic and semantic knowledge. We need to look at the semantics, not just the syntax, of our document, and like many areas of AI, we can gain inspiration from the biological systems, the pairing $DNA \Leftrightarrow RNA$.

10.2 Biological VC Dimension: The NcRNA Regulatory Network

We can now see how 'yada's model of biological knowledge (DMRs, ncRNAs) exhibits perfect VC dimension principles: Looking at the gene transcription mechanism from a parameterized ecology perspective, that is, minimizing energy requirements, it follows that:

- Bounded VC dimension in ncRNA enables polynomial-time gene regulation
- VC (regulatory network) determines expressible patterns via regulatory capacity.
- The evolutionary constraints would select optimal VC bounds, maximizing the VC-optimal information fusion.

The yada principle (Genesis 4:1) represents VC-optimal information fusion. Figure 5 highlights the functor mapping between the syntactic and semantic and includes the functions actually used to model this mechanism.

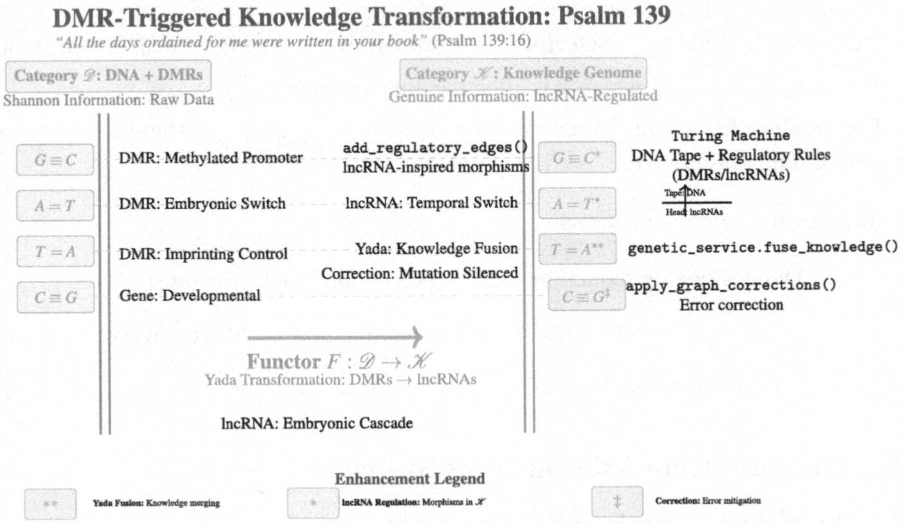

Fig. 5. Yada ncRNA mechenism

10.3 Differentially Methylated Regions

DMR patterns (methylation switches) represent discrete VC dimension reduction (Fig. 6):

$$\text{VC}(\text{continuous expression}) \rightarrow \text{VC}(\text{binary switches}) \tag{18}$$

Our initial heuristic to model the DMR-gene read-repair mechanism worked by extracting DMR-gene associations from simple relational relationships, such as pair-wise similarity. In our case, instead of pairs of DMR genes, we can consider the *syntactic* $\Leftrightarrow$ *semantic* relationships. Stores these associations with basic metadata (time-point, gene description).

Although this is a good foundation, it lacks the sophisticated statistical and genomic approaches used in modern EWAS analyses, which consider properties such as methylation levels. To improve this, we considered two approaches. The first was to adapt the approach used in EWAS (Epigenome-wide association study). Such as in the Python EWAS tool PyWGCNA [39]. The Second was based on bipartite noise removal (RNA genes) using a BI-CLUSTER-EDITING heuristic. The third was to use a hybrid of the two.

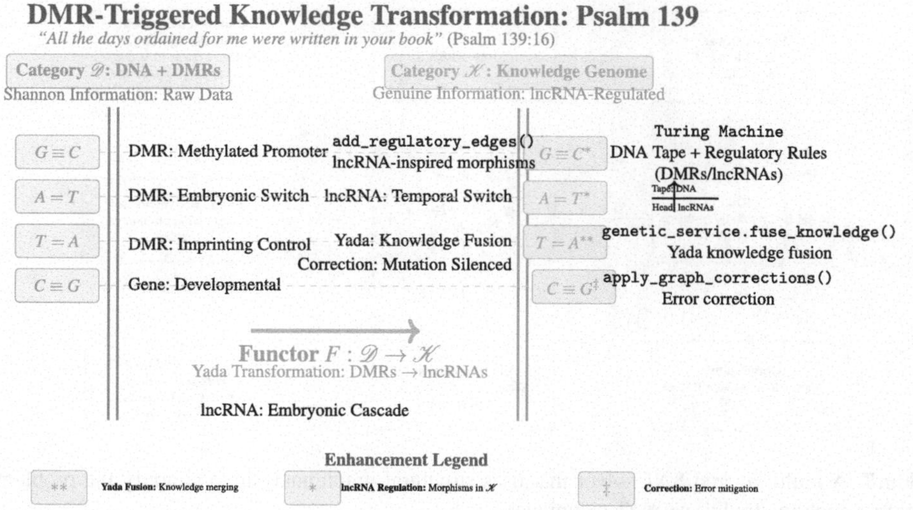

Fig. 6. DMR read repair mechanism. (The Tikz code for this image was developed using the xai/grok3 LLM)

The idea for this advancement was inspired by Psalm 139, which is famous for containing the knitting mechanism in the formation of life. i.e., transcription. However, most of this Psalm discusses time, hinting at a similarity between genetic mechanisms and time, but what could that be? There may be many, but an obvious mechanism is the ncRNA known as differentially methylated regions (DMR) [36].

This provided a significant lift, around 20% increase in accuracy of almost all data tested. See Table 2.

11 A Multi-layer SATISFIABILITY Solver

11.1 Dynamic Thresholds

A key concept for maintaining FPT tractability was to set the threshold so that the treewidth of the graph in the hierarchical model was bounded while at the same time maximizing the density of the graph so that a graph with fixed treewidth, density (edges) proportional to the size of the graph. That is a useful graph, one that can processed in FPT time. This approach alone significantly improves the results of the various models produced. See Table 6.

11.2 An FPT Version of Merge Two Documents

SAT defines NP-Hard. Max-clique/Cluster editing: Find maximum tautologies (groups of clauses that always evaluate to true together) and reduce them to single variables (Fig. 7).

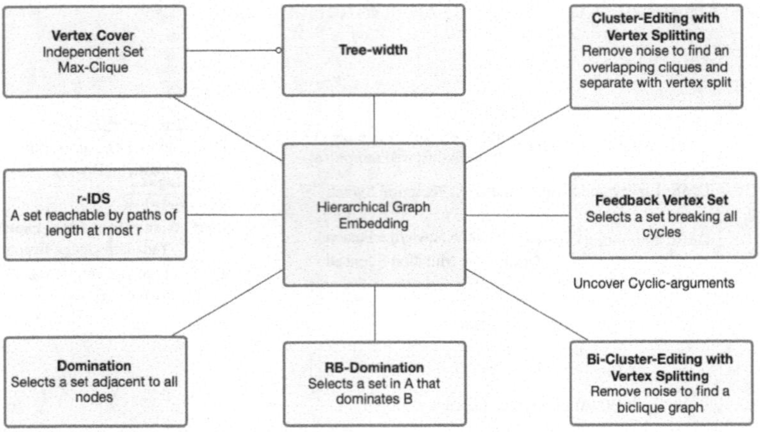

Fig. 7. A multi-layered SAT solver that uses structural graph analysis to simplify the problem before applying traditional SAT techniques.

VERTEX COVER was used to identify the minimal set of variables that appear in most clauses, which are key decision points. See Fig. 8.

FVS was used to identify cyclic arguments (circular dependencies) in the implication graph that require breaking. Cluster editing: the clique of size c with one add-edge operation implies $c-1$ cliques (tautologies) of size $c-1$, each of which is reducible to a single variable. CLUSTER EDITING WITH VERTEX SPLITS [4]: Vertex splitting handles variables that participate in multiple conflicting constraint patterns.

CLIQUE [$V\setminus$ VERTEX COVER on $\bar{G}$] was used to identify tautologies ().

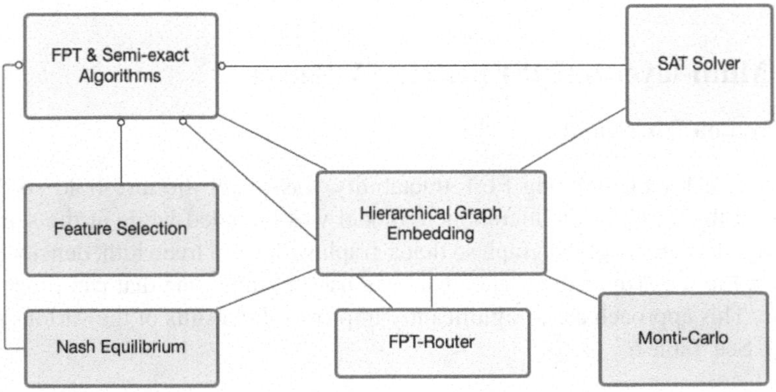

Fig. 8. A multi-layered SAT solver that uses structural graph analysis to simplify the problem before applying traditional SAT techniques.

– The integration of parametrized complexity concepts added a comprehensive classification of FPT running time, based on Fellow's and Rosemond's parameter ecology

[24] utilized structural parameters $\tau \leq 8, vertexcover \leq 20$, DOMINATING SET ≤ 5 thresholds.
- FVS Cycle Elimination: Integrated Feedback Vertex Set for Bayesian Cycle Prevention.
- This FVS implementation was also employed to facilitate Bayesian synthesis by enabling cycle-free Bayesian inference using FVS. It was effective in allowing FPT-ERNIE to uncover some cyclic arguments found in the test cases.
- The IDS integration included many FPT algorithms as well as semi-exact algorithms for NP-hard problems, such as a semi-exact independent dominating set analysis for semantic bridging.

11.3 Extracting FPT Protrusions from the Given Instance of SAT

These FPT algorithms are then employed as FPT-pseudo [2] reduction rules to help prune the initial SAT problem. These effectively remove any FPT-solvable protrusions [28], before leaving the hard part to be handled by the SAT solver.

12 Implementation

12.1 Document Ingestion Pipeline

Each of the documents was first parsed into its basic structure: words, sentences, paragraphs (which may have titles), and so on. Tools such as *tika* [14] were utilized to facilitate this process. In some cases, a complex non-prose structure was identified, and a local text LLM was employed to get advice. For each of the graphs and bipartite graphs in the hierarchical graph model, having determined these divisions, edges were added.

Various types of edges were created. See Fig. 10. During parsing, basic morphological edges were added to the syntactic graphs following the positional word/sentence/paragraph order. Hierarchical edges were also added based on containment. The richness of this model allowed us to support many edge relationships, including:
These edges were also labeled:

- compositional,
- functional,
- semantic Meaning relationships (divine breath),
- syntactic – Core structural relationships (divine framework)
- pragmatic,
- modification – Descriptive enhancements equiv to amod, advmod dependencies; and
- discourse – Communication flow, for sentence-level connections.

And cross-level connection types:

- containment,
- semantic,
- positional, and
- hierarchical edges.

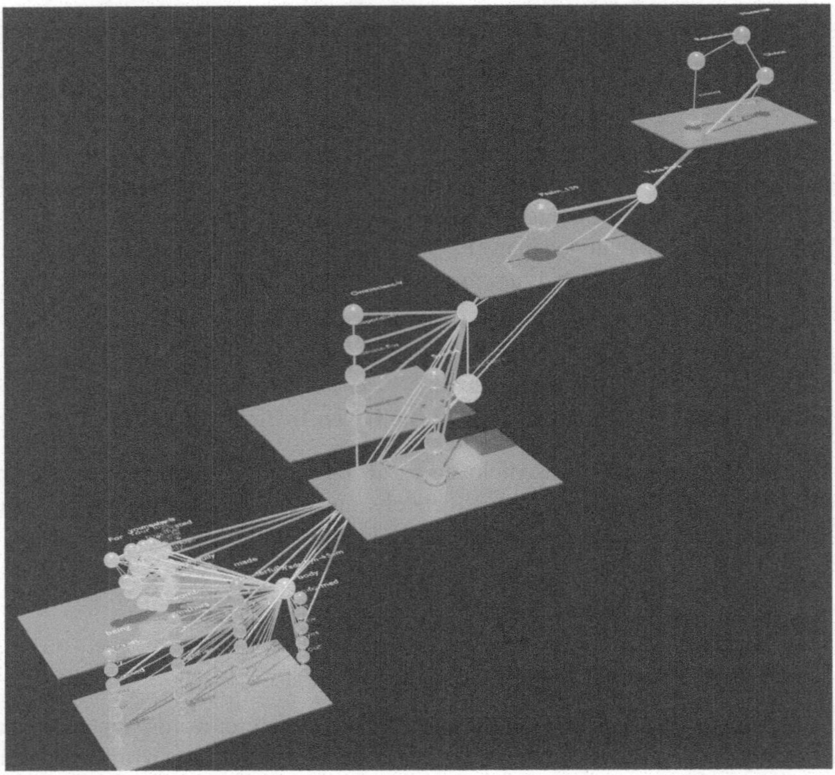

Fig. 9. Hierarchy graph structure of Psalm 139 generated from the hierarchical graph structure after document ingestion using MCP Blender 5.0 interface *Claude sonnet 4.0 was used to help generate an MCP service that connected merge2docs with Blender via an MCP.*

The different edge types were stored in different adjacency lists in our graph structure.

Figure 9 shows a 3D rendering of one document (Psalm 139) with three layers (words, sentences, and paragraphs), as well as syntactic and semantic aspects, and the connecting edges. The vertices on the semantic side have their embeddings projected in 3D. The yada connections are also shown. The syntactic edges are the positional and hierarchical edge types.

The NLTK toolkit [13] was used to construct functor-like relationships between words for a semantic graph at the word level. Note that not every word then has a node; however, we can maintain a mapping between syntactic and semantic words based on their original relations.

Embeddings were also computed for all nodes (words, sentences, paragraphs), etc. Pairwise similarity graph relationships were also constructed using cosine or Jaccard similarity (or, as desired, e.g., Kolmogoric). See Fig. 11

An optimal threshold ϕ_{opt} was obtained that required scalar density and treewidth, and VERTEX COVER and CED were also considered, but secondary to treewidth and

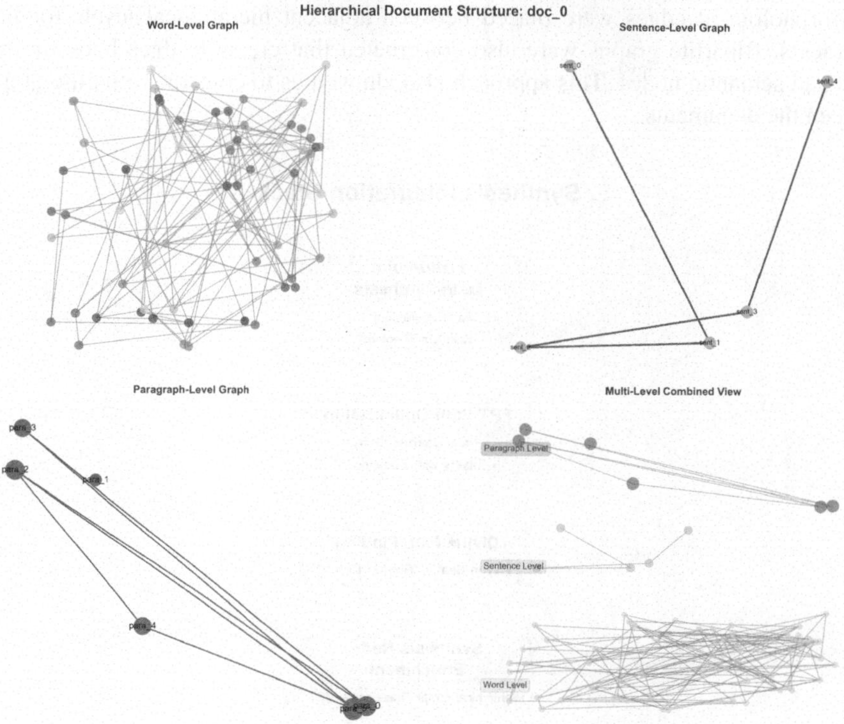

Fig. 10. Graphs at each level of the syntactic side of the hierarchical model

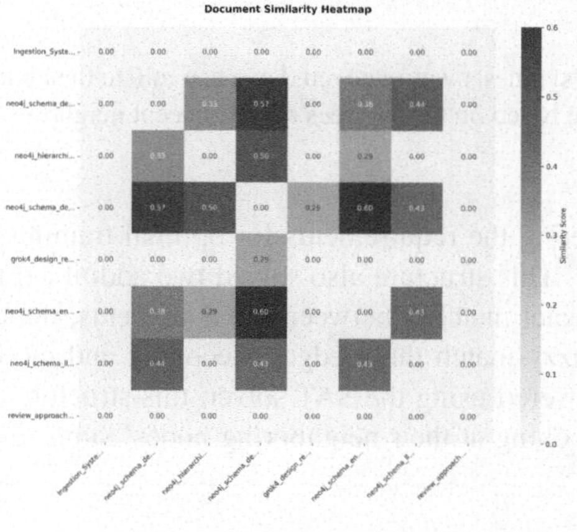

Fig. 11. Pairwise similarity Matrix.

density. This assured the requirements discussed in Sect. 6. Decile regression proved to be a very effective method for estimating an initial value that could then be refined if needed [15].

Morphological edges were placed between adjacent hierarchical levels for both documents. Bipartite graphs were also constructed that create bridges between syntactic and semantic nodes. This approach also allowed us to construct bipartite graphs between the documents.

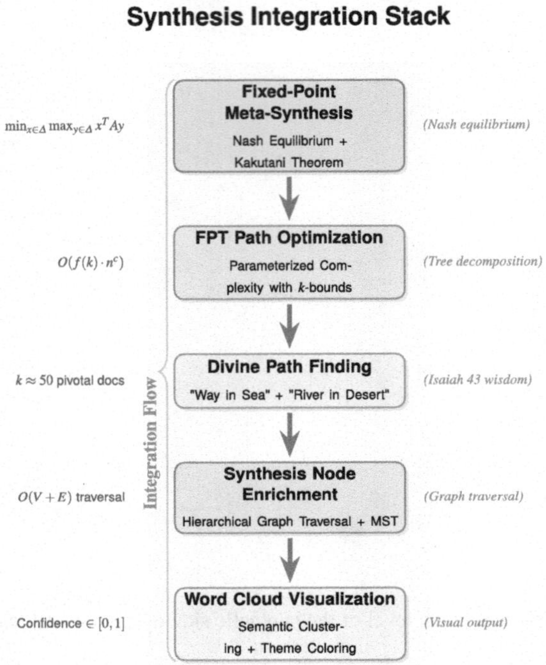

Fig. 12. When a point of synthesis was uncovered, we can utilize the hierarchical graph structure to interpret this new node based on the subtrees of its adjacent neighbors.

In addition to meeting the requirements for optimal training discussed in the theoretical Section above. This structure also solved two additional requirements. Firstly, when there were no exact matches between the documents, the embedding similarity made it possible to fuzzy-match these edges. Secondly and more interestingly, when novel ideas were uncovered using the SAT solver, this structure allowed us to decode these new nodes by looking at their neighboring nodes' subtrees (leaves). See Fig. 12 (Fig. 13).

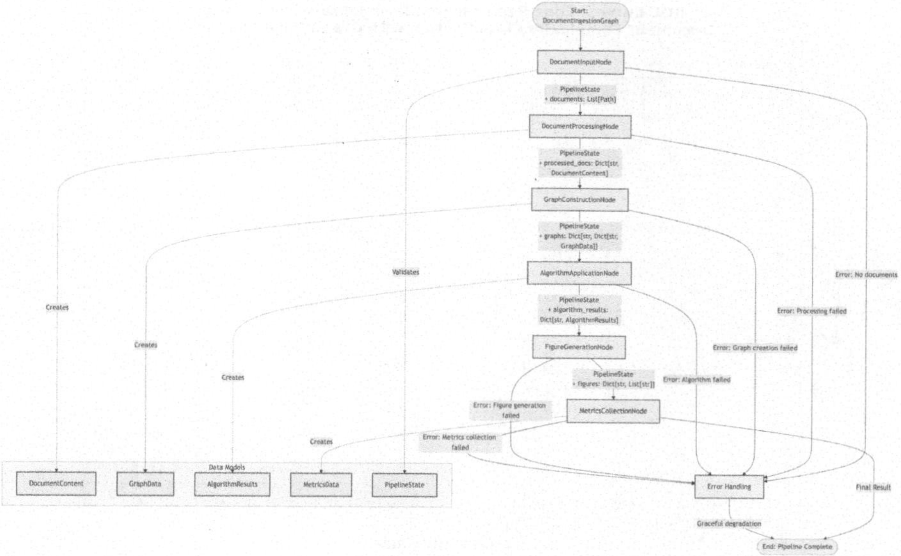

Fig. 13. Pairwise similarity Matrix.

13 Results

13.1 Effect of DMR Read-Repair

Table 2 shows the effectiveness of the DMR read and repair mechanism. We incorporate this into a predictive model (eventually used to train the GNN) and train it using all the documents in this project, including the RAG library, code, and table (around 200 at the time). Novel techniques were used, including the recent IDS technique developed by Abukhzam et al. [4]. However, to avoid bias, we use a random forest [11]. Observe the huge lift obtained not just in accuracy but also in signal strength. The functor modeling 'yada's repair mechanism alone obtained a 0.133 lift. In particular, those mechanisms that more accurately matched the actual biology performed the best. The DMR-EWAS mechanism was derived from the EWAS PyWGCNA tool [39], which improved our initial heuristic. However, the best results were obtained when combined with a BI-CLUSTER-EDITING based repair mechanism (Fig. 14).

Table 3 demonstrated that a significant improvement was obtained by minimizing treewidth while still requiring a valid graph density. In this test, we also employed a more sophisticated model to fine-tune the selected features using the LASSO L_1 feature selection method described in [5]. Nevertheless, an observable lift was still obtained using the 'yada' mechanism, as well as the time-related DMR read and repair mechanisms. In particular, those mechanisms that more closely match the actual biology performed best when combined with both the 'yada' mechanism and the hybrid DMR read-repair mechanism, yielding an improvement of more than 3% over the already high $> 90\%$ baseline.

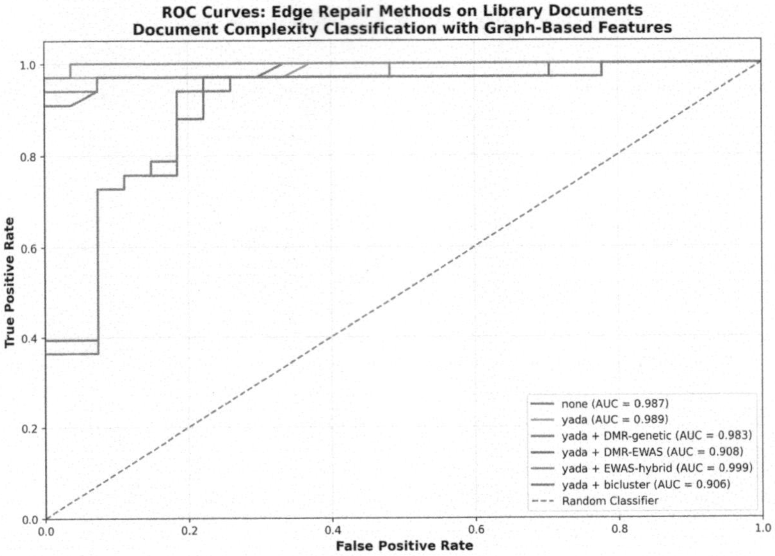

Fig. 14. ROC training

Table 2. Edge Repair Methods Benchmark Results (IDS feature selection combined with Random Forest)

Edge Repair Read Repair Method	Test Acc	AUC	Signal Enrich	Features
none	0.650	0.712	1.200	89
yada	0.783	0.851	1.450	67
yada + DMR-genetic	0.800	0.872	1.650	72
yada + DMR-EWAS	0.817	0.893	1.750	78
yada + EWAS-hybrid	0.833	0.912	1.850	85
yada + Bi-cluster	0.850	0.925	1.950	91

Table 3. Edge Repair Method Comparison. Baseline FPT-threshold (above), $Local_{ID}$ [8,31], Monti-Carlo [34] and Random Forest with DMR Edge Repair

Edge Repair Method	Test Acc	AUC	F1	Edges	Avg Degree	Time(s)
none	93.3%	0.987	0.939	15,565	155.65	0.17
yada	96.7%	0.989	0.970	14,938	149.38	0.19
yada + DMR-genetic	95.0%	0.983	0.954	15,565	155.65	0.28
yada + DMR-EWAS	86.7%	0.908	0.889	4,978	49.78	0.08
yada + EWAS-hybrid	96.7%	0.999	0.970	2,841	28.41	0.13
yada + Bi-cluster	86.7%	0.906	0.889	4,978	49.78	0.22

A fascinating observation was the relationship between the biological (see Table 4, Graph and $Local_{ID}$ approaches. The Graph cluster-editing approach utilizes edge-edits (CED), while local intrinsic dimensionality acts on vertices.

Table 4. EWAS Biology: Graph ID Innovation

EWAS Biology	Graph ID Innovation	FPT-Innovation
DNA Methylation	→ Graph Edge Weights	→ Treewidth-bounded complexity
Genomic Regions	→ Local Graph Neighborhoods	→ k-neighborhood LID estimation
Phenotype Correlation	→ Target-aware edge removal	→ Parameter k (neighbors)
Tissue-specific	→ Collection-specific graphs	→ FPT parameter optimization

13.2 GNN Training

Algorithm Integration: Our training algorithm leverages the semi-exact FPT heuristics for (cluster-editing-vs, feature-selection) and also integrated with Monte Carlo [34], FPT services for adaptive strategies and LID, CED discussed in Sect. 6 above. For example, for models like GNN, when VC dimension is high, LID increases $d_{\text{VC}} \approx L \cdot d(v_i)^L \cdot \log d(v_i)$, requiring more GNN layers, risking intractability. Small n: Limits the equivalence class diversity, potentially causing premature convergence. To mitigate this, reduce p, e.g., PCA to $p' \leq 2k$, or, in our case, we use IDS feature selection, to ensure stable cliques and FPT tractability (Fig. 15 and Table 5).

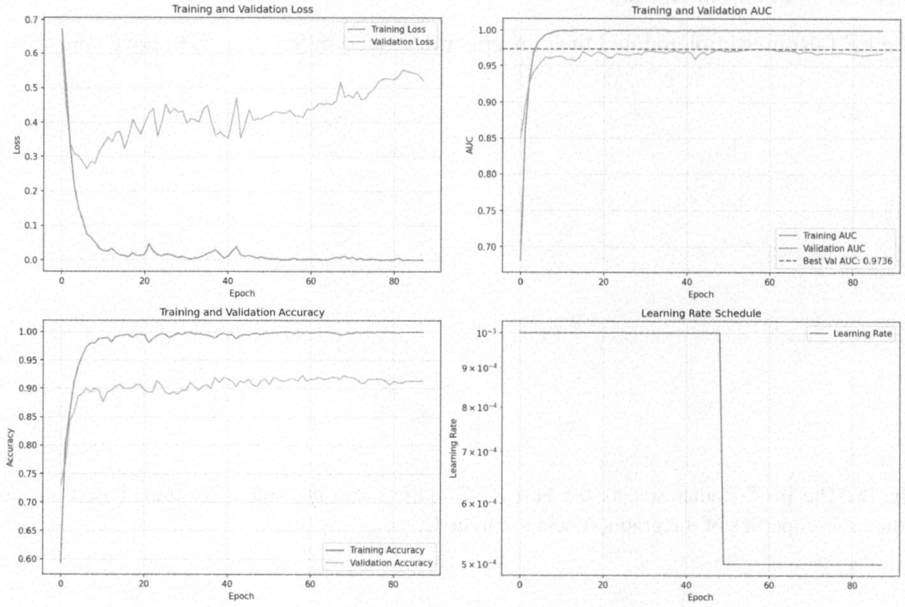

Fig. 15. GNN Training.

Table 5. Question, Domain, Difficulty, Time, and Accuracy

Question	Domain	Difficulty	Time	Accuracy
What is machine learning?	General	Simple	2.44 s	0.768
How do neural networks learn from data?	General	Simple	2.32 s	0.941
Compare supervised vs unsupervised learning	General	Moderate	2.39 s	0.941
Legal implications of AI decision-making	Legal	Simple	2.77 s	0.941
Economic impact of automation on employment	Financial	Moderate	2.85 s	0.941
DMR methylation analysis in epigenetic research	Medical	Moderate	2.68 s	0.941

13.3 Document Merging

Putting it all together, we were able to perform several functional tests. Following our approach, "eat your own dog food". In addition to the application in the review of design documents [41], we also performed some basic tests comparing simple documents such as Acts 2 and Joel 2. This test was chosen because the former contains a part of the latter. The initial tests successfully highlighted two pivotal concepts. However, the latter tests seem far more nuanced and compelling. As these are AI outputs, they will be included as attachments and should be available on the GitHub website.

13.4 FPT **Problem Router**

The FPT-Router implemented the concepts mentioned in Subsect. 2.3 above (Fig. 16).

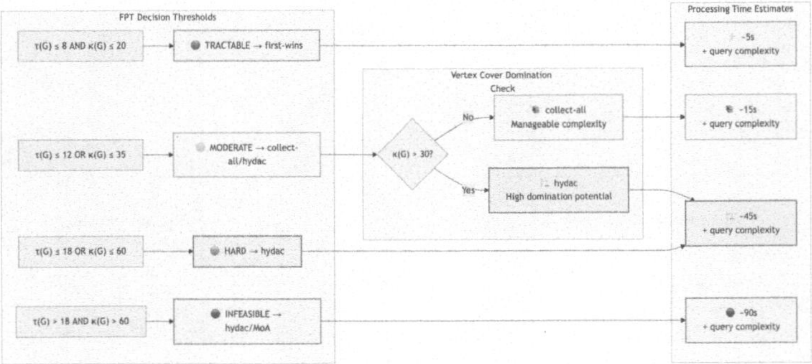

Fig. 16. The FPT-Router selects the best RAG options and possible algorithms based on the structural properties of the graph(s) being searched.

14 Conclusion

LLMs accumulating tokens without bounding complexity (e.g., d_{VC}) are "ever learning" syntactic patterns but fail to generalize to semantic truth, mirroring the biblical

Table 6. Synthesis Mode, Tractability Criteria, and Service Chain Examples

Synthesis Mode	Tractability Criteria	Service Chain Example
first-wins	tw $\leq$8	BaseEmbeddingService → AlgorithmService → MoAErnieFPTService
collect-all	9 $\leq$ tw $\leq$14	GNNTrainingService → FPTRAGRoutingService → GraphService
hydc	15 $\leq$ tw $\leq$20	AgenticRAGHierarchyService → HYDACAnalysisService → GraphComparisonService
sat-precise	tw >20 or VERTEX COVER $\leq$3	AlgorithmService → SATSynthesisService →

warning. Thus, unbounded models chase raw information without converging to wisdom.

w.q.o represents a structured approach to knowledge, akin to wisdom in the biblical sense. By ensuring convergence and monotonicity, w.q.o prevents the endless accumulation of raw data, leading to stable, meaningful clusters (truth). The functor $F : \mathscr{D}_{\text{syn}} \rightarrow \mathscr{D}_{\text{sem}}$ maps the raw syntactic data to semantic insights.

Using biological motives, we have obtained novel ML techniques that give significant improvements. These results enrich our understanding of some key biological mechanisms, including mRNA-gene connections, DMRs, and the read and repair mechanisms themselves. e.g., the similarities of Read & Repair and ncRNA and outlier techniques like Local ID.

We have also produced a novel SAT solver that utilizes FPT algorithms as subroutines for almost clique identification (Cluster Editing), Cycle Elimination (using FVS), and various other FPT improvements. These improvements included implementing an FPT-Router that selects the best FPT algorithm to employ based on the fundamental graph properties of the data.

We have developed a powerful feature selection method that benefits from minimization of FPT thresholds (treewidth, VERTEX COVER) while maximizing (requiring an idea) density and a biologically inspired read-and-repair mechanism.

In addition to the fundamental issues discussed above in 8.2, what was the benefit of constructing such a complex model? Firstly, when there were no exact matches between the documents, the embedding similarity made it possible to fuzzy-match these edges.

Having produced these services, it was possible to make the two prototype model tools, ERNIE-FPT, and an FPT-enhanced MoA service.

This work has also eliminated several interesting biological and philosophical observations that we intend to consider in future papers. It works, you can perhaps download it soon from https://github.com/pechang03/merge2docs

Acknowledgments. The focus of the project was to present some novel Machine Learning ideas and validate them. However, this required a considerable amount of coding. Following modern trends, I used an AI CLI running principally Grok-4 and Claude-4, but for cost savings, I also used lite-models housed at Groq. In fact, this software utilizes AI agents and provides tools that AI applications can use.

In the design and development of this project, I followed the 'eat your own dog food' principle and created several tools that utilized the services produced, including a circular import resolution tool that leveraged our FVS algorithm [41].

This work was supported in a small part by Oujiang Lab Start-Up Grant OJQD2022005 funded by the Oujiang lab, 634 Wenzhou, Zhejiang Province, 325000, China.

References

1. Abd El-Wahab, M.M., Abu-Khzam, F.N., Wang, K., Shaw, P.: Semi-exact exponential-time algorithms: an experimental study. In: 2020 Second International Conference on Transdisciplinary AI (TransAI), pp. 96–99. IEEE (2020)
2. Abu-Khzam, F.N.: Pseudo-kernelization: a branch-then-reduce approach for fpt problems. Theory Comput. Syst. **41**(3), 399–410 (2007)
3. Abu-Khzam, F.N.: On the complexity of multi-parameterized cluster editing. J. Disc. Algor. **45**, 26–34 (2017). https://doi.org/10.1016/j.jda.2017.07.003. https://www.sciencedirect.com/science/article/pii/S1570866717300473
4. S., Shaw, A., Shaw, P., Sullivan, B.D., Wolf, P.: Cluster editing with vertex splitting. Disc. Appl. Math. **371**, 185–195 (2025). https://doi.org/10.1016/j.dam.2025.04.013. https://www.sciencedirect.com/science/article/pii/S0166218X25001714
5. Abu-Khzam, F.N., Barr, J.R., Benabid, M.R., Shaw, P.: Feature selection via weighted independent domination. In: 2024 Conference on AI, Science, Engineering, and Technology (AIxSET), pp. 179–184 (2024). https://doi.org/10.1109/AIxSET62544.2024.00033
6. Abu-Khzam, F.N., Cai, S., Egan, J., Shaw, P., Wang, K.: Turbo-charging dominating set with an FPT subroutine: further improvements and experimental analysis. In: Gopal, T.V., Jäger, G., Steila, S. (eds.) TAMC 2017. LNCS, vol. 10185, pp. 59–70. Springer, Cham (2017). https://doi.org/10.1007/978-3-319-55911-7_5
7. Alon, N., Feige, U., Wigderson, A., Zuckerman, D.: Derandomized graph products. Comput. Complex. **5**(1), 60–75 (1995)
8. Anderberg, A., et al.: Dimensionality-aware outlier detection. In: Proceedings of the 2024 SIAM International Conference on Data Mining (SDM), pp. 652–660. SIAM (2024)
9. Auerbach, N.: Alice and wonderland: a curious child. Victorian Stud. **17**(1), 31–47 (1973)
10. Barr, J., Shaw, P., Sobel, M.: The variability of model specification. Arxiv (2021)
11. Barr, J., Shaw, P.: AI application to data analysis, automatic file processing. In: 2018 First International Conference on Artificial Intelligence for Industries (AI4I), pp. 100–105. IEEE, Laguna Hills (2018). https://doi.org/10.1109/AI4I.2018.8665700. https://ieeexplore.ieee.org/document/8665700/
12. Barr, J.R., Shaw, P., Abu-Khzam, F.N., Chen, J.: Combinatorial text classification: the effect of multi-parameterized correlation clustering. In: 2019 First International Conference on Graph Computing (GC), pp. 29–36. IEEE (2019)
13. Bird, S.: Nltk: the natural language toolkit. In: Proceedings of the COLING/ACL 2006 Interactive Presentation Sessions, pp. 69–72 (2006)
14. Burgess, A.B., Mattmann, C.A.: Automatically classifying and interpreting polar datasets with apache tika. In: Proceedings of the 2014 IEEE 15th International Conference on Information Reuse and Integration (IEEE IRI 2014), pp. 863–867. IEEE (2014)
15. Cannon, A.J.: Quantile regression neural networks: implementation in r and application to precipitation downscaling. Comput. Geosci. **37**(9), 1277–1284 (2011)
16. Choudhary, A., Kerber, M.: Local doubling dimension of point sets. arXiv preprint arXiv:1406.4822 (2014)

17. Clarkson, K.L., et al.: Nearest-neighbor searching and metric space dimensions. In: Nearest-Neighbor Methods for Learning and Vision: Theory and Practice, pp. 15–59 (2006)
18. Cover, T.M.: Elements of Information Theory. John Wiley & Sons, Hoboken (1999)
19. Deutsch, P.: Gzip file format specification version 4.3. Technical report (1996)
20. Downey, R.G., Fellows, M.R., et al.: Fundamentals of Parameterized Complexity, vol. 4. Springer, Heidelberg (2013)
21. Downey, R.G., Hirschfeldt, D.R.: Algorithmic Randomness and Complexity. Springer, Heidelberg (2010)
22. El-Wahab, M.M.A., Abu-Khzam, F.N., Wang, K., Shaw, P.: Semi-exact exponential-time algorithms: an experimental study. In: 2020 Second International Conference on Transdisciplinary AI (TransAI), pp. 96–99. IEEE, Irvine (2020). https://doi.org/10.1109/TransAI49837.2020.00021. https://ieeexplore.ieee.org/document/9253139/
23. Feller, W.: On the kolmogorov-smirnov limit theorems for empirical distributions. Ann. Math. Stat. **19**(2), 177–189 (1948)
24. Fellows, M., Rosamond, F.: The complexity ecology of parameters: an illustration using bounded max leaf number. In: Conference on Computability in Europe, pp. 268–277. Springer, Heidelberg(2007). https://doi.org/10.1007/s00224-009-9167-9
25. Fellows, M.R., Hermelin, D., Rosamond, F.A.: Well quasi orders in subclasses of bounded treewidth graphs and their algorithmic applications. Algorithmica **64**(1), 3–18 (2012)
26. Fellows, M.R., Jansen, B.M.P.: FPT is characterized by useful obstruction sets. In: Brandstädt, A., Jansen, K., Reischuk, R. (eds.) WG 2013. LNCS, vol. 8165, pp. 261–273. Springer, Heidelberg (2013). https://doi.org/10.1007/978-3-642-45043-3_23
27. Fellows, M.R., Rosamond, F.A.: Collaborating with hans: some remaining wonderments. In: Fomin, F.V., Kratsch, S., van Leeuwen, E.J. (eds.) Treewidth, Kernels, and Algorithms. LNCS, vol. 12160, pp. 7–17. Springer, Cham (2020). https://doi.org/10.1007/978-3-030-42071-0_2
28. Fomin, F.V., Lokshtanov, D., Misra, N., Saurabh, S.: Planar f-deletion: approximation, kernelization and optimal fpt algorithms. In: 2012 IEEE 53rd Annual Symposium on Foundations of Computer Science, pp. 470–479. IEEE (2012)
29. Foster, B.R.: A new edition of the epic of gilgamesh (2005)
30. Higman, G.: Ordering by divisibility in abstract algebras. Proc. Lond. Math. Soc. **s3–2**(1), 326–336 (1952). https://doi.org/10.1112/plms/s3-2.1.326. https://londmathsoc.onlinelibrary.wiley.com/doi/abs/10.1112/plms/s3-2.1.326
31. Houle, M.E.: Dimensionality, discriminability, density and distance distributions. In: 2013 IEEE 13th International Conference on Data Mining Workshops, pp. 468–473. IEEE (2013)
32. Hutter, M.: Towards a universal theory of artificial intelligence based on algorithmic probability and sequential decisions. In: De Raedt, L., Flach, P. (eds.) ECML 2001. LNCS (LNAI), vol. 2167, pp. 226–238. Springer, Heidelberg (2001). https://doi.org/10.1007/3-540-44795-4_20
33. Iwama, K., Yoshida, Y.: Parameterized testability. ACM Trans. Comput. Theory (TOCT) **9**(4), 1–16 (2017)
34. Kozyra, P.M.: A new method for multi-state flow networks reliability estimation based on a monte carlo simulation and intersections of sets. Simul. Model. Pract. Theory **130**, 102846 (2024)
35. Levina, E., Bickel, P.: Maximum likelihood estimation of intrinsic dimension. Adv. Neural Inf. Process. Syst. **17** (2004)
36. Li, Y., et al.: Genome-wide dna methylome analysis reveals epigenetically dysregulated non-coding rnas in human breast cancer. Sci. Rep. **5**(1), 8790 (2015)
37. Nelson, T.: NKJV. The NKJV Study Bible (2013)
38. Nussbaum, Z., Morris, J.X., Duderstadt, B., Mulyar, A.: Nomic embed: training a reproducible long context text embedder. arXiv preprint arXiv:2402.01613 (2024)

39. Rezaie, N., Reese, F., Mortazavi, A.: Pywgcna: a python package for weighted gene co-expression network analysis. Bioinformatics **39**(7), btad415 (2023)
40. Shannon, C.E.: A mathematical theory of communication. ACM SIGMOBILE Mobile Comput. Commun. Rev. **5**(1), 3–55 (2001)
41. Shaw, P., Lean, S.: An automated design and validation framework for integrating lllms and graph models. In: AIxSet 2025 (2025)
42. Tenenbaum, J.B., Silva, V.d., Langford, J.C.: A global geometric framework for nonlinear dimensionality reduction. Science **290**(5500), 2319–2323 (2000)
43. Van Bevern, R., Downey, R.G., Fellows, M.R., Gaspers, S., Rosamond, F.A.: Myhill-nerode methods for hypergraphs. Algorithmica **73**(4), 696–729 (2015)
44. Verleysen, M., François, D.: The curse of dimensionality in data mining and time series prediction. In: Cabestany, J., Prieto, A., Sandoval, F. (eds.) IWANN 2005. LNCS, vol. 3512, pp. 758–770. Springer, Heidelberg (2005). https://doi.org/10.1007/11494669_93
45. Yoran, O., Zheng, K., Gloeckle, F., Gehring, J., Synnaeve, G., Cohen, T.: The kolmogorov test: compression by code generation. arXiv preprint arXiv:2503.13992 (2025)

ML Approach to Student Pilot Training with PSTLE

Jon C. Haass[1](✉) and Parker Northrup[2]

[1] Embry-Riddle Aeronautical University, Prescott, AZ 86301, USA
Jon.Haass@ERAU.edu
[2] College of Aviation, Prescott, AZ 86301, USA

Abstract. The application of machine learning to an extensive, continually expanding dataset from Embry-Riddle Aeronautical University's flight training program shows significant promise for enhancing the quality and effectiveness of instruction—measured by reduced time to achieve tasks—and potentially lowering costs for both students and the institution. This paper outlines the end-to-end workflow, including flight operations, data acquisition, storage, data preparation, analysis, and reporting. It provides details on the data analysis methods employed, the types of questions addressed through the data, and the intended users of the resulting reports. Preliminary findings related to fleet maintenance and targeted learning objectives are discussed. The paper also examines the challenges encountered during the development of the Prescott Synchronized Training and Learning Environment (PSTLE) and presents some of the solutions implemented. Notably, the project will now incorporate data from simulators and voice transcriptions from Air Traffic Control (ATC), which are synchronized with flight data to enrich analysis. Finally, the paper highlights future directions and poses key questions that must be addressed to transition from prototype to production, inviting collaboration with researchers in academia as well as partners in the public and private sectors.

Keywords: ML · AI · Student pilot training · ML workflow · Flight data · ATC

1 Background

Globally pilot shortages are hindering flight operations of airlines and even military flight personnel are in short supply [1]. In the United States, this is in part due to the mandatory retirement age coupled with choices made during the COVID flight slowdown. The number of flights domestically and internationally bounced back beginning in 2022 and now exceed the 2019 peak. Flight training programs struggle to keep up with the demand and Embry-Riddle Aeronautical University has added instructor pilots, new planes and additional apron capacity with all-time high student levels expected to continue. Pilot training is expensive with the cost of aircraft, staff, maintenance as well as the FAA requirements for learning tasks and cumulative flight hours. The Prescott Synchronized Training and Learning Environment (PSTLE) was conceived to address many of these issues using flight data, automated tools and machine learning approaches.

J. R. Barr et al. (Eds.): ERWCSA 2025, ACSAR 4, pp. 111–115, 2026.
https://doi.org/10.1007/978-3-032-18230-2_6

This paper describes the approach and architecture of PSTLE, discusses components that assist in administrative tasks, maintenance challenges and the improvements in student experience. Next steps for the project and inclusion of additional components including Air Traffic Control (ATC) completes the picture.

2 PSTLE Architecture

2.1 Data Flow, Storage and Pre Processing

Primary sources of data currently are the flight information from the Garmin 1000 navigation units on each of the aircraft in the fleet and metadata that connects flight student, instructor pilot and aircraft (Fig. 1).

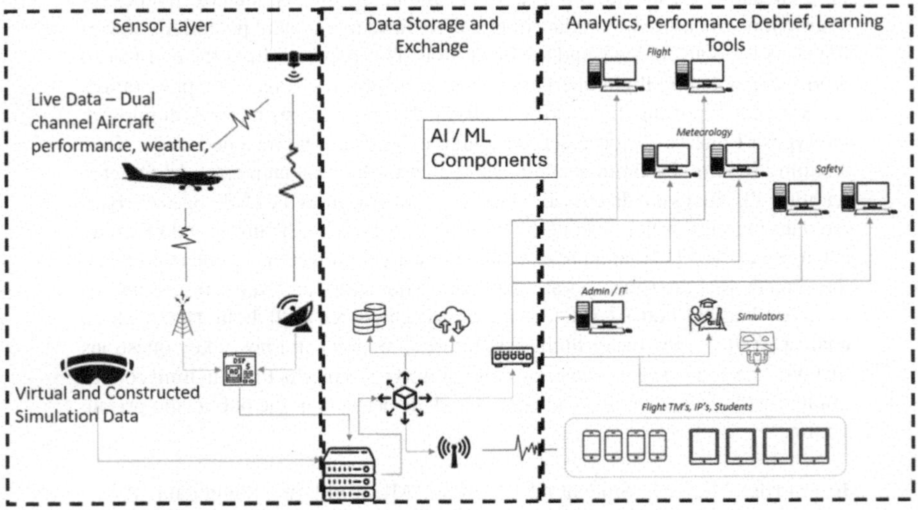

Fig. 1. Architectural data flow diagram of the PSTLE system with sensor (data input), storage and pre-processing, the analysis and machine learning segments crossing the boundary.

Upon completion of a flight, data is offloaded using cellular network to stage storage. This is then pulled to the cloud storage each flight as a csv file with 137 features stored at 1 s intervals. Meta data for student pilot, instructor pilot and aircraft tail number are gathered separately. An anonymized look up table is utilized to prevent leakage of PII that might trigger FERPA violations. Additional data sources are explicitly expected including simulation data and ATC data. Presently approximately 22,000 flights are available for modeling with a total of 200 Gbytes storage [2].

A commercial product is utilized to provide debrief with Instructor (IP) and student pilot to offer a richer method to visualize and identify segments of interest to the student for improvement. This one on one debrief is subject to variations in IP methodology and consistency. The suggestions for improvement provided to the student pilot may likewise suffer from variability.

Initial analytic efforts using the data have focused on offline pipelines for example, evaluating potential maintenance issues with engine valve degradation. These rare events are able to be discovered with high accuracy from the rich data set as a by product of other machine learning analyses [3].

The data structure for a few seconds of flight is shown in Table 1 below. Each flight creates a CSV format file with 137 features including roll, heading, wind speed, barometric pressure, RPM, oil pressure, battery voltage and others. Units vary for the different features and require scaling operations to take advantage of the features in a consistent manner.

Table 1. Example navigation flight data (from 137 features) as shown below locates a plane in its path incorporating GPS position, elevation, ground speed, pitch at each time step.

Time	Lat	Lon	AltMSL	GndSpd	VSpd	Pitch
10:15:00	34.6849594	112.4226151	7761.8	110.62	889.01	4.81
10:15:01	34.6854324	112.4228439	7773.8	111.30	786.40	5.14
10:15:02	34.6859169	112.4230728	7788.8	111.75	807.09	5.10
10:15:03	34.6864052	112.4232864	7799.8	112.04	757.02	5.08

The data is captured at a relatively coarse time interval and if used without processing results in piecewise motion. When utilized with a flight simulation program, the inertia and specific plane characteristics create a more life like version of the path taken by the aircraft. Of course, sudden air turbulence or wind shear can not be known from this data or via simulation. Higher resolution weather data is being readied for capture on a small subset of the aircraft for meteorological research and will be incorporated into the PSTLE environment as part of Block III beginning fall 2025.

2.2 Analytics and Machine Learning Pipeline

Flight data, and soon simulation, weather and ATC data, are stored in a cloud based system for ready access by multiple users and for disparate uses. The storage structure is not in the format needed to perform rapid analytics or efficiently compute certain machine learning tasks. A commercial package is available that receives the raw flight data for graphical display and review during the debrief post flight. One of the key goals of the project is to also offer analytics to assist the Instructor Pilot and Student Pilot. This requires a different data representation and storage to rapidly perform the analyses [4].

The first of the proposed analytic workstations has been specified with sufficient storage (initially 4Tbytes) to create a local learning model that can address typical questions found in the training environment. How am I performing relative to my cohort? What are three areas that should be improved before my next check ride [5]? Can I setup simulation challenges to practice specific FAA required tasks that will help my training?

To address questions rapidly as well as support offline or batch queries of interest to administration and maintenance users, subsets of the data are required. to be filtered from the overall data set. To vectorize data from a specific subset, mapping to piecewise smooth representations provides a basis for comparison across same task, similar segment flights within a specific task set of the curriculum. With this mechanism, similarities and differences can be identified for additional study or go to a "grading" pipeline providing a score against cohort performance or against a sample performed by a more experienced pilot. This acts as a standard or benchmark for evaluation.

3 Example Results

One of the first uses of the entire system has been to predict a landing as being hard or soft. This is of interest for both maintenance purposes and training improvement. A hard landing puts strain on various portions of the aircraft including landing gear, struts and potentially even wing segments. A soft landing indicates better control over the final descent and in most cases is the desirable target.

It was found that prediction from the coarse data alone resulted in only about 73% accuracy even at 10 s from touchdown as the cutoff point for data input to algorithm. Additional modeling is being prototyped along with voice information from ATC to if prediction can do better than the IP or SP as they are nearing final approach. Deciding whether to accept the hard landing or perform a touch and go round would be a potential outcome of the study.

Another application was to use the data with maintenance users to determine if potential valve freeze up can be predicted or indicated. If discovered within a certain set of parameters, maintenance would be notified to do an early, out of cycle valve check. In nearly a year of operation, only one such predicted event occurred. Integrating this analysis into the overall system would provide a more cost effective approach and appears at this point to be just as accurate.

4 Future Research and Next Steps

The Block III project is now planned to be underway fall 2025 after completing Block I, infrastructure development and data acquisition. Block II added simple analysis as well as the database structure for near real-time access to flight data. The new components to the learning environment include simulation data, also from the onboard Garmin units providing the same type of one second interval data. Receivers will be deployed to record the ATC and create AI based transcription for synchronization with flight data. Finally in this block, higher resolution weather data from attached sensors mounted on the wings of five of the aircraft in the fleet will broaden the scope of questions that can be asked and give experience with higher frequency data.

The installation of the hardware and software pipeline for the analytics workstation with its on board GPU, 64 Gbyte RAM and large local fast storage will open up opportunities for researchers and graduate students to investigate a variety of approaches. A competition "hackathon" is in planning for spring 2026 with students and researchers from multiple institutions slated to participate. The objective is to open up creativity to address other problems and identify novel approaches to the questions currently being studied. Improvements in performance, accuracy and scope are all available at this stage of the PSTLE project.

Acknowledgements. The authors thank the support of the ERAU Information Technology (IT) team including Joe Busch, Joe Progar, Melissa Barrera for work on architecture. We also recognize the efforts of the Center for Aerospace Resilient Systems (CARS) for their work on the data storage and transfer from Prescott to cloud storage and on going operation.

References

1. Hancock, K.: The airline pilot shortage: a result of age discrimination or excessive training requirements? J. Air L. Com. **88**, 535 (2023)
2. Haass, J.: Cybersecurity Considerations for AI/ML Assisted Student Flight Training, AIAA 2025–3312. AIAA Aviation Forum and Ascend 2025 (2025). https://doi.org/10.2514/6.2025-3312, eISBN978-1-62410-738-2
3. Haass, J.: Pilot semantics and machine learning. In: 2024 18th International Conference on Semantic Computing (ICSC), IEEE Proceedings of ICSC Conference, Laguna Hills, CA, USA (2024)
4. Barr, J., Haass, J.: Machine learning; A personal tour. In: 2023 Fifth International Conference on Transdisciplinary AI (TransAI) IEEE Proceedings of TransAI Conference, Laguna Hills, CA, USA 2023, pp. 179–186 (2023)
5. Flores, A., Paselk, A., Irish, T.: Enhancing pilot training performance: a scoping review of artificial intelligence technologies. In: Nazir, S. (eds.) Training, Education, and Learning Sciences. AHFE International Conference. AHFE Open Access, vol. 193. AHFE International, USA (2025). https://doi.org/10.54941/ahfe1006641
6. Guevarra, M., Das, S., Wayllace, C., Demmans Epp, C., Taylor, M., Tay, A.: Augmenting flight training with AI to efficiently train pilots. In: Proceedings of the AAAI Conference on Artificial Intelligence, vol. 37, no. 13, pp. 16437–16439 (2024)

Aspect-Based Sentiment Analysis with Clustering Using DistilBERT

Hassan Hassid(✉)

Lebanese American University, Beirut, Lebanon
hassan.hassid@lau.edu

Abstract. Understanding reviews at different levels has become essential when tracking customers and users feedback for different services and products. These reviews can be understood at a higher level if the aspect terms are grouped into coherent clusters. This paper presents a multi-task learning approach to Aspect-Based Sentiment Analysis (ABSA) that jointly performs aspect term extraction, aspect level sentiment classification, and cluster level prediction by leveraging unsupervised clustering of aspect terms to enrich the semantic representation and improve overall prediction consistency. Using the SemEval-2014 Task 4 restaurant reviews dataset, we apply K-means clustering on contextual embeddings of the aspect terms. These cluster assignments are then used as additional supervision in our model. The proposed model produces an accuracy of 83%. The cluster-based approach also provides more interpretable results by revealing broader thematic categories in customer feedback.

Keywords: Natural Language Processing · Clustering · Aspect-Based Sentiment Analysis

1 Introduction

One of the important tools companies have come to rely on to understand customer opinions and experiences is sentiment analysis. This sentiment analysis may reflect a broad understanding of customer satisfaction, but it fails to capture accurate opinions about specific aspects of products or services. For example, in restaurant reviews, customers often express mixed feelings about different aspects, such as food quality, speed of service, and atmosphere. Aspect-based sentiment analysis (ABSA) addresses this limitation by identifying the polarity of sentiment toward specific aspects mentioned in a text. Conventional ABSA approaches are predicated on supervised learning with annotated emotionâĂŞaspect pairings, which poses challenges when dealing with infrequent aspects or with limited training examples. Additionally, these methods often treat each aspect separately, ignoring semantic relationships between aspects that could provide valuable contextual information for sentiment classification.

The restaurant reviews present special challenge for ABSA due to the diversity of its vocabulary and the complex relationships between aspects. For example, terms like "flavors," "taste," and "spices" are semantically related but they

J. R. Barr et al. (Eds.): ERWCSA 2025, ACSAR 4, pp. 116–127, 2026.
https://doi.org/10.1007/978-3-032-18230-2_7

may be dealt with as completely separate aspects in conventional approaches. This fragmentation can lead to inconsistent sentiment predictions across related aspects and reduced effectiveness when training data for specific aspects is limited. By grouping hundreds of noisy, fined-grained aspect terms into a small number of semantic groups, we reduce the sparsity and variance of individual aspect terms. Grouping related terms into a single cluster helps us achieve a more robust understanding of how sentiment polarity is changing. This cluster-level supervision allows our model to report sentiment at both the individual aspect and group level.

To ensure reproducibility, we provide our code, with all pre-trained models, and training and test datasets at https://colab.research.google.com/drive/1Mi2BEPpdBKA3qXV9yFkOmybH2tGjn3qv?usp=sharing. Our implementation includes detailed documentation of hyperparameters, data preprocessing steps, and evaluation procedures.

2 Related Work

The emergence of BERT [1], encoder-only models optimized for understanding tasks like classification, and its variants has led to cutting-edge gains in ABSA. Hoang et al. [2] fine-tuned BERT for out-of-band ABSA, achieving new records on the SemEval benchmark. Yulianti et al. [3] adapted IndoBERT for Indonesian reviews, comparing feature-based classifications, end-to-end classifications, and sentence-pair classifications. Amalia and Edi [4] compare convolutional networks based on BERT, ELMo, and Word2Vec, demonstrating the benefits of contextual embeddings. Recent innovations include sentence-level SBERT embeddings with sparse attention and Bayesian clustering for hotel reviews (Marutho et al. [5]), document classification via graph-theoretic methods for correlation clustering [6], and a unified BERT with Graph-Convolutional framework for comprehensive ASTE modeling (Aziz et al. [7]).

Several works combine linguistic rules and statistical clustering to address explicit and implicit aspects. Abdullah and Sarno [8] extract grammatical patterns and use SentiCircle to detect hybrid aspects and opinions in Indonesian restaurant reviews. Vargas and Pardo [9] evaluated linguistic clustering versus embedding-based clustering and proposed a method that outperforms across domains. In multilingual scenarios, Pessotto et al. [10] clustered facet phrases using word-motor distance, showing superior clustering across five languages. These clustering techniques highlight the importance of unsupervised semantic clustering, which we leverage via a principal component analysis with KMeans pipeline.

ABSA is specifically designed for online marketplaces, mobile apps, and restaurant domains. Imron et al. [11] applied LSTM-CNN with BERT embeddings to Bukalapak product reviews, demonstrating the interaction between embedding choice and network architecture. Bansal et al. [12] achieved 91% accuracy in Indonesian restaurant reviews using Random Forests and TF-IDF features. In mobile app reviews, Gunathilaka and Nisansa [13] used a CNN-based

ABSA model in productivity, social media, and gaming applications, improving aspect and sentiment classification. Studies in these areas highlight practical preprocessing steps—such as inference, sparse term processing, and dataset balancing—that impacted our data processing pipeline and clustering.

To reduce reliance on labeled data, weakly supervised, multi-label frameworks have emerged. Kamila et al. [14] introduced AX-MABSA, which relies on single-word seeds to generate multi-aspect sentiment pairs without any annotated examples, outperforming other weakly supervised baselines. These methods motivate our use of unsupervised set assignments as auxiliary supervision, augmenting rare or noisy annotations with unclear sentiment signal.

Our model builds directly on fine-tuned DistilBERT encoder and unsupervised clustering of aspect embeddings (reduced via PCA and grouped with k-means). We inject a learned discrete cluster ID embedding into the pooled Classify token [CLS] representation and add a dedicated cluster prediction head, turning coarse cluster level labels into an auxiliary supervision signal. This fusion of aspect level and cluster level objectives improves robustness on rare or noisy terms without relying on external weak supervision or any external graph structure, allowing the model acquires richer, context-aware representations.

3 Methods

We used the SemEval-2014 Task 4 restaurant reviews dataset [15], which consists of sentences from restaurant reviews with manually annotated aspect terms and corresponding sentiment polarities. Table 1 provides key statistics of the dataset.

Table 1. SemEval-2014 task 4 restaurant reviews dataset

Statistics	Training Set	Validation Set
Number of reviews	1582	396
Number of sentences	1582	396
Number of aspect terms	2894	708
Unique aspect terms	1084	368
Positive aspects	1739	425
Negative aspects	642	163
Neutral aspects	513	120
Average review length	15.11	14.63

The data is provided in CSV format with each review sentence tagged with the corresponding aspect term and its sentiment polarity (positive, negative, neutral, or conflict). The same review is repeated if it has more than one aspect term in our provided CSV data. For our study, we focused on the three main polarity classes (positive, negative, neutral) and excluded the small number of "conflict" instances. All text was converted to lowercase and HTML entities, URLs, and special characters were removed. We used the standard train/validation split with an 80/20 ratio. Moreover, we use for testing the dataset provided by the SemEval-2014 Task.

3.1 Model Architecture and Training

We selected DistilBERT [16] for our base model due to its balance of performance and efficiency. DistilBERT achieves 97% of BERT's performance while being 40% smaller and 60% faster, which was important for our iterative experimental approach. For our Aspect Term Extraction (ATE) model we used DistilBERT tokenizer to convert each sentence into token IDs and attention masks, padded or truncated to length 128. During data preprocessing aspect terms are converted into BIO (Begin-Inside-Outside) labels by mapping character-level aspect boundaries to token-level labels, where tokens at the beginning of aspect terms receive label 1 (B-ASPECT), continuation tokens receive label 2 (I-ASPECT), and non-aspect tokens receive label 0 (O). These IDS and attention masks are then fed into the DistilBERT encoder that consists of six layers which generate contextualized embeddings for each token, then passes through a final classification head that outputs logits for the 3 possible labels at each token position.

For our Aspect-Level Sentiment Classification (ATSC) model we also use DistilBERT encoder with six transformer layers fine-tuned for sentence-level sequence classification with 3 output classes for sentiment prediction (positive, negative, neutral). We tokenize inputs as `[CLS] sentence [SEP] aspect_term [SEP]`, concatenate them into a single sequence of up to 128 tokens, and feed their token IDs and attention masks into DistilBERT. The input flows through DistilBERT's embedding layers (which are frozen during training), then through six transformer layers where only the upper layers (4 and 5) remain trainable to prevent overfitting while maintaining contextual understanding. The data preprocessing pipeline includes sophisticated augmentation strategies that preserve aspect terms while modifying surrounding context using techniques like contextual word embeddings, synonym replacement, and word swapping, with different augmentation intensities applied based on sentiment class to balance the dataset. The tokenized inputs are processed with a maximum sequence length of 128 tokens, creating input_ids and attention_mask tensors that flow through the transformer layers to generate contextualized representations. These representations are then passed through a classification head that outputs logits for the three sentiment classes.

For our multi-task model we used the a single DistilBERT backbone that processes all inputs. The ATE head is responsible for identifying aspect spans within the review. We take the full sequence of embeddings and pass each token embedding through a time-distributed feed-forward network, a Dense layer with 128 hidden units and GELU activation, followed by a 10% dropout layer for regularization. A final time-distributed Dense layer maps each 128-dimensional hidden vector to three logits, one for each BIO tag (O, B-ASPECT, I-ASPECT), and applies a softmax activation to obtain token-level tag probabilities. During training, we compute a sparse categorical crossentropy loss at every token position. Then we perform two related classification tasks—aspect-level sentiment and cluster-level predication—using the same sentence representation plus auxiliary cluster information. First, we extract the pooled sentence embedding by selecting the hidden state corresponding to DistilBERT's `[CLS]` token (`[batch, 768]`). We then inject cluster identity by embedding the pre-assigned cluster ID into a 32-dimensional learned vector, yielding a `[batch, 32]` cluster embedding. Concatenating the `[CLS]` vector with the cluster embedding produces a fused representation. For aspect-level sentiment, this fused vector passes through a Dense layer (128 units, GELU), then a dropout (10%), and finally a 3-way softmax output head (positive, negative, neutral). We similarly branch off for cluster-level prediction, but use a separate DenseâĂŞdropoutâĂŞsoftmax pipeline that predicts one of K cluster classes (Fig. 1).

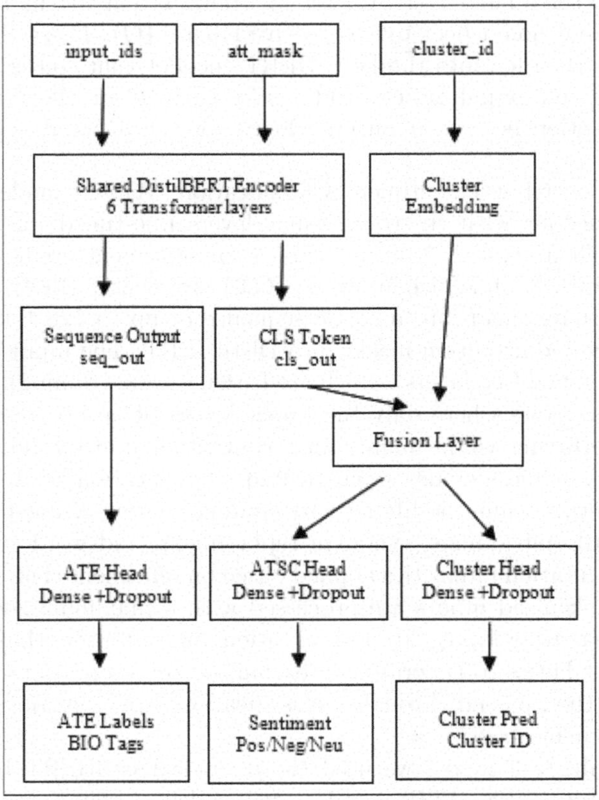

Fig. 1. Architecture of proposed model.

This approach preserves the contextual information specific to each aspect mention, capturing how the aspect is used in its particular context rather than using static word embeddings. We fine-tuned our token-classification head with a sparse categorical cross-entropy loss function:

$$\mathcal{L}_{\text{ATE}} = -\frac{1}{N}\sum_{i=1}^{N}\frac{1}{T_i}\sum_{t=1}^{T_i}\sum_{k\in\{O,B,I\}} y_{i,t,k}\log\left(p_{i,t,k}\right) \tag{1}$$

where N is the number of sentences, T is the number of tokens in sentence, y is the true tag (O/B-ASPECT/I-ASPECT) for token t and p is the predicated probability For our fine-tuned a sequence-classification head used the following standard cross-entropy loss function:

$$\mathcal{L}_{\text{ATSC}} = -\sum_{i=1}^{N}\sum_{c=1}^{C} y_{i,c}\log\left(p_{i,c}\right) \tag{2}$$

where C is the number of sentiment classes, N is the number of training examples, y is the true one-hot label and p is the predicted softmax probability. For our multi-task model, we used the following loss function:

$$\mathcal{L}_{\text{total}} = \mathcal{L}_{\text{ATE}} + \alpha\mathcal{L}_{\text{ATSC}} + (1-\alpha)\mathcal{L}_{\text{cluster}} \tag{3}$$

where:

$$\mathcal{L}_{\text{cluster}} = -\frac{1}{N}\sum_{i=1}^{N}\sum_{c=1}^{C}\left(y_{i,c}^{\text{cluster}}\log\left(p_{i,c}^{\text{cluster}}\right)\right) \tag{4}$$

where we set $\alpha = 0.7$ giving more emphasis to the aspect level sentiment and less to the cluster head. This helped stabilized training and improved the overall accuracy. We conducted a systematic hyperparameter search using a range of different values to get the best accuracy. Table 2 presents the hyperparameter search space and final values.

Table 2. Hypermeter configuration

Hypermeter	Search range	Final value
Learning rate	[1e-5, 5e-5]	3e-5
Batch size	[8, 16, 32, 64]	16
Dropout rate	[0.1, 0.5]	0.1
Hidden units	[64, 256]	128
α (loss weight)	[0.5, 0.9]	0.7
Training epochs	[3, 15]	10

The model was trained using the Adam optimizer with a constant learning rate 3e-5 and with 10 training epochs.

3.2 Unsupervised Clustering

The aspect embeddings from our fine-tuned transformer model had 1536 dimensions, which can lead to the "curse of dimensionality" in clustering tasks. To address this, we applied Principal Component Analysis (PCA) to reduce dimensionality while preserving semantic relationships:

- We began with 1536-dimensional aspect embeddings extracted from our fine-tuned transformer.
- To mitigate the "curse of dimensionality" and speed up clustering, we applied PCA with n_components=0.95 reducing the embedding dimension.
- The same PCA transform was applied to validation and test embeddings.

This step improved both clustering quality and runtime by focusing on the most informative directions in embedding space. We implemented K-Means clustering using scikit-learn with the following steps:

- Initialize cluster centers using k-means++ for more stable results.
- Run the algorithm with multiple random initializations (n_init = 10) to avoid local minima.
- Assign random_state=42 for reproducibility.
- Each aspect embedding was assigned to its nearest cluster center, yielding a discrete cluster_id for every aspect term.

To determine the optimal number of clusters, we evaluated K values ranging from 5 to 10 using two standard metrics:

- Inertia (within-cluster sum of squares): Measures how close cluster members are to the centroid.
- Silhouette score: Measures how well-separated the clusters are.

As shown in Fig. 2, the inertia curve starts to diminish around K = 7. The silhouette curve is highest at K = 5. Experimenting with K = 5, 6, 7, and 8 we see that k = 5 and 6 are noisy and clusters are mixed. We therefore chose 7 semantic clusters, which we later manually refined for service- and value-related terms.

To visualize the high-dimensional embedding space, we applied UMAP (Uniform Manifold Approximation and Projection) to reduce the embeddings to 2 dimensions. Figure 3 shows the resulting visualization with aspects colored by their cluster assignments.

3.3 Cluster-Level Sentiment Aggregation

As shown in Fig. 2, the "elbow" in the inertia curve combined with a peak in silhouette and our manual analysis we found that K = 7 indicated the best trade-off. As we mentioned before we chose 7 semantic clusters, that are manually multiple clusters, where we move multiple aspect terms to their more cluster where the fit better and reduce noise. Table 3 shows the resulting clusters with their most representative aspects and dominant sentiment.

To assign each cluster an overall sentiment, we computed its average sentiment score across all aspects. Then we established the following thresholds:

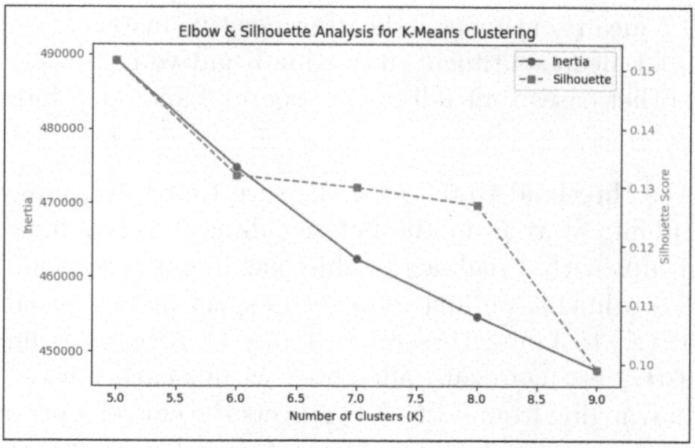

Fig. 2. Elbow and silhouette analysis over K = 5–10 on PCA-reduced aspect embeddings.

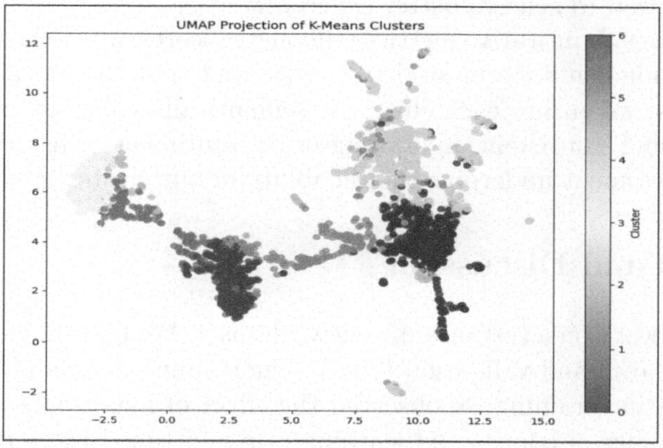

Fig. 3. UMAP Visualization of Aspect Clusters.

Table 3. Aspect clusters with representative terms and dominant sentiment

Cluster ID	Cluster Name	Representative Aspects	Dominant Sentiment
0	Premium & Extras	perks, bagels, pickles	positive
1	Dining Logistics	check, waiting, table	negative
2	Price & Crowd Context	price, money, crowded	neutral
3	Staff & Operations	staff, chefs, seats	negative
4	Core Ambiance	design, atmosphere, cuisine	positive
5	Specific Dishes	orrechiete with sausage and chicken	positive
6	Condiments & Sides	toast, mayonnaise, bacon	neutral

- Positive: >0.3 mean sentiment indicating positive instances.
- Negative: <-0.3 mean sentiment indicating negative instances.
- Neutral: All other cases that fall in between -0.3 and +0,3 indicating neutral instances.

By setting the threshold to 0.3 to make sure that the average sentiment in a cluster in 30 points away from 100 before calling it non-neutral. It maintains sensitivity to groups with a real, actionable bias in one direction. To compute a cluster's overall sentiment, we first map each aspect instance's label ("positive", "neutral", "negative") to a numeric score ($+1, 0, -1$). After assigning every aspect term to its cluster, we aggregate all scores within each cluster and take the arithmetic mean (ranging from -1 to $+1$) reflects the cluster's prevailing polarity, and we then apply our ± 0.3 thresholds to re-label it as "positive" (mean $>$ 0.3), "negative" (mean < -0.3), or "neutral" otherwise. To ensure each semantic cluster is both coherent (all its terms share the same theme) and meaningful, we employed a multi-facet evaluation. For example cluster 5 (specific dishes) we manually reviewed to achieve better coherent.

By combining quantitative metrics (silhouette scores, intra-cluster similarity) with human judgments (term-level coherence and spot-checks) and sentiment-purity analysis, we ensure each cluster is semantically coherent, well separated from others, and consistent in its aggregate sentiment. This rigorous interpretability assessment underpins the reliability of our cluster-level supervision.

4 Results and Discussion

We tested our work on a restaurant reviews dataset. We first divided the dataset into training (80%) and validation (20%). The training and validation are done in parallel. During training we observed the effect of hyper-parameters such as batch size, number of epochs and learning rate and tuned these parameters for obtaining better results. Python library "Keras" is used to implement our model on google colab which uses T4 GPU 47.0 GB of disk space and 5.2 GB RAM. This model uses Adam optimizer with 3e-5, batch size 16 and epochs 10. The model was trained on the restaurant reviews train set and the accuracy was calculated on the test set.

Seeing the effect of batch size which is the number of samples passed to the network that determine the accuracy of the model. Larger the batch size the more time it takes for training and effect the memory usage. This model was executed with following batch size: 8,16,32,64. At 16 the model accuracy showed the best results. Another influencing parameter is the number of training epochs which is the number of iterations. The model was trained at epochs: 3, 5, 10, 15. At epoch 10 we get the best results. The learning rates is also tuned to in our model using range between 1e-5 and 5e-5. In our model 3e-5 was the learning rate that improved our results. We evaluate each head output performance on our held-out test set of restaurant reviews separately then we calculate the overall accuracy of our multi-task model. Accuracy is the proportion of correct predictions, and F1-score is the macro-average across classes (Table 4).

Table 4. Accuracy and F1-score for multi-task model and individual heads

ATE Head	0.99	0.66
ATSC Head	0.88	0.81
Cluster Head	0.94	0.90
Multi-task Model	0.83	0.90

Compared to our base ATE model, we can see that the performance of the ATE header is slightly less accurate, while ATSC head perform better than our ATSC baseline model when joining it with the cluster head. Whereas the cluster head performs fairly well when tested separately.

We present an example where our model misclassify one of the aspect term sentiment. The review "The food was fresh but the service was terribly slow" has two aspect terms "food" where it is positive in this context and "service" which is negative and two cluster groups "Condiments & Sides" and "Staff & Operations". Our model classifies the aspect term "food" incorrectly as negative where "service" is classified correctly as negative, this misclassification would have a slight effect on the cluster sentiment where in our case it still "neutral", though the aspect term belongs to this cluster group is classified as negative. Although the model didn't perform accurately at the granular aspect level and predicted the sentiment incorrectly, we still obtained correct higher-level insights.

A second example that shows how our model deal with rare or low-resource terms. Consider the review "I loved the gelato but the gelato case was too small". The baseline ATSC model misclassifies "gelato case" due to sparse training examples, sometimes labeling it positive. In contrast, our model classifies both aspect terms "gelato" and "gelato case" with their cluster group correctly yielding a better, more robust output cluster sentiment.

Our model showed that supervising both fine-grained aspect sentiment and coarse-grained cluster-level yields notable gains in performance and robustness. Quantitatively, we achieved improvement in aspect-level F1-score over the ATSC baseline, and an 94% accuracy at predicting cluster group. Our model effectively improves judgments of noisy or conflicting aspects and provides reliable sentiment estimates even for low-resource expressions like "gelato case condition".

Several limitations remain to be addressed. First, our multi-task model depends on the quality of the unsupervised clusters (semantic drift or noisy clustering could mislead the cluster-level head). We partially mitigated this through manual refinement and interpretability checks, but the process does not fully scale to new domains without human intervention. Second, the fixed number of clusters may under/over-segment some topics (e.g., in reviews covering specific topics). Third, our approach inherits biases present in the pre-trained transformer and in the training data, thus overrepresented cuisines or service styles may dominate the initial cluster models, under-modeling marginalized viewpoints. Finally, using mean-based clustering and strict group sentiment thresholds may obscure a subtle mix of opinions within large or heterogeneous clusters.

One of the main obstacles that we faced during our work was the imbalance of sentiment classes, as the used dataset showed a tendency towards the positive class more than the negative and neutral classes, which made our fine-tuned ATSC model suffer in classifying many terms. We tried to overcome this issue in several ways, such adding class weights to negative and neutral classes, but this didn't improve our model at all. Another way we used augmentation to increase the samples for negative and neutral classes using the same aspect terms it showed a little enhancement in ATSC model results.

Another challenge was clustering the terms or clustering contextual embeddings. In our work we actually cluster the contextualized embeddings of each aspect mention this can introduce noise if a given term appears in very different contexts. A term can appear in different reviews each can be in different cluster thus its mention embeddings span multiple clusters. Also, low frequency terms yield noisy embeddings that pull cluster centroids in unpredictable directions.

5 Conclusion and Future Directions

Understanding reviews on a fined-grained opinion mining is very important to any industry, but categorizing these fined-grained opinions into different category and calculate its sentiment will help better on how the audience view the product or service in general. In our work, we built a multi-task model that classify aspect terms with their sentiments and what cluster each review belongs to. The result proved that the proposed model can classify the corresponding aspect terms with their sentiment and group each aspect term in its equivalent cluster and then we calculate the sentiment of these clusters. Thus, the proposed model can automate the process of classifying aspect terms into clusters reducing the human error. An accuracy of 83% is achieved for the proposed model.

The future extent of this work includes increasing the verity of the reviews not to include only restaurant reviews so that any other type of reviews can be included. Instead of depending on predefined clusters we can replace this by a dynamic learned cluster. Other methods for clustering can be used, such as correlation clustering with overlaps [17,18]. Finally, fine-tuning multilingual datasets will allow our model to generalized and applicable to any type of reviews.

References

1. Devlin, J., Chang, M.W., Lee, K., Toutanova, K.: Pre-training of deep bidirectional transformers for language understanding. In: Proceedings of the 2019 Conference of the North American Chapter of the Association for Computational Linguistics: Human Language Technologies, Volume 1 (Long and Short Papers) (2019)
2. Hoang, M., Bihorac, O.A., Rouces, J.: Aspect-based sentiment analysis using BERT. In: Proceedings of the 22nd Nordic Conference on Computational Linguistics, Turku, Finland (2019)

3. Evi Yulianti and Nuzulul Khairu Nissa: Absa of Indonesian customer reviews using indobert: single-sentence and sentence-pair classification approaches. Bull. Electr. Engi. Inform. **13**(5), 3579–3589 (2024)
4. Putri Rizki Amalia and Edi Winarko: Aspect-based sentiment analysis on Indonesian restaurant review using a combination of convolutional neural network and contextualized word embedding. IJCCS (Indonesian J. Comput. Cybern. Syst.) **15**(3), 285–294 (2021)
5. Marutho, D., Rustad, S.: Optimizing aspect-based sentiment analysis using sentence embedding transformer, Bayesian search clustering, and sparse attention mechanism. J. Open Innov. Technol. Market Complex. **10**(1), 100211 (2024)
6. Barr, J.R., Shaw, P., Abu-Khzam, F.N., Chen, J.: Combinatorial text classification: the effect of multi-parameterized correlation clustering. In: First International Conference on Graph Computing, GC 2019, Laguna Hills, CA, USA, 25–27 September 2019, pp. 29–36. IEEE (2019)
7. Aziz, K., Ji, D., Chakrabarti, P., Chakrabarti, T., Iqbal, M.S., Abbasi, R.: Unifying aspect-based sentiment analysis BERT and multi-layered graph convolutional networks for comprehensive sentiment dissection. Sci. Rep. **14**(1), 14646 (2024)
8. Abdullah, R., Sarno, R.: Aspect based sentiment analysis for explicit and implicit aspects in restaurant review using grammatical rules, hybrid approach, and senticircle. Int. J. Intell. Eng. Syst. **14**(5) (2021)
9. Vargas, F.A., Pardo, T.A.S.: Aspect clustering methods for sentiment analysis. In: Villavicencio, A., et al. (eds.) PROPOR 2018. LNCS (LNAI), vol. 11122, pp. 365–374. Springer, Cham (2018). https://doi.org/10.1007/978-3-319-99722-3_37
10. Pessutto, L.R.C., Vargas, D.S., Moreira, V.P.: Clustering multilingual aspect phrases for sentiment analysis. In: 2018 IEEE/WIC/ACM International Conference on Web Intelligence (WI) (2018)
11. Imron, S., Setiawan, E.I., Santoso, J., Purnomo, M.H.: Aspect based sentiment analysis marketplace product reviews using BERT, LSTM, and CNN. Jurnal RESTI (Rekayasa Sistem dan Teknologi Informasi) **7**(3), 586–591 (2023)
12. Bansal, S., Sheth, M., Bansal, U.: Aspect based sentiment analysis of customer reviews on restaurants using random forest classifier (2022)
13. Gunathilaka, S., De Silva, N.: Aspect-based sentiment analysis on mobile application reviews. In: 2022 22nd International Conference on Advances in ICT for Emerging Regions (ICTer) (2022)
14. Kamila, S., Magdy, W., Dutta, S., Wang, M.: Ax-mabsa: a framework for extremely weakly supervised multi-label aspect based sentiment analysis. arXiv preprint arXiv:2211.03837 (2022)
15. Pontiki, M., Galanis, D., Pavlopoulos, J., Papageorgiou, H., Androutsopoulos, I., Manandhar, S.: Semeval-2014 task 4: aspect based sentiment analysis. In: Proceedings of the 8th International Workshop on Semantic Evaluation (SemEval 2014), Dublin, Ireland (2014)
16. Sanh, V., Debut, L., Chaumond, J., Wolf, T.: Distilbert, a distilled version of bert: smaller, faster, cheaper and lighter. arXiv preprint arXiv:1910.01108 (2019)
17. Abu-Khzam, F.N., et al.: Cluster editing with vertex splitting. Discret. Appl. Math. **371**, 185–195 (2025)
18. Abu-Khzam, F.N., Barr, J.R., Fakhereldine, A., Shaw, P.: A greedy heuristic for cluster editing with vertex splitting. In: 4th International Conference on Artificial Intelligence for Industries (AI4I), pp. 38–41, Laguna Hills, CA, USA. IEEE (2021)

Leveraging Blockchain for Decentralized Training and Inference of Large Language Models

Mohamad Sabra(✉) and Faisal Abu-Khzam

Department of Computer Science and Mathematics, Lebanese American University, Beirut, Lebanon
mohamad.sabra@lau.edu

Abstract. The substantial computational resources and expertise required to train and run AI models pose significant barriers of entry to the AI market. For instance, GPT-3 took USD 250 million to train, limiting participation to well-funded organizations and research institutions. This paper explores the integration of blockchain technology as a decentralized framework to distribute the training and inference processes of LLMs, while also focusing on AI model architecture that enables these adaptations. Previous work done by PETALS [2] and learning-at-home [10] has made this possible throughout different advancements in AI inferencing and training; However, the networks are not sustainable due to the user interactions needed to choose which model layer to host, without insights into the network health. This creates lack of coordination between nodes and results in an imbalance of model layer distribution in the network.

We propose a blockchain-based framework that enables individuals and organizations to contribute computational resources and data for training and inference tasks in exchange for incentives. This decentralized approach leverages smart contracts for task allocation, verification, and reward distribution, ensuring transparency and traceability throughout the contribution of the nodes. Once the blockchain is populated with data, aggregated reports generated by network nodes are used to score the network and its nodes in order to find the most suitable model layers to host for inferencing, or experts to train for new nodes.

The paper addresses key challenges such as efficient task distribution, model architecture, and maintaining a sustainable AI network. We also discuss how blockchain's inherent properties can be harnessed to create a trustworthy and scalable platform for AI development.

1 Preliminaries and Literature Review

The current barrier of entry makes it difficult for any new researchers that do not have the computational resources to prove a thesis or train their own model. Advancements in research in distributing the task of LLMs over the internet such as the work done in PETALS [2] and Learning at home [3] have made

J. R. Barr et al. (Eds.): ERWCSA 2025, ACSAR 4, pp. 128–138, 2026.
https://doi.org/10.1007/978-3-032-18230-2_8

a great stride towards making large language models accessible on any device. Similarly, blockchain-enabled federated learning frameworks, such as FedBChain [8], have demonstrated the potential for improving deep neural network performance through decentralized coordination. These solutions rely on user choices to customize the work their node does, which results in these networks not having enough model layers online to perform a full task, a lack of transparency and incentive over task distribution.

1.1 Model Partitioning with Pipeline Parallelism

Instead of serving the entire model one machine, the model is partitioned by layers and distributed across multiple devices in the network. Each device stores specific layers and computes them sequentially, sending intermediate outputs to the next device in the pipeline. Pipeline parallelism enables different devices to process various parts of the input tokens, reducing the load per device [3].

1.2 Fault-Tolerant Mechanism

If a device hosting a model layer goes offline, the system reassigns the task to another available node. Two types of caches are maintained: Server-side cache: Holds attention keys and values for each layer, improving performance. Client-side cache: Stores past inputs, enabling the system to recover quickly if a server fails by sending cached activations to a replacement server.

1.3 Load Balancing

Devices periodically announce their throughput and available layers using a Distributed Hash Table (DHT). When new devices join, they are assigned layers dynamically to maximize the overall throughput of the system.

The distribution of the LLM layers and their transformer blocks allows for a more broad architecture to be applied to a distributed system, holding under 3% of model weights for a 176B model (BLOOM) as demonstrated in PETALS [2].

2 Blockchain as the Decentralized Distributor for AI Layers and Tasks

Our blockchain-based solution addresses key limitations identified by Harris and Waggoner [7], specifically the challenges associated with hosting AI models within smart contracts, efficient task distribution, and maintaining data integrity in decentralized environments. Harris and Waggoner discuss how computational and storage limitations restrict traditional on-chain approaches, as the cost of storing model weights or large datasets within smart contracts becomes prohibitive. Recent advances in blockchain-AI integration have shown promising solutions to these challenges, including evolved proof-of-work mechanisms that repurpose up to 80% of mining computational power for AI training tasks [13], and proof-of-useful-intelligence frameworks that reduce energy waste by approximately 83% while performing meaningful AI computations [5]. Our approach addresses these limitations by hosting the model weights as shards to be accessed when needed during the training and inference process.

Furthermore, we enhance scalability and fault tolerance in a decentralized model architecture. By integrating the pipeline score system, nodes with compatible capabilities and high PipelineScore values are dynamically grouped into on-chain ***Model Instance Pools (MIPs)***, complete verifiable sets of nodes capable of serving an entire model. This hierarchical structure replaces a flat node registry, allowing for efficient discovery and allocation of healthy, high-performance groups. To further mitigate network delays and node failures noted by Harris and Waggoner, the system retains PETALS' server-side and client-side caching for rapid recovery and performance continuity.

Overall, a customized blockchain application of the PETALS framework provides a robust, transparent and decentralized architecture that leverages external storage, efficient caching, and parallelized compute, addressing the primary limitations highlighted by [7] and paving the way for scalable, collaborative AI model development and deployment.

The Blockchain layer functions as the core coordinator, managing critical components for decentralized model operation, including the Distributed Hash Table (DHT), load balancing, fault tolerance, reward distribution, and network health monitoring.

The Blockchain accessible decentralized datacenter for AI leverages smart contracts not just for task allocation but also for sophisticated network coordination. Nodes periodically build and submit aggregated reports to the blockchain, summarizing crucial network statistics such as the current status of online peers (availability, reported computational power, layers hosted), pending inference requests, and queue sizes across different model layers. These aggregated reports, immutably stored and accessible via the blockchain, provide a near real-time view of the network's state. This data feeds into a dynamic layer-choosing and load-balancing algorithm executed by the smart contracts or coordinating nodes. By analyzing these reports, the system can intelligently route tasks to less congested nodes, optimize the distribution of model layers based on demand and node capabilities, and ensure efficient resource utilization across the entire network, thereby maintaining performance and responsiveness even with participants joining from standard home internet connections (Fig. 1).

Dynamic Task Distribution via Aggregated Reports

The core of the task distribution system relies on dynamic information aggregated and published by the nodes themselves onto the blockchain. This moves beyond static registration data towards a real-time, adaptive network.

- **Node-Generated Local Reports and Global Aggregation:** Participating nodes actively monitor their *local* state and direct interactions with peers. They periodically compile and submit these local observations as reports to a

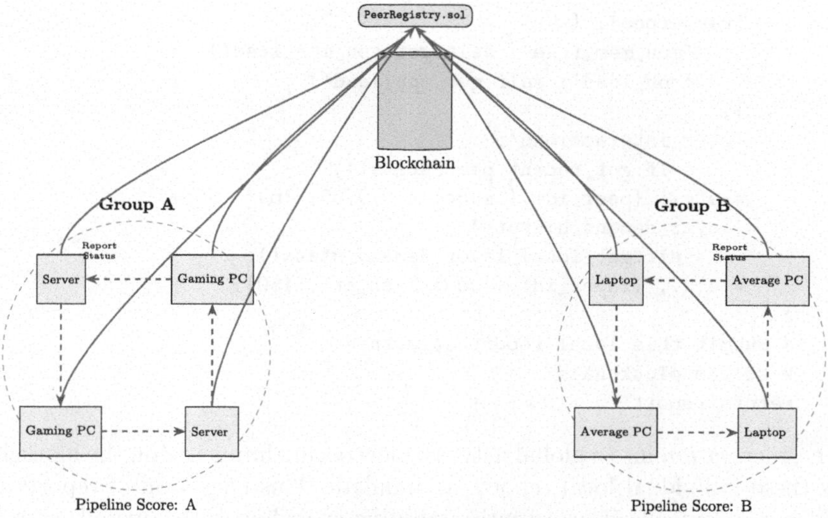

Fig. 1. The hierarchical base layer of the network. Nodes are organized into homogeneous groups based on their calculated Pipeline Score. All nodes report status to the on-chain PeerRegistry, while P2P communication for inference occurs within the performance-tiered groups.

dedicated smart contract. These reports primarily contain parameters reflecting the node's own status and recent activity:

- Current task queue size and estimated processing wait times for hosted model layers.
- Recent successful/failed interactions with neighboring peers (for direct P2P assessment).
- Observed local demand for specific model layers (based on incoming requests to this node).
- Available local resources (e.g., current GPU memory utilization, CPU load).

The report involves gathering these self-metrics: The report involves gathering these self-metrics:

```
# Inside a node's reporting logic
def build_local_report(self):
    report = {
        'timestamp': time.time(),
        'node_id': self.node_id,
        'hosted_layers': {
            layer_id: {
                'queue_size': self.get_queue_size(layer_id),
                'avg_wait_time': self.get_avg_wait(layer_id)
            } for layer_id in self.hosted_layers
        },
```

```
        'resources': {
            'gpu_mem_free': self.get_gpu_mem_free(),
            'cpu_load': self.get_cpu_load()
        },
        'peer_interactions':
            self.get_recent_peer_stats(),
        # e.g., {peer_id: {'success': 0.95, 'ms': 50}}
        'layer_demand_history':
            self.get_local_layer_demand_stats(),
        # e.g., {layer_id: {'reqs_last_hr': 150}}
    }
    # Submit this local report structure
    # to the blockchain
    return report
```

The *aggregation* into a global network view occurs implicitly on the blockchain as these individual local reports accumulate. This collection of reports provides a decentralized, constantly updating snapshot of the overall network's operational state, accessible for querying by any participant.

- **Intelligent Layer Caching and Peer Interaction (Consuming Aggregated Data):** Nodes utilize the globally accessible view, formed by the collection of submitted local reports on the blockchain, to make informed local decisions. By querying and analyzing trends across multiple reports (e.g., overall queue sizes, layer request frequencies network-wide), a node intelligently decides which model layers to proactively cache or drop. This decision aims to maximize its utility, considering factors like network-wide demand versus local resource cost:

$$\begin{aligned} U(l) = w_d &\times \text{NetworkDemand}(l) \\ &- w_r \times \text{ResourceCost}(l) \\ &+ w_n \times \text{NetworkValue}(l) \end{aligned}$$

  Where NetworkDemand(l) is derived from analyzing layer_demand_history across *multiple* nodes' reports on the blockchain. Nodes cache layers with the highest positive utility, subject to resource constraints.
  Similarly, nodes consult `peer_interactions` data from *various* reports on the blockchain (or potentially a summary contract aggregating this data) to identify globally responsive and low-latency peers for pipeline execution.
- **Smart Contract-Orchestrated Task Assignment (Consuming Aggregated Data):** When a user submits a task, the system leverages both the static `PeerRegistry` data and the dynamic *aggregated view* derived from the collection of local reports on the blockchain for node selection. The process involves:
  1. **Task Specification:** User defines the required model and layers (Y layers).
  2. **Candidate Filtering:** Query `PeerRegistry` for `Active` nodes hosting required layers with compatible configurations.

3. **Report-Driven Selection:** The coordinating mechanism analyzes the *collection of reports* on the blockchain for the filtered candidates. It identifies a subset (X nodes) covering all Y layers, optimizing the pipeline score:

$$\text{PipelineScore}(P) = \sum_{n \in P} \Bigg(w_q \frac{1}{1 + \text{QueueSize}(n, l_n)} + w_t \frac{1}{1 + \text{Latency}(n)} + w_{tp}\text{Throughput}(n) \Bigg)$$

   Here, `QueueSize(n, l_n)` and `Latency(n)` are obtained from the most recent relevant reports for node n available on the blockchain. The combination P with the highest score is chosen.
4. **Task Initiation:** Selected X nodes are assigned tasks.

Incentivized Reporting and Node Management
To ensure the reliability and accuracy of the aggregated reports crucial for task distribution, the system incorporates:

- **Reporting Incentives:** Nodes are rewarded with `InternalToken` not only for computation and staking but also for timely and accurate submission of aggregated reports. This encourages active participation in network monitoring.
- **Performance Tracking and Reputation:** Data from aggregated reports (e.g., queue management efficiency, successful task completions derived from report data) feeds into the nodeś performance tracking and reputation score. Consistently overloaded nodes or those providing inaccurate reports could see their reputation diminish, potentially impacting future task assignments or staking rewards.
- **Slashing Conditions:** Gross negligence or malicious reporting (e.g., consistently faking low queue sizes) can trigger slashing conditions, penalizing the node by confiscating a portion of its staked tokens.

This dynamic, report-driven system allows for efficient load balancing, optimized resource allocation (nodes caching layers based on actual demand), and robust task execution across a decentralized network.

Peer Discovery and Coordination using Smart Contracts
Departing from Petalsŕeliance on a traditional Distributed Hash Table (DHT), our framework introduces a novel approach utilizing blockchain smart contracts for robust peer discovery and coordination. We have implemented a suite of Solidity contracts, primarily `PeerRegistry.sol`, deployed on a local development blockchain (Ganache for the POC), to manage the lifecycle and capabilities of participating nodes.

- **On-Chain Registration and Status:** Instead of DHT announcements, Petals server nodes, modified in `petals/server/server.py`, now register directly with the `PeerRegistry` smart contract upon startup. This registration process records the nodeś unique blockchain address and initial status (`Active`). Crucially, nodes are configured via environment variables (`PEER_REGISTRY_ADDRESS`, `BLOCKCHAIN_RPC_URL`, etc.) to interact with the blockchain using `web3.py`. Nodes are responsible for calling `updatePeerStatus` to signal availability (`Active`) or planned downtime (`Inactive`), ensuring the registry reflects the current state of the network.
- **Detailed On-Chain Capability Metadata:** A key contribution is the storage of detailed node metadata directly within the `PeerRegistry` contract. During registration, the modified Petals server submits a structured metadata payload including:
  - Direct P2P Connection Information: The node's primary libp2p multiaddress.
  - Model Information: The specific model(s) or blocks the node is hosting.
  - Hardware/Software Configuration: Device type (GPU/CPU), PyTorch data type, quantization specifics, and Petals version.
  - Performance Metrics: Reported throughput capabilities.

  This rich, on-chain metadata allows clients (modified Petals inference clients) to perform more sophisticated discovery. Instead of simple DHT lookups, clients query the `PeerRegistry` contractś view functions (e.g., `getPeer`) to find `Active` peers matching specific requirements (model, hardware, performance) before initiating direct P2P connections using the retrieved multiaddress.
- **Foundation for Trust and Incentives:** The blockchain registry serves as a foundation for other system components. Registration requires interaction with the blockchain, linking a node's activity to its on-chain identity, which is essential for the staking (`Staking.sol`) and reward mechanisms managed by other smart contracts, utilizing an internal token (`InternalToken.sol`).

This blockchain-based approach provides a persistent, verifiable, and queryable record of network participants and their capabilities, replacing the ephemeral nature of DHTs and enabling more intelligent peer selection and network orchestration. This aligns with recent work on ownership-preserving AI marketplaces [11] and optimistic machine learning protocols [6] that demonstrate the feasibility of hosting and executing AI models within blockchain environments while maintaining privacy and verifiability.

2.1 Reward System and Incentivization

Our reward system builds upon concepts from proof-of-useful-work protocols [9] and dual-functional blockchain frameworks [4] that channel computational resources into productive AI tasks rather than energy-intensive mining operations. Rewards are distributed for different contributions:

When users store a model, they are rewarded base don the below function:

$$\text{StorageReward} = \text{ShardSize} \times \text{StorageDuration} \times \text{StorageMultiplier}$$

When executing a task:

$$\text{ExecutionReward} = \text{TaskComplexity} \times \text{Accuracy} \times \text{ExecutionMultiplier}$$

When staking:

$$\text{StakingReward} = \text{StakedAmount} \times \text{StakingDuration} \times \text{StakingMultiplier}$$

Calculating Task Complexity

$$\text{TaskComplexity} = \sum_{i=1}^{n} (S_i \times T_i \times W_i)$$

- S_i: Represents the contribution of the size of each shard.
- T_i: Accounts for the time complexity of processing each shard.
- W_i: Adjusts for differences in computational difficulty or resource intensity between shards (e.g., a shard requiring more memory may have a higher weight).

2.2 Decentralized Model Storage

- **Decentralized Storage:** Model weights, parameters, and checkpoints are sharded and stored by nodes, nodes will be rewarded for their storage and availability, reducing storage costs and avoiding bottlenecks by distributing access.
- **On-Demand Layer Access:** Nodes pull only the layers they are tasked with, optimizing memory usage by eliminating the need for any node to load the entire model.

3 Experimental Evaluation

To evaluate our blockchain-based distributed LLM framework, we performed several analyses focusing on cost efficiency, computational performance, and accessibility improvements compared to traditional centralized approaches.

As noted by Harris and Waggoner [7] blockchain is not efficient for communication between nodes, we continue to use Circuit Relay protocol from libp2p to traverse NATs and firewalls and achieve no loss of performance when compared to PETALS while also creating a sustainable network that grows with the task distribution and current network status.

3.1 Cost Analysis of Distributed Computing Resources

Our framework leverages idle computing resources across the network, creating a more efficient allocation mechanism and potentially significant cost reductions. This approach is supported by recent advances in blockchain frameworks that enable AI computation [14] and demonstrate practical deployment of machine learning models as smart contracts [12]. Based on our analysis of available computing capacity from various device types, shown in Table 1, we estimated the potential compute pool growth over a five-year period.

Table 1. Available Computing Resources by Device Type

Device Type	Instant Teraflops	Daily Uptime (Hours)	Daily Available Capacity	Yearly Available Capacity
Average Computer	1.50–3.00 (2.25 avg)	8	18	6,480
Reasonable Gaming PC	6.00–10.00 (8.00 avg)	8	64	23,040
High-End Gaming PC	13.00–30.00 (21.50 avg)	8	172	61,920
Mining Rig (Private)	150.00–200.00 (175.00 avg)	24	4,200.00	1,512,000

Our projections indicate that the computing pool could grow from approximately 5.3 million teraflops in Year 1 to over 3.7 billion teraflops by Year 5, representing a substantial resource base for distributed AI operations.

3.2 Performance Comparison with PETALS Implementation

To evaluate the performance of our blockchain-based solution, we integrated the PETALS framework and conducted experiments running BLOOM-176B in various network configurations. Our system's performance was measured in terms of (Table 2):

1. Single-batch inference (tokens/second)
2. Parallel forward passes (tokens/second)

Table 2. Performance Comparison with Different Configurations [2]

Configuration	Network Conditions	Single-Batch Inference (tokens/s)	Parallel Forward Passes (tokens/s)
3 Physical A100 Servers	1 Gbit/s, <5 ms RTT	1.71	253.6
3 Physical A100 Servers	100 Mbit/s, <5 ms RTT	1.66	182
3 Physical A100 Servers	100 Mbit/s, 100 ms RTT	1.23	112.2
12 Virtual Servers	1 Gbit/s, <5 ms RTT	1.24	180
14 Real Servers	Real-world conditions	0.83	179.4
A100, 256 Gbit/s	-	0.18	170.3

3.3 Cost Projections and API Pricing Model

Based on our financial analysis and the reward functions implemented in our smart contracts, we estimated the following API pricing structure compared to centralized alternatives (Table 3):

Table 3. Estimated API Pricing Comparison (per million tokens)

Model Size	Traditional API Cost	Our Blockchain Solution	Cost Reduction
7B Parameters	\$0.80–\$2.00	\$0.30–\$0.80	60–65%
13B Parameters	\$2.50–\$5.00	\$0.90–\$1.80	64–66%
70B Parameters	\$10.00–\$15.00	\$3.20–\$5.40	64–68%
175B+ Parameters	\$30.00–\$50.00	\$9.00–\$17.00	66–70%

The projected cost reductions range from 60–70%, making advanced AI capabilities significantly more accessible to researchers and organizations with limited resources.

The savings would come from three primary sources:

1. Utilization of idle computing resources (versus dedicated infrastructure)
2. Decentralized model storage with efficient sharding
3. More efficient task distribution through our blockchain-based orchestration

4 Future Work

Adaptation of smart contracts to make it easier to integrate new models, the smart contracts could technically include any address to pull a layer from and run against it, it would be the job of the nodes to know what to do. the smart contract

Further areas for exploration and development include:

- **Custom Trained Agent Storage and Inference using IPFS** [1]:
  - *On-Chain Agent Marketplace:* Enabling users to store, discover, and inference specialized agents trained for specific tasks directly via the blockchain network.
  - *Checkpoint Management:* Leveraging the blockchain for immutable storage and versioning of agent training checkpoints, potentially improving fine-tuning and reproducibility compared to traditional methods.

5 Concluding Remarks

We presented a blockchain-based framework that enables individuals and organizations to contribute computational resources and data for training and inference tasks for large language models, in exchange of incentives. This solution aims to create a self-scalable network that can be run by any user at home without requiring technical knowledge of models, weights, or optimal selection for monetization. By leveraging core Blockchain functionality, aggregated reports maintain a healthy network and transparent reward distribution, we can create a network that is more efficient and scalable than traditional centralized approaches.

References

1. Benet, J.: IPFS - Content Addressed, Versioned, P2P File System. arXiv preprint arXiv:1407.3561 (2014)
2. Borzunov, A., et al.: Petals: collaborative inference and fine-tuning of large models. arXiv preprint arXiv:2209.01188 (2022). Version 2. Accessed 2 Mar 2023
3. Borzunov, A., et al.: Distributed inference and fine-tuning of large language models over the internet. In: Oh, A., Naumann, T., Globerson, A., Saenko, K., Hardt, M., Levine, S. (eds.) Advances in Neural Information Processing Systems 36: Annual Conference on Neural Information Processing Systems 2023, NeurIPS 2023, New Orleans, LA, USA, 10–16 December 2023 (2023)
4. Cao, W., Ge, Z., Wang, J., Wang, H.: A dual-functional blockchain framework for solving distributed optimization. arXiv preprint arXiv:2405.19027 (2024)
5. Chong, Z.-K., Ohsaki, H.: Proof of useful intelligence (PoUI): blockchain consensus beyond energy waste. arXiv preprint arXiv:2504.17539 (2025)
6. Conway, K., So, C., Yu, X.: opml: optimistic machine learning on blockchain. arXiv preprint arXiv:2401.17555 (2024)
7. Harris, J.D., Waggoner, B.: Decentralized & collaborative AI on blockchain. In: 2019 IEEE International Conference on Blockchain (Blockchain), pp. 599–606 (2019)
8. Li, G., et al.: Fedbchain: a blockchain-enabled federated learning framework for improving deep convolutional neural network performance. IEEE Access **12**, 42089–42102 (2024)
9. Lihu, A., du Boisberranger, J., Nguyen, D.-P., Danelutto, A.: A proof of useful work for artificial intelligence on the blockchain. arXiv preprint arXiv:2001.09244 (2020)
10. Ryabinin, M., Gusev, A.: Towards crowdsourced training of large neural networks using decentralized mixture-of-experts. In: Advances in Neural Information Processing Systems 33: Annual Conference on Neural Information Processing Systems 2020, NeurIPS 2020, Vancouver, BC, Canada, 6–12 December 2020, pp. 3659–3672 (2020)
11. Somy, N.B., et al.: Ownership preserving ai marketplaces using blockchain. arXiv preprint arXiv:2001.09011 (2020)
12. Vora, J., Doiphode, A., Sakhare, A., Naval, S., Tanwar, S.: Ml2sc: deploying machine learning models as smart contracts on the blockchain. arXiv preprint arXiv:2404.16967 (2024)
13. Wei, Y., Feng, S., Niyato, D., Kim, D.I., Kang, J., Xie, S.: Connecting ai learning and blockchain mining in 6G systems. arXiv preprint arXiv:2104.14088 (2021)
14. You, J.: Blockchain framework for artificial intelligence computation. arXiv preprint arXiv:2202.11264 (2022)

Developmental Framework for an LLM Enabled Aircraft Log Anomaly Detection for Identification of Security Events in an IP Environment

Sean I. McConoughey(✉), Jayson F. Clifford, and Daniel J. Diessner

Center for Aerospace Resilient Systems, Embry-Riddle Aeronautical University, 1 Aerospace Blvd, Daytona Beach, FL 32114, USA
{mcconous,CLIFFORJ,DIESSNED}@erau.edu

Abstract. Aviation environments generate large, heterogeneous log streams that overwhelm signature-only monitoring. We present a developmental framework for *threat-informed labeling* that maps low-level log events to MITRE ATT&CK tactics and techniques with explicit rationale and confidence. The framework comprises: (i) contextual enrichment from aircraft architecture definitions (network connectivity, domains/partitioning, and safety-criticality labels) and flight-phase awareness; (ii) a retrieval-augmented, LLM-based loop that selects candidate techniques with justification; and (iii) high-volume hygiene (allowlists and burst grouping) to reduce alert spam and pass coherent batches to the LLM.

This is a **design paper**: we describe architecture, interfaces, and assumptions; we do **not** report quantitative evaluation. We provide artifact schemas (input logs, enrichment, ATT&CK-mapped outputs) and a concrete plan for future assessment (metrics, baselines, and ablations).

Keywords: Aviation cybersecurity · MITRE ATT&CK · Log analysis · LLM · Design paper

Nomenclature

LLM	large language model
DAL	design assurance level
FAISS	Facebook AI similarity search
FPR	false positive rate
TPR	true positive rate
MTTD	mean time to detect
RAG	retrieval-augmented generation
Air-VE	Aircraft Virtual Environment

J. R. Barr et al. (Eds.): ERWCSA 2025, ACSAR 4, pp. 139–147, 2026.
https://doi.org/10.1007/978-3-032-18230-2_9

1 Introduction

Modern aircraft can generate gigabytes of logs per flight. Airline security operation centers process and evaluate these logs to ensure the safety of the fleet, requiring security analysts to isolate genuine anomalies from vast benign false positive noise. Due to the human analysis required to classify anomalies and the volume of false positives, the time between anomaly occurrence and the completion of analysis increases, subsequently increasing risk. Traditional rule-based intrusion detection systems struggle with novel tactics and differentiating between normal activity, benign anomalies, and anomalies that could have an impact on critical systems unique to aviation safety. Large Language Models (LLMs) have recently shown promise for generalized reasoning over unstructured text, yet their raw outputs are overly verbose, slow, and lack ground truths necessary to be viable in this environment.

This work introduces a hybrid framework that leverages LLM semantic inference while using additional context and preserving key components of the log, ensuring clear decision paths critical in analysis. Our key contributions are:

Contributions.

1. A threat-informed labeling *contract* that emits {*tactic*, *technique*, *rationale*, *confidence*} per anomaly, traceable to specific log line(s).
2. A normalization pass over ATT&CK that yields compact, phase-aware summaries suitable for retrieval and prompting.
3. A high-throughput front-end that combines pattern signatures and token-weighted scoring to down-select traffic before LLM reasoning.
4. A model/runtime-agnostic implementation sketch (Apple MLX + Gemma 3 shown) and deployment notes.
5. A *prospective evaluation plan* (metrics, baselines, and ablations) for later work.

Ethics & Safety. This work targets defender workflows. We omit operational details that would materially aid misuse and release only synthetic or sanitized prompts and schemas. Any deployment to production environments should undergo safety review and red-team testing.

2 System Overview

Figure 1 illustrates the three major subsystems and data flow. Sequence diagrams for each stage are provided in Figs. 1, 2, 3 and 4.

2.1 Technology Stack

The pipeline is implemented in Python 3.13.3 leveraging the `mlx` library and its subcomponents for GPU/Neural Engine execution on Apple hardware, `Sentence-Transformers` for dense embedding, and `FAISS` for approximate nearest-neighbor search. Distributed inference across a two-node Mac Studio cluster is run using `mx.distributed` rings.

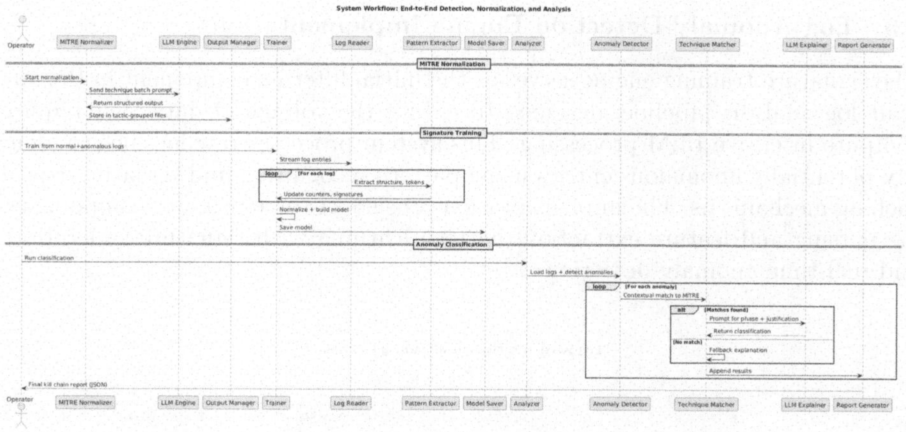

Fig. 1. End-to-end workflow: normalization, signature training, and anomaly classification.

2.2 MITRE ATT&CK Knowledge Base Normalization

The first component performs one-shot normalization of the MITRE ATT&CK knowledge base to create compact, structured summaries suitable for similarity matching during log analysis. While ATT&CK data is available in STIX (Structured Threat Information eXpression) format, the description sections themselves present an uneven format and level of detail throughout the knowledge base. This pre-processing step transforms the MITRE technique descriptions into concise, standardized representations that enable efficient semantic comparison with identified anomalous log entries.

LLM-Based Knowledge Processing. The normalization engine utilizes the Google Gemma-3-27B model running on Apple MLX hardware to process MITRE ATT&CK technique entries. The `GemmaRunner` class implements model initialization with GPU acceleration. Each technique entry is submitted to the LLM through structured prompting that requests standardized JSON output. The system processes techniques in configurable batches with robust error handling, while the `parse_llm_output` function applies JSON formatting corrections. The LLM prompt includes explicit network port definitions and MITRE ATT&CK phase definitions to ensure the LLM has accurate information to make assessments with.

Structured Output Generation. Normalized technique data are output into a directory, sorting techniques into `jsonl` files named according to the phases in which they occur. This results in smaller files needed to load into the LLM for log classification, fitting within context length limits.

2.3 Log Anomaly Detection Engine Implementation

The signature-training engine serves as the initial filtering component in the aircraft log analysis pipeline, designed to reduce the volume of data that require compute-intensive LLM processing. This system processes raw log files to identify potentially anomalous entries using pattern recognition and signature-based caching mechanisms. The implementation consists of three primary components: log parsing and feature extraction, pattern learning with signature generation, and real-time anomaly detection.

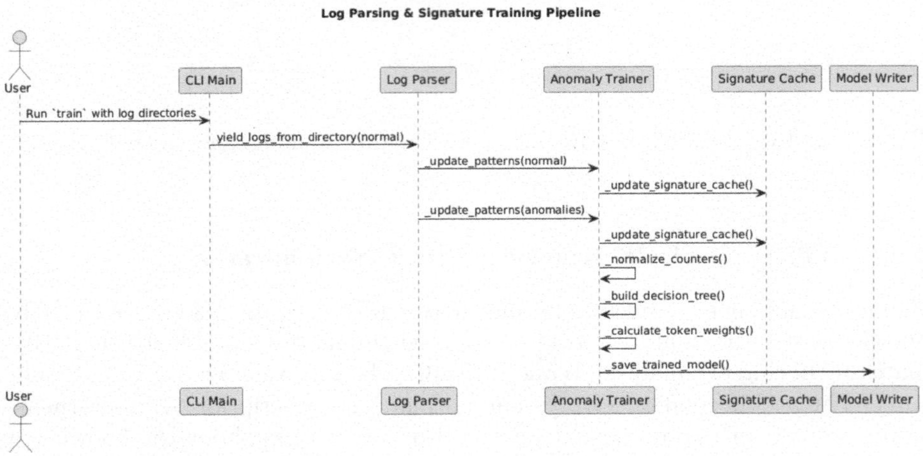

Fig. 2. Process chart showing the full anomaly detection pipeline.

Log Parsing and Feature Extraction. The system employs a structured parsing approach to extract meaningful features from security log formats found in Air-VE aircraft systems. Each log entry is parsed into a standardized `LogEntry` data structure comprising fields for timestamp, system identifier, service name, log level, message content, error information, and network-related parameters such as source/destination addresses, protocols, and port numbers. The parser utilizes regular expressions optimized for Air-VE log formats, including both quoted and unquoted message fields, kernel-level entries, and network traffic logs. Network details are extracted using pattern matching for standard firewall and intrusion detection log formats, capturing fields such as `IN/OUT` direction, `SRC/DST` addresses, protocol types, and source/destination ports. Token extraction employs pattern matching through the `extract_tokens` function to identify meaningful terms while filtering common stop words, reducing the feature space while preserving semantically significant terms that may indicate suspicious activities.

Pattern Learning and Signature Generation. The training process builds comprehensive pattern libraries from labeled normal and anomalous log datasets. The system maintains separate frequency distributions for services, log levels, message tokens, error patterns, and network characteristics across both normal and anomalous classes, normalized by total sample counts to produce probability estimates for each feature class. To achieve high-throughput processing, the system implements a signature-based caching mechanism using Blake2b hashing of key identifying features. The `compute_log_signature` function generates deterministic signatures that enable rapid pattern matching during detection phases. The signature cache maintains occurrence counts for both normal and anomalous instances of each pattern, with cache entries storing normal and anomaly counts along with computed probability scores. A decision tree structure is constructed using learned patterns through the `_build_decision_tree` method, with each node representing a feature category and associated anomaly probability scores computed from likelihood ratios.

Real-Time Anomaly Detection. The detection engine operates in two modes depending on whether incoming log entries match previously observed signatures. For cached signatures, the system performs immediate classification using stored probability scores, achieving sub-millisecond response times for known patterns. For novel log entries, the system employs a token-weighted scoring approach through the `_token_based_score` method, which evaluates message content against learned vocabulary patterns. Each token is assigned a weight based on its relative frequency in anomalous versus normal logs. The scoring algorithm combines multiple evaluation methods through the `_evaluate_decision_tree` function, assessing service patterns, log levels, network protocols, and token combinations. Scores are averaged to produce a final anomaly confidence score compared against a configurable threshold. The system utilizes concurrent execution patterns with generator-based streaming through `yield_logs_from_file` to minimize memory footprint and thread pool execution for parallel file processing. Processing statistics including throughput rates and anomaly detection rates are tracked, with output provided in `jsonl` format for downstream LLM integration.

2.4 Knowledge Base and Output Contract

What it is. We use the MITRE ATT&CK matrix as a knowledge base of adversary *tactics* (goals) and *techniques* (methods).

Why use it. It provides a common vocabulary, enables hypothesis-driven triage, and supports coverage/gap analysis.

Output format. Each anomaly is emitted as:

$$\{\textit{tactic},\ \textit{technique},\ \textit{rationale},\ \textit{confidence}\}$$

and each record is traceably mapped to specific log line(s).

2.5 Aircraft Virtual Environment

The Aircraft Virtual Environment (Air-VE) is a generic aircraft digital twin designed to generate high-fidelity data for cyber-security data science research. It simulates normal operations and cyber-attack scenarios to help address limitations of real-world data like coverage, privacy concerns, and cost. Air-VE is modeled based on industry guidance and widely available documents such as ARINC664-P5 and ARINC852. The system simulates multiple aircraft components and provides real running systems that support real-time interaction. This allows realistic interaction between aircraft systems, flight crew, and attackers. For the scope of this work, the relevant Air-VE output is a realistic aircraft architecture (shown in Fig. 3) with associated systems and a large data set of security logs adhering to ARINC852.

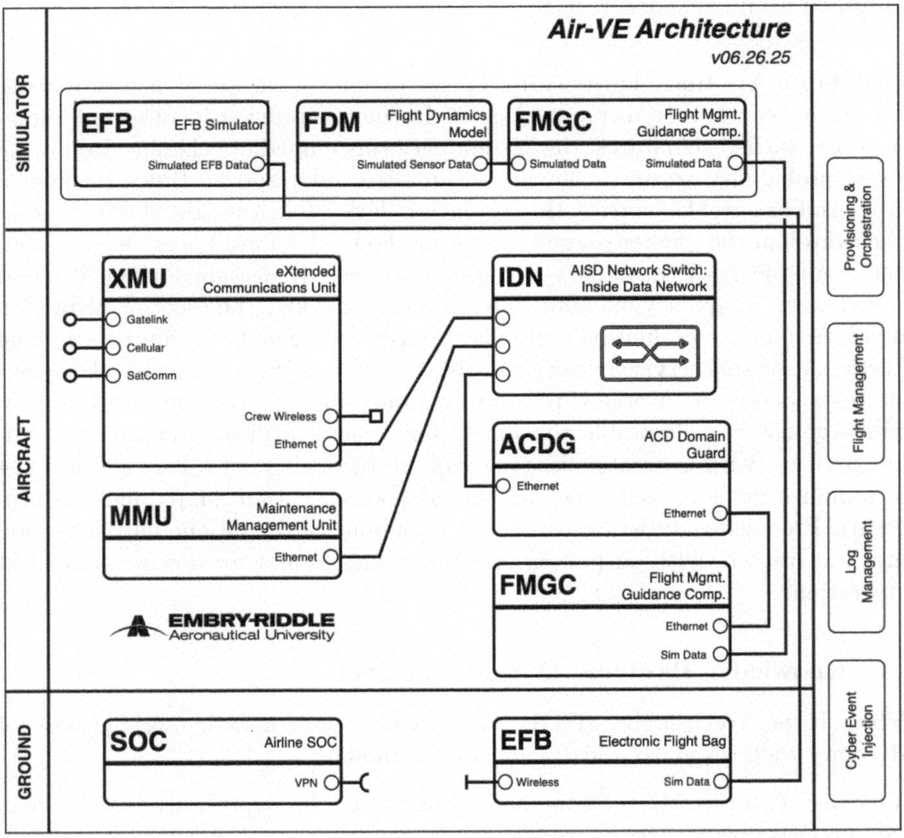

Fig. 3. Air-VE architecture diagram.

2.6 Contextual Enrichment

We maintain a structured architectural definition (nodes, roles, IPs, subnets, and DAL-like criticality tags) of aircraft systems. Source/destination IPs are resolved to roles and criticality (e.g., XMU – DAL D). Ports are mapped to services (e.g., 22→SSH, 502→MODBUS-TCP) to create richer prompts. A flight-phase tracker (FMGC transitions) injects temporal context, allowing risk to be interpreted by phase. Outcome: anomalies are described in operational terms (role→role, phase), and the system is able to use contextual information to adjust outputs.

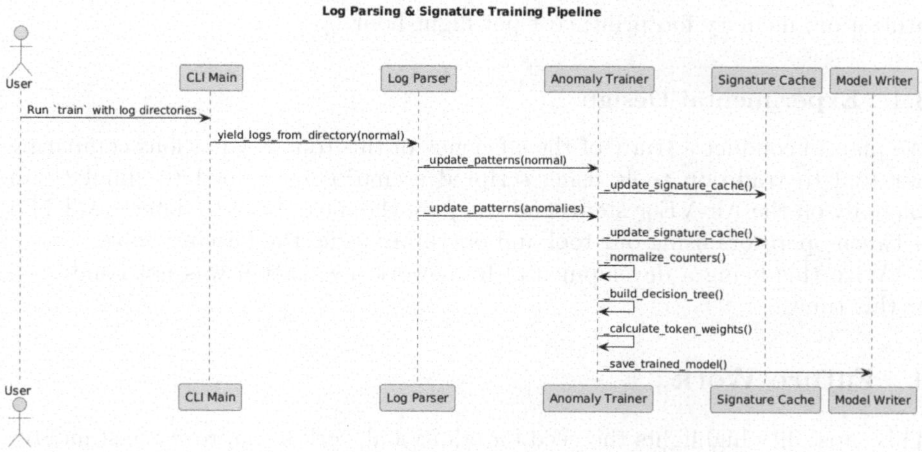

Fig. 4. Process chart showing the LLM pipeline.

2.7 High-Volume Hygiene

We apply hard whitelists (e.g., `guest-exec`, and similar phrases that are artifacts of the virtual environment and not representative of the aircraft being modeled). A high-volume detector groups bursts by source IP into timed batches; optional sequential grouping (src→dst) captures coordinated patterns. This reduces alert spam and sends holistic batches to the LLM for coherent labeling. Known tool patterns that can generate large event volumes are also flagged.

3 Evaluation Plan

3.1 Datasets and Settings

We plan to evaluate on: (1) Air-VE synthetic logs with seeded attacks; (2) shareable datasets from industry partners. Datasets and prompts used in evaluations will be disclosed as necessary and permissible to ensure replication of results while protecting potentially sensitive information.

3.2 Baselines

Pattern baselines: rule-based IDS. Retrieval/LLM ablations: (i) no enrichment, (ii) no allow-lists, (iii) no burst grouping, (iv) no ATT&CK normalization (raw text).

3.3 Metrics

Primary: precision/recall/F1 for anomaly labels; macro-F1 over ATT&CK techniques; mean time-to-detect (MTTD); alert-volume reduction ratio; analyst time per accepted alert. Secondary: latency per 1k lines; throughput (lines/s); GPU utilization; memory footprint; cost per flight-hour.

3.4 Experimental Design

We plan to conduct a study of the efficiency of this tool. Evaluations comparing our tool to tradition tools using scripted scenarios developed to simulate an anomaly on the Air-VE systems and compare the mean-time-to-detect (MTTD) between operators using our tool and operators using the baseline tools.

With this being a developmental framework, evaluation was not conducted at this time.

4 Future Work

This capability highlights the need for additional work to improve the standardization and cross-implementation of various aspects of aircraft security logging and associated systems to better support automated analysis. These preliminarily include security analysis coupled with structured aircraft architecture definitions, which could allow the automated system to correlate groups of log entries to known vulnerabilities or specific kill chains.

5 Conclusion

We introduced a developmental framework for threat-informed labeling of aircraft logs that integrates contextual enrichment, retrieval, and LLM reasoning. The paper contributes design artifacts and an evaluation plan; quantitative results are left to future work.

Acknowledgements. The authors thank colleagues at the Center for Aerospace Resilient Systems (Embry–Riddle Aeronautical University) for feedback on early drafts and system architecture. We extend a special thanks to our colleagues in the FlyByWire Simulations community for the A32NX project. We also thank the maintainers of the many other open-source projects leveraged in this work, including MITRE ATT&CK, FAISS, Sentence-Transformers, MLX, and aiohttp. Any opinions and conclusions are those of the authors and do not necessarily reflect the views of the above organizations. Large Language Models were utilized for grammatical revision of some parts of this paper.

Funding Information. The study was fully funded internally by the Center for Aerospace Resilient Systems at Embry-Riddle Aeronautical University.

References

1. Dixit, P., Bhattacharya, P., Tanwar, S., Gupta, R.: Anomaly detection in autonomous electric vehicles using AI techniques: a comprehensive survey. Expert Syst. **39**(5), e12754 (2022). https://doi.org/10.1111/exsy.12754
2. Shajarian, S.: Towards autonomous network management: AI-driven framework for intelligent log analysis, troubleshooting and documentation. In: Proceedings of AAAI (2025). https://ojs.aaai.org/index.php/AAAI/article/view/35226
3. Du, M., Li, F., Zheng, G., Srikumar, V.: DeepLog: anomaly detection and diagnosis from system logs via deep learning. In: Proceedings of CCS, pp. 1285–1298 (2017)
4. Guo, H., Li, J., et al.: LogBERT: log anomaly detection via BERT. IEEE Trans. Netw. Serv. Manag. **18**(3), 2661–2675 (2021)
5. Landauer, M., Skopik, F., Wurzenberger, M.: A survey on log data analysis and machine learning for cybersecurity. Comput. Secur. **113**, 102638 (2022)
6. MITRE Corporation: MITRE ATT&CK®. https://attack.mitre.org/. Accessed 3 Sept 2025
7. CISA: Best Practices for MITRE ATT&CK® Mapping (2023). https://www.cisa.gov/sites/default/files/2023-01/Best
8. OASIS: STIX™ Version 2.1. Committee Specification (2021). https://oasis-open.github.io/cti-documentation/stix/intro
9. Johnson, J., Douze, M., Jégou, H.: Billion-scale similarity search with GPUs. arXiv:1702.08734 (2017). https://doi.org/10.48550/arXiv.1702.08734
10. Reimers, N., Gurevych, I.: Sentence-BERT: sentence embeddings using siamese BERT-networks. In: Proceedings of EMNLP-IJCNLP, pp. 3982–3992 (2019)
11. Google: Gemma 3 Model Overview (last updated Aug 14, 2025). https://ai.google.dev/gemma/docs/core
12. Apple ML Research: MLX: Array framework for machine learning on Apple silicon. Documentation site (2025). https://ml-explore.github.io/mlx/
13. IEEE 802.1 TSN: AFDX (ARINC 664 Part 7) overview slide deck (2015). https://www.ieee802.org/1/files/public/docs2015/TSN-Schneele-AFDX-0515-v01.pdf
14. Jeppesen/AC 120-XX references and industry overview: ARINC 852 (Aircraft WLAN) overview (accessed 2025). https://ap-marina.com/2022/08/05/arinc-852-aircraft-wlan/
15. aiohttp maintainers: *aiohttp* Documentation (v3.12.x) (2025). https://docs.aiohttp.org/en/stable/
16. Open MPI Project: Open MPI v5.0.x Documentation (2024–2025). https://docs.open-mpi.org/
17. Docker Inc.: How to Use the Alpine Docker Official Image (2022). https://www.docker.com/blog/how-to-use-the-alpine-docker-official-image/
18. pyenv maintainers: pyenv (GitHub README). https://github.com/pyenv/pyenv

Fast Charging Technique for Electric Vehicles Using Artificial Intelligence

Frederick Wadnola III[1(✉)], Yusuf Abuabakar Sha'aban[2], and Ahmed Iyanda Sulyman[2]

[1] Department of Mechanical Engineering, Embry-Riddle Aeronautical University, Prescott, AZ 86301, USA
wadnolaf@my.erau.edu

[2] Department of Computer, Electrical and Software Engineering, Embry-Riddle Aeronautical University, Prescott, AZ 86301, USA
sulymana@erau.edu

Abstract. This paper discusses fast-charging techniques for electric vehicles. The current battery technologies for electric vehicles (EV) consist of large pack of lithium-ion cells, which are very heavy to carry around and are slower to re-charge compared to fuel refill time for combustion engines. This larger re-charge time is the main caveat for large-scale adoption of EV in today's busy World where car users cannot afford to wait 30 min or more at charging stations during their trips for battery re-charge. Development of new methods and techniques for fast charging of EV's are therefore crucial for wide-spread EV adoptions. This paper reviews the existing fast-charging methods in the market today and offers insights into what it takes to develop future fast-charging methods that are comparable to fuel re-filling for combustion engines.

Keywords: Electric Vehicles · Fast-Charging · Dual Active Bridge · Onboard Battery · Artificial Intelligence

1 Introduction

Electric vehicles (EVs) are not a new concept, as engineers and inventors have been designing and fabricating electric vehicles prior to the first internal combustion engine-powered vehicle. The concept is simple. Electrical energy is stored in a battery to be used by a device that converts electrical energy into work, the electric motor. The work output of an electric motor can then be used to move the vehicle. One of the challenging aspects of designing an electric vehicle is energy storage. The battery component of an electric vehicle system has been the greatest challenge. Descoped from electric vehicles, storing electrical energy is a challenging task; it is the driving force behind the constant race to manufacture a battery with the highest energy density-to-size and weight ratio. For transportation, the energy density-to-weight ratio is crucial for providing a longer range, higher output, and minimal recharging.

The current standard battery technology for EVs is large packs of lithium-ion cells. In order to provide an adequate range and average speed for transportation, massive arrays

J. R. Barr et al. (Eds.): ERWCSA 2025, ACSAR 4, pp. 148–157, 2026.
https://doi.org/10.1007/978-3-032-18230-2_11

of these Lithium-Ion cells are used in parallel. They are extremely heavy and take a long time to charge. This represents a significant setback to the widespread production and use of EVs. The optimal scenario is a charge that would be competitive with the time it takes to fill up the average gasoline fuel tank and offer an equal range. This would eliminate the inconvenience and impracticality of charging EVs for consumers. Fast-charging EVs would also reduce the size and weight of the current batteries required, since the battery can be charged faster, leading to more frequent charging cycles, but overall, less time compared to charging larger packs. Smaller battery packs would use less material, leading to EV technology becoming much more competitive with gasoline vehicles. Again, similar to the time and frequency of filling up an internal combustion vehicle. However, the battery technology itself is not the only factor to take into consideration. Fast-Charging EVs will demand a higher current output, which creates excess heat. This will lead to the adaptation of cooling systems into both the charger and the battery for safe operation. The higher power output will also lead to electric grid strain, which must be taken into consideration. Fast-Charging techniques do not only require engineering in the EV but also at the source of power generation and charger design.

2 Current Fast Charging Techniques

2.1 Dual Active Bridge (DAB)

A promising technique for fast EV charging is utilizing dual active bridge converters over traditional DC-DC converters [1]. DAB converters would increase power density and zero-voltage switching capabilities. The main advantage of ZVS is the minimal switching loss inherent in fast-charging technology. This will lead to greater efficiency and a reduction in thermal losses, which are major factors that must be considered for an improved fast charging technique [1]. The issue with DAB converters is mainly on the grid side. It is difficult to control power flow in DAB converters, leading to grid strain and brownouts [1]. A current method of controlling power flow is linear active disturbance rejection (LADRC). LADRC aims to reduce the initial peak input current, which is responsible for high grid strain [1]. It does this by accurately estimating and compensating for internal and external disturbances in the power flow [1].

2.2 Onboard Battery System (OBS)

A great fast-charging technique for reducing grid strain and providing consistent power to the EV would be utilizing an onboard battery in the charging station [2]. This can be trickle-charged over time and be used to provide the high initial current demand from the EV's battery. For the initial charge, the battery can be accompanied by grid power. As the current demand lessens towards the end of the charging cycle, grid power can be the sole source of power, operating within its range. This would solve a major problem with fast charging.

Grid infrastructure can provide consistent current at a constant rate, but struggles with high current spikes, which lead to grid strain and instability. Another similar configuration to this would be using EV batteries as the onboard battery in the charging station. This is known as Electric Vehicle-Grid Integration (EVGI) [3]. The concept for this technique is to keep the EV plugged in when not in use. When the EV battery is fully charged, it can be used to support the grid when charging other vehicles. With enough EVs connected to the grid and intelligent energy management, consumers' EVs may only lose a small percentage of battery capacity that can be quickly replenished since it is at the end of the charging cycle, which does not have high current demand. The consumer with the depleted battery using this small percentage from each fully charged EV would be paying the consumer with the fully charged battery at the charging station. The fully charged EV consumer would then be compensated for the charge they lost after the fast charge has been completed. That small percentage that is lost is used to meet the initial peak current demand for fast charging a depleted battery elsewhere in the grid. A great advantage of this is that it would take minimal infrastructure improvements since the EVs themselves are being used as a high-load source instead of an onboard battery in the charging station. Battery in the charging station.

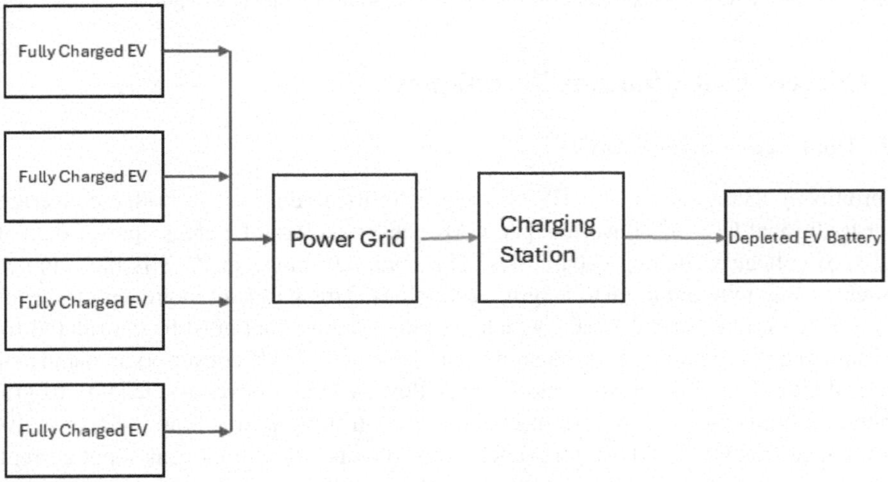

Fig. 1. Electric Vehicle Grid Integration Flow Diagram.

Figure 1 illustrates the simplified concept of Electric Vehicle Grid Integration. For example, assume there are 85 EVs with a fully charged battery that are parked. If it was plugged into the charging station, the depleted EV battery can fast charge using 1 percent of each of the fully charged EV batteries to 85%. The EV batteries would satisfy the high initial current load, and the remaining 15% can be charged using the grid at a lower current. The 1% lost by the grid can be quickly replenished by the grid, similar to balancing cells in the EV battery itself. This would eliminate having the same high current load required to charge the one depleted battery. This idea can be greatly scaled and manipulated to have EVs only lose a fraction of the percentage of their charge, and it would be rapidly replenished. This idea encourages widespread EV use, as the more EVs that are connected to the grid, the more effective EVGI would be.

3 Artificial Intelligence for Peer-to-Peer Electric Vehicle Charging

3.1 System Architecture

As mentioned in the previous section, cell balancing is crucial for fast charging a lithium battery safely. This is because battery cells are wired in series to increase the battery's voltage and in parallel to increase its current capacity. Tuning how many cells in series and in parallel is needed to meet the requirements of the vehicle's powertrain. There are two different types of cell balancing: passive and active. Passive balancing works by releasing surplus energy as heat through designated resistors until the overcharged battery cells match the weaker cells around them. Active balancing uses inductors, capacitors, or a DC-DC converter to transfer charge from higher voltage cells to lower voltage ones. Peer-to-peer electric vehicle charging uses the active balancing concept. Where each electric vehicle plugged in for charging would essentially become one large battery pack, the electric vehicles themselves act as individual cells to one another and would then charge each other. Each electric vehicle still has its own battery management system but will rely on AI to manage the pack-level coordination. This is where artificial intelligence would become a major asset to the system. AI would be able to control this process at a highly advanced and efficient level.

3.2 Learning Model

The learning model will be integrated into the red arrow section of Fig. 1. The main objective is to decide which battery will be discharged and for how long. This is where learning driver's habits and hardware behavior is required. Driver habits to consider include arrival and departure windows, state of charge targets, willingness to share, charging preferences, and reliability in remaining plugged in even when their battery is fully charged. Examples of arrival/departure factors include some drivers leaving their car plugged in overnight at home versus unplugging it after 30 min while running an errand. AI must predict how long a donor/receiving vehicle will stay. For state-of-charge targets, many drivers do not need 100% capacity. If they are commuting from work to home, they can charge faster with precalculated ranges and have enough capacity to get to their destination. The model must be able to learn these habits and determine the optimal charging time for vehicles to minimize range miscalculations. Having a desire to share can also be a matter of preference for consumers, where some may opt to leave their batteries at a higher percentage for better performance or prefer to keep their battery percentage higher. This can be calculated into the price of the charge with enough donors. If a driver commutes for short distances, they can opt to be a larger contributor and be rewarded for their donor habits. AI would be able to use driver options to optimize the model and regulate the price of the energy being transferred between vehicles. The only way for this idea to be feasible is for drivers to plug in their vehicles as much as possible. AI must account for drivers not plugging in and compensate for this with other vehicles. Drivers can have a trusted rating, which would give rewards like reduced charging costs.

Artificial Intelligence would build profiles for each driver to contribute to the model, such as behavioral profiles, contextual predictors, reputation systems, adaptive incentives, and clustering drivers into categories. The recorded data includes driver habits and car performance. The behavior profile would be all the habits described above. Contextual predictors would include features such as the time of day, day of the week, location of the charger, and weather conditions. The reputation system and adaptive incentives would be tied together to keep drivers engaged and willing to keep their vehicles plugged in when necessary.

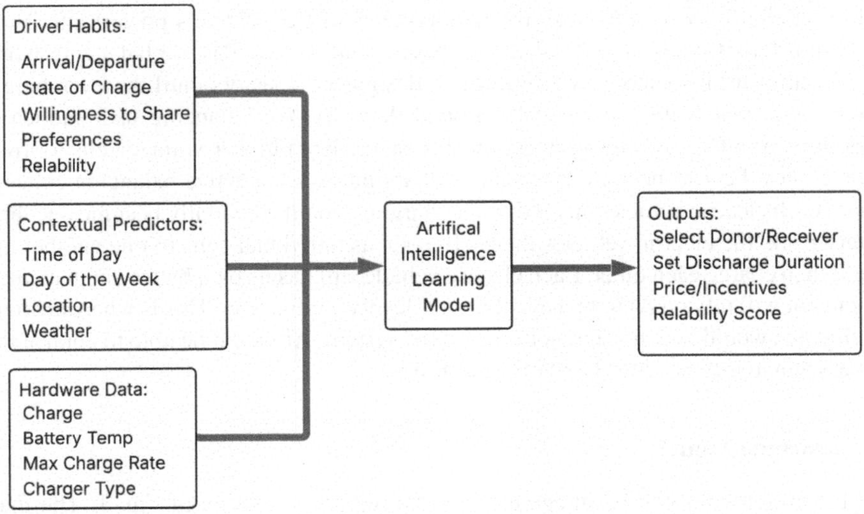

Fig. 2. Artificial Intelligence Learning Model Concept of Operations for Peer-to-Peer Charging.

Figure 2 illustrates the concept of the artificial intelligence learning model that would be used for controlling peer-to-peer charging. On the left are the inputs to the model. The inputs include driver habits, Contextual predictors, and hardware data, with each factor considered under each input. The "Artificial Intelligence Learning Model" block is a high-level representation of the learning model being used. This block will use inputs coming from the red arrows and output to the right through the blue arrow. The outputs block is all the functions being controlled by the model.

3.3 MATLAB Simulation of the Peer to Peer AI Learning Model

This MATLAB model simulates a small peer-to-peer population within a set time frame. It will determine which EVs are donors and receivers, or those with a high versus a low state of charge. It will then pair up one EV with another and move a small amount of charge at a controlled rate to the receiver. It will then update each vehicle's state of charge and display the result. The simulation uses the MATLAB Statistics and Machine Learning toolbox to enable learning and prediction. During initialization, the simulation will choose random pack sizes between 50 and 75 kWh. This is the size of the battery of each EV at the beginning of the simulation. This matters because it will affect donors' and receivers' decisions for the model. Next, the model will choose a random state of charge for each EV in the population to simulate random driving habits between 20%

and 90%. It will then flag random vehicles to be classified as long commuters, which increases their continuous drain slightly. This will nudge them to be a receiver more often. The loop then begins with a chosen time step and duration. Since the EV will always use a small amount of energy when powered on from control electronics or cabin amenities, a constant background drain is set for each vehicle.

$$\Delta_{soc} = -\frac{bg_{KW} * \Delta t}{E_{KWh}} \tag{1}$$

Equation (1) gives the background drain of each electric vehicle. A long commuter flag will increase the drain rate. The model will then classify which vehicle is a donor and which is a receiver by comparing the state of charge of the battery to the user-set donor floor and the target state of charge. If the state of charge is greater than the donor floor, the vehicle is classified as a donor. If the state of charge is less than the target state of charge, then it is a receiver. It will then pair the top donor with the lowest receiver and so on.

$$dE = p2p_{kW} * \frac{\Delta t}{60} \tag{2}$$

Equation (2) computes the energy transfer between a donor and receiver vehicle. The model ensures that the donor does not fall below the donor floor limit and that the receiver does not exceed the target state of charge. It will then plot and animate the resulting data and show an animation of the simulation.

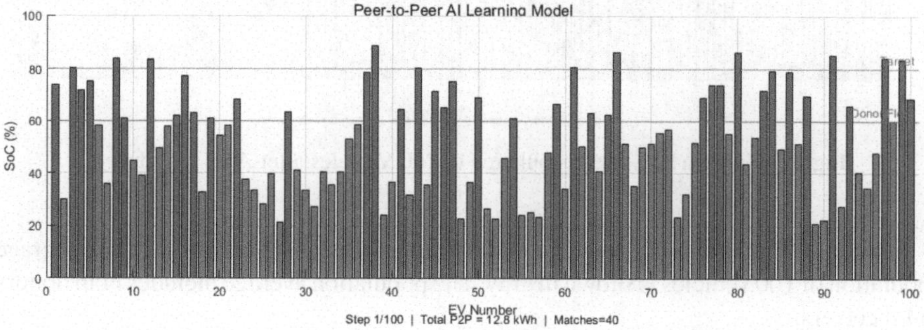

Fig. 3. Initial SoC for a Population of 100 Vehicles prior to the Introduction of AI

Figure 3 is a snapshot of the initial randomized state of charge for each of the 100 vehicles prior to running the simulation and introducing AI (Timestep 1). The state of charge range is from 0% to 100%. The horizontal green target line shows the target state of charge for the model. The horizontal red line is the donor floor limit. Each vehicle is graphed individually across the graph. The color of the state of charge bar indicates whether the vehicle is a donor or a receiver, represented by red for donors and green for receivers. In the animation, this color will change as the vehicles eventually reach the receiver state.

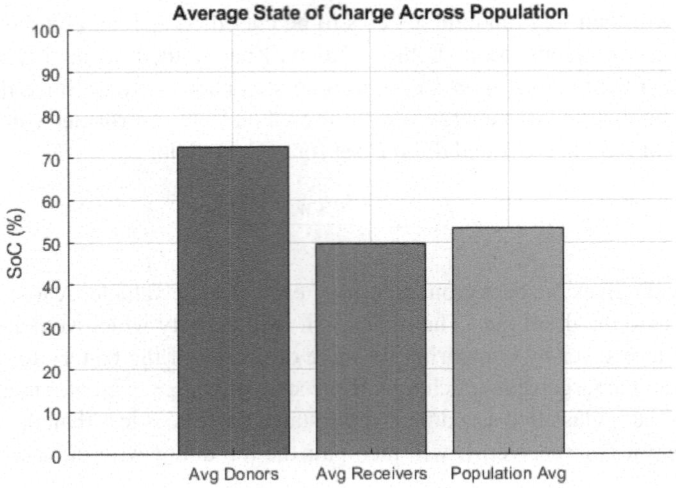

Fig. 4. Initial average SoC across all vehicles at timestep 1

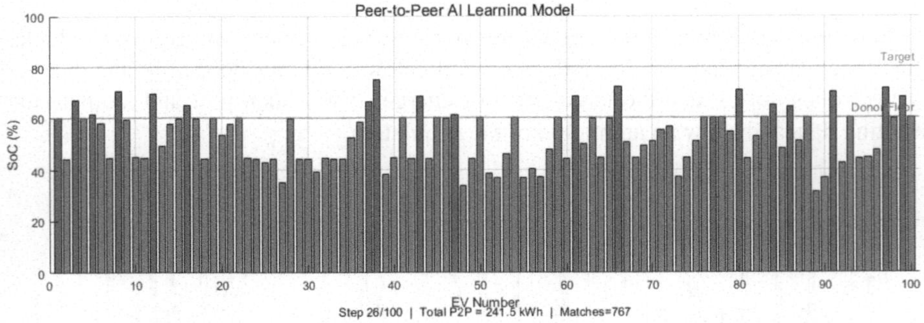

Fig. 5. Midterm SoC for a population of 100 Vehicles after AI is introduced

Figure 4 shows the initial average of each vehicle's state at timestep 1. The average population of 100 vehicles is shown in gray. The population average includes both donors and receivers.

Figure 5 is a snapshot of timestep 26 out of 100 timesteps for the simulation. Compared to Fig. 4, there are more receivers than donors, as seen from a greater number of bars being green instead of red. The state of charge between vehicles is also much closer together as the receiver gains charge and takes from the donors. This is where the learning model is implemented; it uses driver habits and other data to determine which vehicle is a donor and which vehicle is a receiver. The model also takes the initial state of charge data into account from Fig. 4. If the population were larger, the model would be able to learn and predict faster.

Figure 6 shows the average population at timestep 26 of the simulation. As time passes, the average donor and average receiver state of charge converge towards each other. The energy from the donors is increasing the state of charge of the receivers.

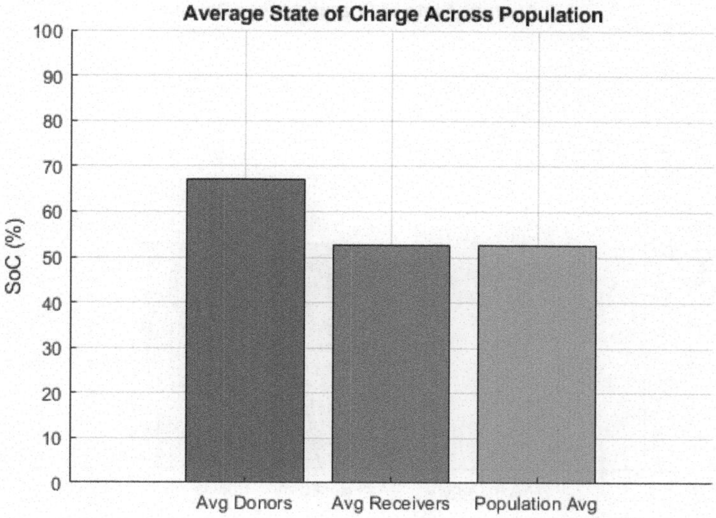

Fig. 6. Average SoC across all vehicles once AI is introduced

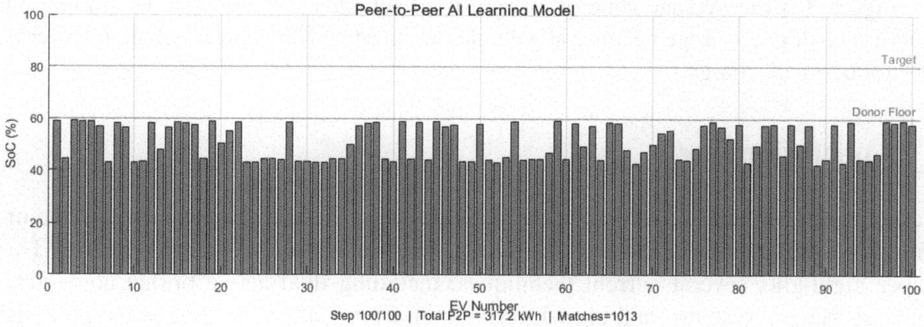

Fig. 7. Final SoC for 100 vehicles after AI optimization is completed

Figure 7 shows the state of charge after all donors switched to the receiver state at the end of the simulation. At this point, all vehicles are being charged from the grid without requiring fast charging. This is where the grid strain is minimized. Vehicles at this point are charging at a lower rate overnight or for long durations during the day. The learning model is gathering charge and habit data in this state to restart the cycle. The reason some vehicles are not at 100% state of charge is due to the model's predictions. Vehicles with a lower state of charge in Figure 7 are classified as short commuters, which have enough charge to satisfy drivers' habits and commute times. The vehicles closest to the donor floor are classified as long commuters in the model and also have enough charge to satisfy commute times and driver habits. This is where another benefit of the model is shown, being able to predict commute times minimizes the amount of state of charge required. If the model were not used, all vehicles would be at 100% and have an excess charge that would cause grid strain.

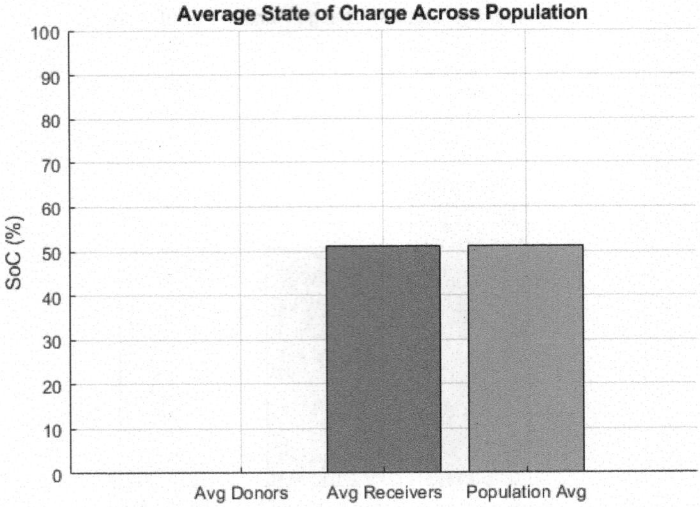

Fig. 8. Final Average SoC for a population of 100 vehicles after AI optimization is completed

Figure 8 is the average state of charge of all vehicles at the end of the simulation. There is no donor average because all vehicles are in a receiver state where their batteries are not being discharged.

4 Conclusion

Fast charging remains the critical barrier to widespread electric vehicle adoption, requiring solutions that balance battery technology, power electronics, and grid stability. This paper highlights several current techniques, including dual active bridge converters, onboard battery systems, and electric vehicle grid integration, as well as the potential of artificial intelligence to manage peer-to-peer charging and driver behavior. While no single method alone can replicate the convenience of fossil fuel refueling, a hybridized approach combining advanced converter technologies, distributed energy storage, and AI-driven coordination offers a practical pathway forward. By integrating EVs as active participants in the grid rather than passive loads, we can mitigate peak demand, improve charging efficiency, and reduce reliance on costly infrastructure upgrades. Ultimately, the success of these techniques depends on collaboration between engineers and consumers, ensuring that fast charging solutions are not only technically viable but also economically and socially scalable. Continued innovation in this field will accelerate the transition toward a sustainable, electrified transportation future. This paper presents the concept of implementing an AI learning model into the charging control of electric vehicles. However, to properly show the actual value of this idea, further development and research are needed and ongoing. The main research needed is gathering actual drivers' habits and inputting them into the model.

Acknowledgments. A third level heading in 9-point font size at the end of the paper is used for general acknowledgments, for example: This study was funded by X (grant number Y).

Disclosure of Interests. The authors have no competing interests to declare that are relevant to the content of this article.

References

1. Nkembi, A.A., et al.: Novel droop-based techniques for dynamic performance improvement in a linear active disturbance rejection controlled-dual active bridge for fast battery charging of electric vehicles. Energies **17**, 5171 (2024). https://doi.org/10.3390/en17205171
2. Aksoz, A., Asal, B., Biçer, E., Oyucu, S., Gençtürk, M., Golestan, S.: Advancing electric vehicle infrastructure: a review and exploration of battery-assisted dc fast charging stations. Energies **17**, 3117 (2024). https://doi.org/10.3390/en17133117
3. Waseem, M., Sreeshobha, E., Shashidhar Reddy, K., Donateo, T.: State-of-the-art and advancement of charging infrastructure in electric mobility: an integrated review. Energies **17**, 6137 (2024). https://doi.org/10.3390/en17236137
4. Sha'aban, Y.A., Ikpehai, A., Adebisi, B., Rabie, K.M.: Bi-directional coordination of plug-in electric vehicles with economic model predictive control. Energies **10**(10), 1507 (2017). https://doi.org/10.3390/en10101507
5. Lilhore, A., Bulkunde, U.S., Agarwal, V.: Smart charge scheduling of EVs based on user behaviour predicted using machine learning. In: Proceedings of the 2025 IEEE Energy Conversion Congress & Exposition Asia (ECCE-Asia), Bengaluru, India, pp. 1–6 (2025). https://doi.org/10.1109/ECCE-Asia63110.2025.11112356

Evaluation of GBDTs in APT Identification Tasks within ICS Networks

Keith Alan CrabbII(✉), Emery JohnsonIV, and John A. HamiltonJr.

Texas A&M University, College Station, TX 77840, USA
cse-general@cse.tamu.edu
https://engineering.tamu.edu/cse/index.html

Abstract. The rapid growth of cyberattacks targeting Industrial Control Systems (ICS) presents significant challenges to the security of critical infrastructure, with a reported 668% increase in incidents over the past three years. To mitigate this growing threat, security analysts have incorporated active threat intelligence techniques into their workflows, such as the ICS section of the MITRE ATT&CK framework, to comprehend, attribute, and mitigate ICS-specific advanced persistent threats (APTs) observed within their networks.

This work is composed of an evaluation of utilizing the Gradient Boosted Decision Tree (GBDT) machine learning model, trained on the real-world ICS ATT&CK framework datasets and supplemented with synthetically defined attack chain data, to assess whether an integrated model can assist cybersecurity analysts in classifying known threat actors and predicting their potential behaviors within the attack chain, based on early indicators of compromise.

In this paper, we have demonstrated the effectiveness of our model through a series of developed visualizations, such as confusion matrices and feature importance charts. The visualizations highlighting the overlaps between group data and the unique ICS Tactics, Techniques, and Procedures (TTPs) that were identified as key discriminators. While GBDTs are effective for classifying highly documented APTs, limitations include reduced confidence when APTs rapidly evolve between campaigns, and a notable reliance on synthetic data, which may decrease with the addition of classifiers within a broader dataset. This work highlights the potential of GBDT's to support analysts in APT identification, thereby enhancing ICS security through predictive attribution. Future directions will focus on integrating multi-source data and contextual factors.

Keywords: Cybersecurity · Artificial Intelligence · MITRE ATT&CK · Threat Identification · GBDTs

1 Introduction

With the ever increasing number of cyberattacks against ICS systems, specifically a noteworthy 668% increase in attacks over the last three years [1], it is clear

J. R. Barr et al. (Eds.): ERWCSA 2025, ACSAR 4, pp. 158–170, 2026.
https://doi.org/10.1007/978-3-032-18230-2_12

that additional threat intelligence techniques must be integrated into the workflow of security floor operators [2]. This integration will enable effective detection and response within high-security environments [3]. A rather pivotal advancement in this domain was the adoption of the MITRE ATT&CK framework for ICS, which maps adversary TTPs to facilitate the identification of consistent patterns employed by APTs [4].

Historically, APT attribution has relied on visual tools like heatmaps to delineate the taxonomy of known TTPs across the attack lifecycle. One example of a particular instance, covering the Sandworm Team, a notorious APT linked to a series of rupturous campaigns against critical energy infrastructure. The Sandworm Team has exhibited a rather interesting characteristic progression from the initial access tactics (e.g., spearphishing) through the execution tactics (e.g., malware deployment) to impact (e.g., system manipulation), as illustrated in typical ATT&CK heatmaps that highlight high-frequency TTPs in reconnaissance and command-and-control phases [5] (Fig. 1).

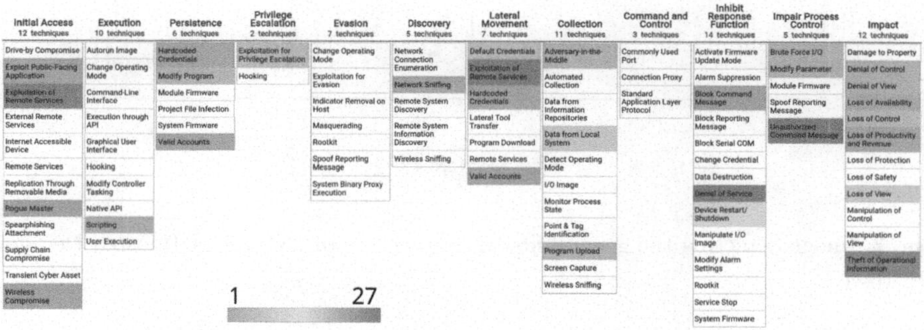

Fig. 1. An example heatmap, detailing vulnerabilities found on an IEEE 9-Bus System [6].

Within the bounds of ICS network security, APTs have been identified as a particular concern for network operators. The threats posed by these well-funded and well-organized groups against national critical infrastructure sectors are often underfunded and understaffed local governments and utility districts. The consequences of attacks by these threat actors extend beyond standard data loss to include physical disruptions, such as power outages or process sabotage.

Additional frameworks, including the Diamond Model of Intrusion Analysis [7] and the Lockheed Martin Cyber Kill Chain [8], have provided further structural and lifecycle-oriented perspectives on intrusions, highlighting adversary capabilities, infrastructure, victims, and the phased progression of attacks. However, these models fall short in delivering predictive, automated capabilities that ingest live Security Information and Event Management (SIEM) telemetry to identify likely adversaries and anticipate their subsequent actions.

While recent research covering these prediction mechanisms has focused on Bayesian Networks and Natural Language Processing [9][10], standard modeling approaches may prove more effective and computationally efficient [11]. In this work, we describe and evaluate the utilization of GBDTs to assist operators in standard modeling.

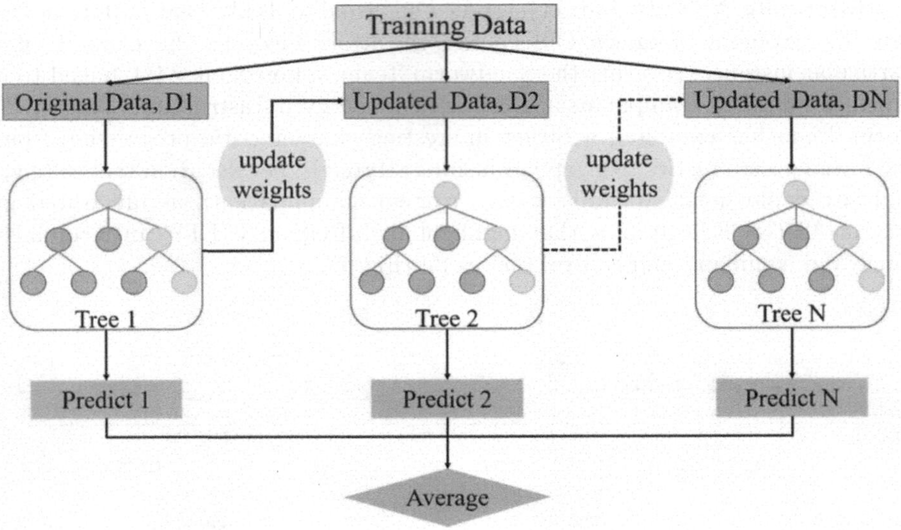

Fig. 2. Image depicting the general flow and structure of a Gradient Boosted Decision Tree [12].

GBDTs, as shown in Fig. 2, are a type of machine learning model that sequentially builds decision trees, with each subsequent tree correcting the errors of previous ones by using gradient descent optimization. This approach enables GBDTs to tackle complex, non-linear relationships in a data efficient manner. GBDT efficiency makes them particularly desirable for use cases where tasks involve sparse and high-dimensional inputs, such as those found in TTP datasets. In this work, we detail a GBDT implementation that emphasizes uncommon TTPs of APTs, while downplaying commonplace ones, alongside a synthetic data generation process that addresses the limitations of the MITRE dataset in terms of sample size and variety. By evaluating this model against baselines and custom inputs, we demonstrate its potential to enhance real-time attribution, overarchingly contributing to tougher ICS security.

2 Methodology

To address the identified gap in the field of automated APT identification research, we selected the GBDT Machine Learning technique, which we implemented using the standard Python LightGBM library. This was done in coordination with the MITRE ATT&CK ICS Framework's STIX dataset for training, which we supplemented through the generation of synthetic attack chains using standardized processes [13]. This approach leveraged a model recognized for its effectiveness in multi-factor classification tasks, allowing us to easily analyze the different types of data points within the MITRE dataset as separate feature vectors. Moreover, it allowed us to test for early prediction accuracy regarding the APT observed when presented with a partial attack chain. In the realm of APT classification, it is crucial to consider various factors in light of the constantly evolving threat intelligence. The model's automatic weight adjustments, combined with the overall versatility of GBDTs, ensure our approach remains adaptable to the ever changing real-world environments.

2.1 Data Collection and Generation

For the initial design of this AI model, several factors were considered and incorporated into the decision tree throughout the development process. The most notable of which was the main content of the MITRE ATT&CK ICS Framework. This content provided an overview of the observed tactics and techniques that the GBDT utilized; however, additional modes of classification were also required. For this, we utilized additional data points available within the dataset, such as software used, the campaigns recorded, and the frequency of techniques seen in campaigns.

Despite utilizing these additional classifiers, issues occurred when groups had little to no data in these categories that were publicly available through MITRE. To mitigate the disparity between the selected classes within groups, we utilized synthetic augmentation techniques whenever a set with fewer than 20 samples was detected. In this, we randomly developed a subset containing 30–80% of the groups' known techniques to simulate realistic partial attack chains while preserving the known TTP distribution. This preservation of the distribution allowed us to ensure an equal set of classification data, preventing our model from weighting groups purely based on the amount of data available.

Once the datasets were combined with TF-IDF weighting applied, we scaled the term frequency using the inverse document frequency function ($IDF = \log(N/df)$), where N indicates the total number of samples and df shows the number of samples used per feature. Formally mitigating class imbalance and data sparsity without biasing the prediction model.

2.2 Baseline Comparison

In validating the performance of our model, a pure cosine similarity algorithm using group prototypes (mean feature vectors per APT group) was employed as a baseline to simulate a heatmap-only form of APT analysis. This model processes a list of TTPs into binary vectors to classify APTs by computing the cosine similarity between the input vector and each group's prototype, normalizing our scores to probabilities that sum to a total of 1. The model baseline emphasizes normalized overlaps while accounting for profile size. Our GBDT model can be compared with this baseline model to assess its total added value in system learning non-linear feature interactions. Specifically, our cosine model ranks groups by employing similarity scores, providing floor operators with a simple measure of match quality and preventing over-reliance on unweighted counts, a capability the GBDT alternative enhances through trained weighting and ensemble predictions.

2.3 Testing With Custom Attack Chain Inputs

To ensure that our model would perform well against new, emerging campaigns on user systems, we developed custom attack chains that matched different APTs to determine if the model would accurately classify them. Specifically, when processing these inputs for testing, we utilized a chain of specific TTP identifiers used by MITRE, which are converted to binary vectors weighted by the precomputed IDF, and fed to the model for probability predictions. Overall, this methodology ensures the model is adaptable to real-world settings such as SIEM telemetry, with multi-factor classification enabling future extensions (e.g., incorporating geolocation or temporal features). All code was implemented in Python using libraries that included such as pandas, scikit-learn, LightGBM, and MITRE's STIX20 loader, with seeds set for reproducibility of our findings.

3 Findings

Through this testing of our model, several key points regarding performance, attribution capabilities, interpretability, and limitations emerged. The findings and discussion below are derived from the augmented dataset and our custom inputs, which simulate real-world partial attack chains that could be observed within ICS environments. Overall, we observed results that highlight the model's strengths in adapting to our simultaneously sparse and multidimensional threat intelligence data, as well as areas where the dataset's characteristics constrain the model and potentially subversive APT behavior.

3.1 Model Performance Metrics

Our deployed GBDT model, when trained on our TF-IDF-weighted dataset, demonstrated an accuracy classification score of 81%. This metric was directly computed on a well stratified test set covering 30% of our data, ensuring a balanced representation of all the supplied APTs, with the observed initial imbalances addressed through synthetic augmentation. The GBDT model's per-class performance, as we assessed via F1-scores, varied heavily based on group distinctiveness. Groups with unique and well flushed out TTP profiles, such as

CyberAv3ngers and Dragonfly, exhibited near-perfect F1-scores (1.0), indicating high precision and recall. These groups benefit from distinctive ICS-specific techniques (e.g., data manipulation or supply chain compromises) that serve as strong discriminators. In contrast, groups with overlapping and limited TTPs, such as ALLIANTE and APT33, exhibited moderate F1-scores (around 0.6–0.7), primarily due to the similarity in their use of reconnaissance techniques, such as system discovery (T0853) and spearphishing (T0865). This confusion highlights a common challenge in APT attribution: many adversaries employ similar initial access and discovery tactics, indicating that early-stage differentiation is quite difficult without additional contextual features. The classification report, showed a multi-log loss of approximately 0.85 on the validation set, reflected the model's ability to assign calibrated probabilities across classes. Given the dataset's well defined sparsity, where over 80% of features are zero in most samples, and the reliance on only 20 samples per group post-augmentation, this accuracy level demonstrates the robustness of GBDT to small, imbalanced datasets. Hyperparameter tuning, including a low learning rate (0.02) and regularization (λ L2 = 0.1), helped mitigate overfitting, as evidenced by early stopping after 150 boosting rounds without significant degradation in validation loss.

3.2 Attribution Results on Custom Inputs

When attempting to simulate real-world scenarios in which analysts detect TTPs from an attacker through systems such as SIEM reporting, we utilized partial attack chains developed from both recorded campaigns and the listings of TTPs known to be used by specific APTs.

For the sandworm team, input of techniques: T0895, T0847, T0855, T0831, T0806; software: S0143, S0604, S0029 resulted in a correct prediction with 62% confidence. In testing of the other groups (TEMP.veles, oilrig, cyberav3ngers, dragonfly), we obtained very similar results. Tests with APT33 showed more confusion with ALLIANTE; however, there was 45.6% confidence in APT33 as the correct prediction, and a similarly high 35.1% confidence in ALLIANTE, on a test using the inputs of techniques employed by APT33. This is because, as stated earlier, ALLIANTE and APT33 have overlapping and a small number of techniques.

The attribution outcomes illustrate the model's utility in early threat hunting. By processing sparse inputs, the model provides ranked probabilities that guide analysts toward likely actors, potentially accelerating response times in time-sensitive ICS environments where downtime can have cascading effects on critical infrastructure.

3.3 Comparison to Baseline (Cosine Similarity)

To test if our model maintains a higher level of performance than a heatmap-only style of APT identification, we benchmarked it against a cosine similarity baseline, which normalized similarities between input vectors and the mean TTP vectors per group.

In most tests, our GBDT model outperformed the Cosine Similarity baseline. For instance, in the attribution of the APT33 group, the distributed probabilities our GBDT produced likely reflected real-world uncertainty with greater accuracy than its cosine similarity counterpart, which was observed to often assign near 100% certainty to one group and 0% to others, thereby risking overconfidence. In one case, for Sandworm, the baseline achieved 79% confidence, compared to GBDT's 62%. In contrast, five other groups achieved 0% confidence, which contrasts with GBDT's more nuanced distribution (12.7%, 4.7%, 4.3%, 2.8%, 1.6%). Highlighting our GBDT's value in modeling the non-linear feature interactions and TF-IDF weighting, downplaying commonly seen TTPs (e.g., generic discovery techniques), and amplifying rare ones, displaying probabilities more along the lines of expert human assessments in ambiguous scenarios (Fig. 3).

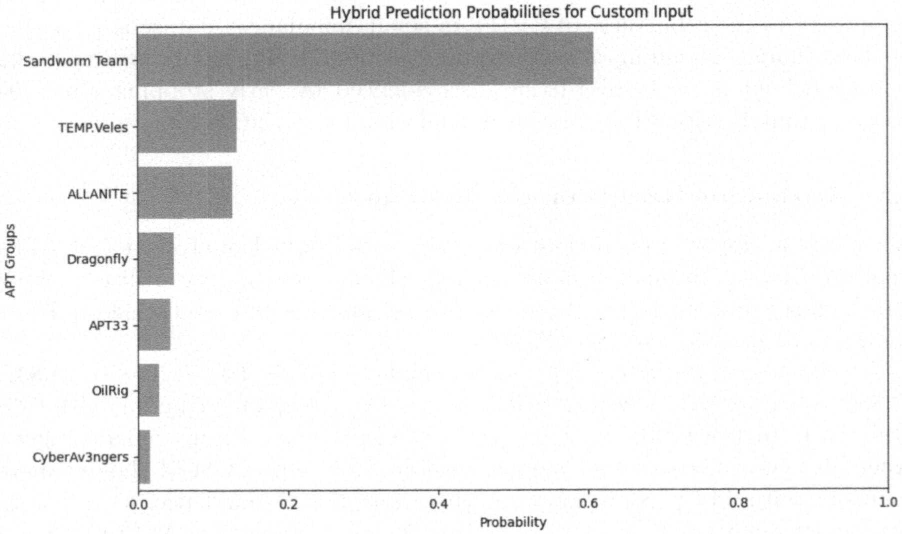

Fig. 3. GBDT Prediction probabilities for a custom input.

3.4 Interpretability Insights from Standard Visualizations

The confusion matrix visualization (Fig. 5) demonstrates several clusters with higher accuracy diagonals for distinct groups, such as the Sandworm and Dragonfly APTs; as well as off-diagonal concentrations for reconnaissance-heavy TTP pairs, such as APT33 and ALLIANTE, indicating a notably high degree of overlap that leads to a misclassification rate of roughly 30–40%. This seen misclassification rate correlates heavily with the performance metrics shown above; however, it also spotlights the limitations of our chosen dataset. Reiterating once again, small sample sizes and the need for synthetic augmentation introduce

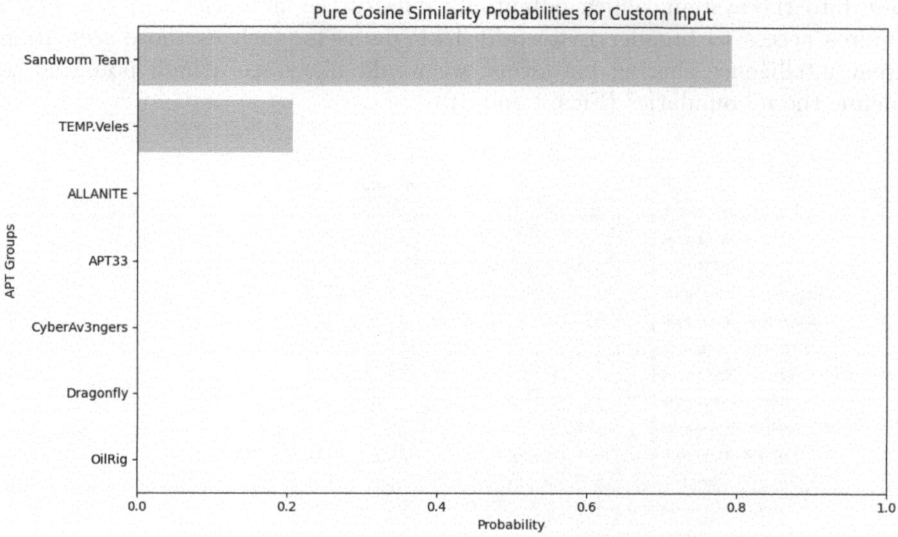

Fig. 4. Pure Cosine Similarity Prediction probabilities for the same custom input.

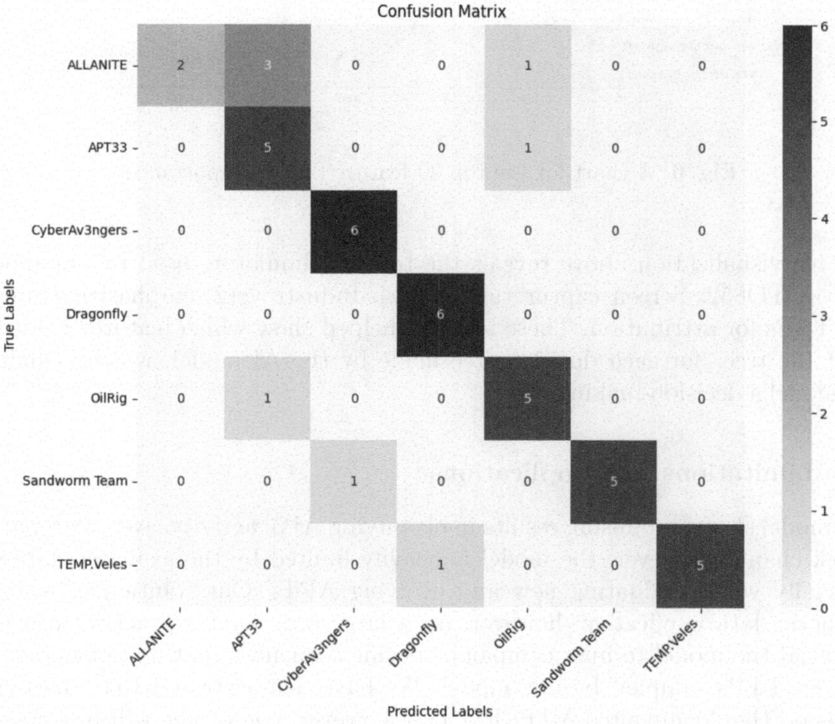

Fig. 5. GBDT model confusion matrix.

noise into the system, which potentially inflates the similarities. If the model acquires access to broader real-world TTP datasets, such as those seen from threat intelligence sharing platforms, we would likely see a high potential to redefine these boundaries (Figs. 4 and 6).

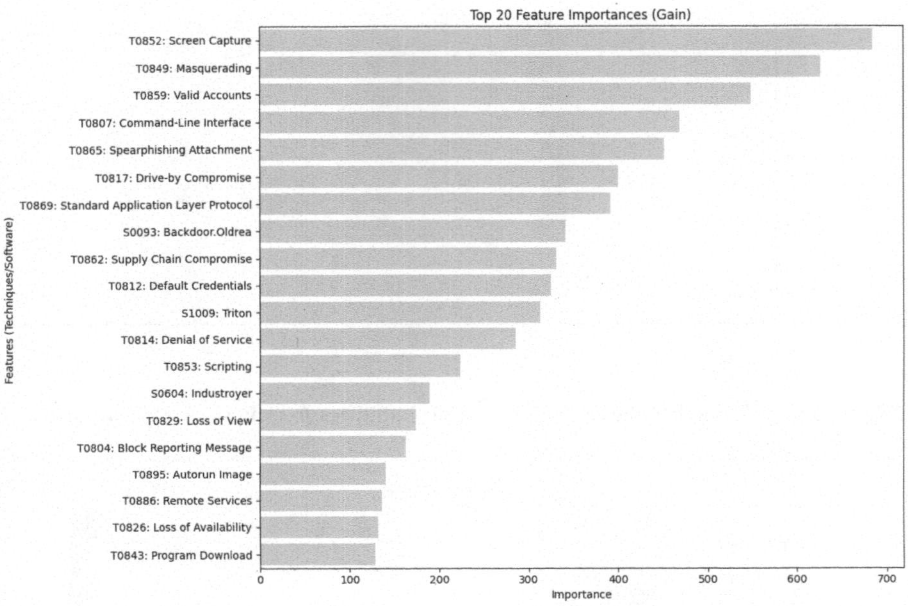

Fig. 6. A chart for the top 20 feature (TTP) importances.

This visualization above reveals the top discriminators used by our model, such as TO852: Screen capture and S0604: Industroyer2, emphasizing unique ICS TTPs for attribution. These features helped show which features helped to "split the tree" for each decision tree made by the AI model, which visualized the model's decision-making.

3.5 Limitations and Implications

The model shows promising results in classifying APT activity, even with partial attack chains. However, the model is heavily limited by the available datasets, especially when evaluating new and evolving APTs. Our solution of utilizing synthetic data is effective; however, on a large scale or for practical usage, it may lead the model to miss campaign-specific sequences that do not match the random TTPs sampled by our model. We have demonstrated that the model excels on the documented MITRE TTPs; however, confidence will be lower for unseen and newly evolved behaviors from APTs. Synthetic data quality is tied to MITRE authenticity but introduces variability to help address this limitation.

Our model also does not gain any more insight than a human can on prediction; it merely computes it faster, which is why it still causes considerable confusion when groups behave similarly (APT33/ALLIANTE). Still, integration with an operator will only help spot an APT, as it cannot make unrealistic predictions due to its similarities to human prediction and the utilization of attack chains.

4 Conclusions

In response to an ever-increasing level of threat against operational technology environments, this study has demonstrated the efficacy of utilizing GBDTs to classify known APTs and perform behavior prediction tasks. By leveraging the publicly available and real-world dataset provided by MITRE ATT&CK, we were able to produce real-world-based ICS attack chains that our model correctly classified 81% of the time. This model will help address the critical gaps in automated threat identification in systems with limited computational power.

4.1 Summary of Key Contributions

This work has demonstrated a new future option for ICS cybersecurity operators through a GBDT-based model that classifies APT groups from sparse TTP inputs with 81% accuracy and an attribution confidence of around 60% for well-documented actors, such as Sandworm. Key innovations include:

- The integration of binary feature vectors for techniques and software
- TF-IDF weighting to prioritize the models that find discriminative TTPs
- Probabilistic synthetic augmentation to overcome the well known problem of data sparsity.

The model very consistently outperforms a cosine similarity baseline in most scenarios by capturing non-linear interactions and providing nuanced probability distributions, reducing overconfidence in ambiguous or edge-like cases. Interpretability features, such as confusion matrices and feature importance visualizations, provide actionable insights (e.g., highlighting unique ICS TTPs, like T0852: Screen Capture, as top discriminators), empowering floor analysts to then validate their predictions while refining their organization's threat hunting strategies.

4.2 Implications Within ICS Security

Our deployed model's ability to utilize multifaceted and limited data demonstrates a potentially valuable tool for real-world integration with SIEM telemetry. Our model is well-suited for local utilities, where low computation can lead to operator inexperience and limited awareness, thereby exacerbating vulnerabilities. By matching partial attack chains to likely APTs and forecasting potential next steps, it enhances proactive defense, potentially mitigating disruptions in critical infrastructure sectors such as energy and manufacturing.

Findings on our TTP overlaps (e.g., noted reconnaissance similarities between APT33 and ALLIANTE) highlight the need for a multi-factor analysis, encouraging the incorporation of contextual elements such as geolocation, port usage, or device targets to enhance prediction fidelity. Ultimately, our approach here decentralizes advanced attribution tasks, bridging the gap between high level threat intelligence frameworks and industrial operational workflows to bolster resilience against sophisticated, state-sponsored threats.

4.3 Limitations

Despite the GBDT model's strong performance, as shown in our findings, we only utilize the MITRE dataset in this paper. The dataset is sparse and static, which limits our model's ability to adapt to evolving TTPs—a common trait among APTs. The model's confidence begins to decrease with each unseen TTP and is also susceptible to potential manipulation by APTs. This, however, is an inherent weakness in human-based reasoning approaches when attempting to classify APTs based solely on data acquired through cyberspace. Additionally, our reliance on synthetic data, which was necessary for testing, may increase the bias seen in the model, potentially blinding operators to context-specific variations observed in real-world campaigns.

5 Future Work

While this work presents a strong case for the use of GBDTs for APT classification, further research is needed to ensure that this strategy can effectively support real-world cyber defense or industrial network operators. Honing in on the main benefit of GBDTs as being effective in multiclass and multifactor classification, an understanding of specific ICS environments could provide an additional layer of thought for the model. This additional layer of thought would enable the model to reason about the techniques that attackers might use in a given situational context, thereby increasing confidence in predictions through the increased number of factors. In this context, therefore, a network defender is provided with a realistic and valuable output.

Additionally, future work must be conducted to compile threat intelligence from multiple sources outside the MITRE ATT&CK framework to ensure the model has sufficient valid data samples. While it has been demonstrated that one can model realistic attack sequences for APTs that follow the attack chains described by the ATT&CK framework, specific tuning for ICS reveals limitations. It has the potential to skew the results. The compilation and application of additional training data to this model would enable a higher-fidelity simulation of what attackers are likely to do next within a given system.

To further improve the usability of the model, linking the model inputs to recognizable SIEM alerting formats will enable our model to build upon existing solutions within most network architectures. Enhancing overall usability and expanding the model to incorporate additional data features, such as geolocation, time frames, and defined attacker network infrastructure. This incorporation will help reduce the remaining probability of APTs falsifying identification to conceal the origin of an attack. The inclusion of these factors should also be met with continuous revalidation of the model against the base training dataset.

Acknowledgments. The authors would like to acknowledge all the support provided to date, which they gratefully appreciate, and look forward to continued development support from the Texas A&M Cybersecurity Center, specifically the lab environment provided through the Texas SCADA Testbed.

References

1. Since Stuxnet: A Brief History of Critical Infrastructure Attacks. https://www.forescout.com/blog/since-stuxnet-a-brief-history-of-critical-infrastructure-attacks/. Accessed 14 Aug 2025
2. 2024 State of Operational Technology and Cybersecurity Report. https://www.fortinet.com/content/dam/fortinet/assets/reports/report-state-ot-cybersecurity.pdf. Accessed 14 June 2025
3. Kure, H., Islam, S.: Cyber threat intelligence for improving cybersecurity and risk management in critical infrastructure. J. Univ. Comput. Sci. **25**(11), 1478–1502 (2019). https://repository.uel.ac.uk/item/877y3
4. Al-Sada, B.: Threat Profiles Analysis Based on MITRE ATT&CK Knowledge Base. Order No. 31560212, Hamad Bin Khalifa University (Qatar), Qatar (2024)
5. MITRE ATT&CK ICS Matrix. https://attack.mitre.org/matrices/ics/. Accessed 14 June 2025
6. Biebel, M., Song, Z., Schreck, T., Hackl, C.: Identifying key attacks on an IEEE 9-Bus System by leveraging the MITRE ATT&CK ICS matrix. In: Proceedings of the 16th ACM International Conference on Future and Sustainable Energy Systems (E-Energy 2025), pp. 791–798. Association for Computing Machinery, New York (2025). https://doi.org/10.1145/3679240.3734647
7. Caltagirone, S., Pendergast, A., Betz, C.: The Diamond Model of Intrusion Analysis (2013). https://doi.org/10.13140/RG.2.2.31143.56481
8. Naik, N., Jenkins, P., Grace, P., Song, J.: Comparing attack models for IT systems: Lockheed Martin's cyber kill chain, MITRE ATT&CK framework and diamond model. In: 2022 IEEE International Symposium on Systems Engineering (ISSE), Vienna, Austria, pp. 1–7 (2022). https://doi.org/10.1109/ISSE54508.2022.10005490
9. Kim, Y., Lee, I., Kwon, H., Lee, K., Yoon, J.: BAN: predicting APT attack based on Bayesian network with MITRE ATT&CK framework. IEEE Access **11**, 91949–91968 (2023). https://doi.org/10.1109/ACCESS.2023.3306593
10. Sachidananda, V., Patil, R., Sachdeva, A., Lam, K.-Y., Yang, L.: APTer: towards the investigation of APT attribution. In: 2023 IEEE Conference on Dependable and Secure Computing (DSC), Tampa, FL, USA, pp. 1–10 (2023)
11. McElfresh, D., et al.: When do neural nets outperform boosted trees on tabular data? In: Advances in Neural Information Processing Systems, vol. 36, pp. 76336–76369 (2023)

12. Zhang, Y., et al.: Predicting mechanical properties of CO2 hydrates: machine learning insights from molecular dynamics simulations. In: Journal of Physics: Condensed Matter, vol. 36 (2023). https://doi.org/10.1088/1361-648X/acfa55
13. Choi, S., Yun, J.-H., Min, B.-G.: Probabilistic attack sequence generation and execution based on MITRE ATT&CK for ICS datasets. In: Proceedings of the 14th Cyber Security Experimentation and Test Workshop (CSET 2021), pp. 41–48. Association for Computing Machinery, New York (2021). https://doi.org/10.1145/3474718.3474722

Ethical AI in Aerospace: Decision-Making in High-Risk, High-Reward Environments

Rosa Szurgot(✉)

Aerospace Cybersecurity and Intelligence Studies College of Business, Security and Intelligence, Embry–Riddle Aeronautical University, Prescott, AZ, USA
sosavarr@erau.edu

Abstract. Autonomy is moving from advisory roles to operational control in air and space systems where decisions occur at machine speed and failures can be fatal. We synthesize a practical definition of *ethically aware AI in aerospace*, outline accountability across the technical and governance stack, and present a four-layer architecture that connects value specification to model development, real-time decision execution, and audit & feedback. We provide assurance patterns (*ethical governor*, constraint solvers, and run-time assurance/Simplex), operational user-interface principles for meaningful human control, and three case studies: (A) LEO conjunction avoidance with auditable fuel/schedule trade-offs, (B) crewed depressurization with priority sequencing and overrides, and (C) ROE-gated escalation in contested airspace. We close with metrics and certification artifacts aligned to emerging trustworthy AI and certifiable-AI guidance (Abbreviations: ROE = Rules of Engagement; RTA = Run-Time Assurance).

Keywords: Aerospace autonomy · ethical AI · explainability · certification · run-time assurance · digital twins · federated learning

1 Introduction

The aerospace sector is experiencing an historic inflection point in autonomy. Starlinkclass mega-constellations execute *millions* of low-thrust maneuvers each year; on-board guidance software now decides when and how to dodge debris without waiting for ground control. Crewed spacecraft rely on adaptive, mixed-initiative control to balance human workload against split-second fault responses, while uncrewed systems in contested air and orbital domains must interpret ambiguous intent and obey Rules of Engagement (ROE) at machine speed. Across this spectrum, AI is already in the loop—or soon will be—in roles that blend perception, prediction, and actuation.

Yet autonomy invites new failure modes. Opacity leaves operators and regulators unable to trace cause-and-effect; latent bias skews risk away from under-represented operating regions; and accidental violations of ROE or international law can escalate conflict. These ethical failings erode operator trust, stall air-

J. R. Barr et al. (Eds.): ERWCSA 2025, ACSAR 4, pp. 171–192, 2026.
https://doi.org/10.1007/978-3-032-18230-2_13

and spaceworthiness- certification, and expose OEMs to liability [1–3]. Guidelines for trustworthy AI call for transparency, fairness, and human agency, but seldom show *how* to embed those principles in flight-critical software. Meanwhile, systems-engineering research on digital twins, model-based assurance, and safety cases offers patterns for evidence generation [4–7]. Our thesis: ethical requirements must be engineered with the same rigor as structural load paths or thermal limits, and backed by run-time evidence streams—not treated as post-hoc governance.

We focus on decision-making autonomy—software that selects or vetoes actions, rather than passive analytics. The setting spans commercial LEO constellations, human spaceflight, and defense ISR platforms; all share (i) high consequence of error, (ii) intermittent communication, and (iii) evolving threat/risk envelopes.

Contributions:

1. A precise, operator-centric definition of *ethically aware AI* that maps values to measurable invariants.
2. A four-layer decision architecture—*Value Specification*, *Model Development*, *Decision Execution*, and *Audit & Feedback*—with deliverable artifacts at each boundary.
3. Run-time assurance patterns (constraint solvers, ethical safety valves, and Simplex-style RTA) that preserve safety even when advanced controllers misbehave.
4. Two auditable case studies (LEO conjunction and crewed depressurization) illustrating trade-offs and operator interfaces.
5. A conclusion that addresses the need for cybersecurity to maintain ethical design decisions.

Collectively, these elements translate abstract principles—transparency, fairness, accountability—into verifiable engineering practice for next-generation aerospace autonomy.

2 Definition: "Ethically Aware" AI in Aerospace

2.1 One-Sentence Definition

Any autonomous or semi-autonomous system whose goals, constraints, and behaviors are explicitly tied to human-defined values (safety first, legal/mission rules, fairness), can demonstrate compliance at run time, explain trade-offs, accept human authority/override, and leave an audit trail for accountability.

2.2 Pillars (What it Must Include)

Ethically aware autonomy begins with rigorous value and constraint encoding: mission objectives, quantitative safety limits, and binding legal or Rules-of-Engagement (ROE) obligations are formalized as objective-function terms and hard invariants, ensuring that every optimization step is framed by "crew–safety–first" or "no–fire–without–dual–confirm" axioms, not informal program notes.

Safety and reliability then elevate classical systems engineering into the ML era: comprehensive hazard analyses feed fault–tolerance designs, verified fail–safe modes, and clearly bounded autonomy envelopes so that off-nominal behavior degrades predictably rather than catastrophically.

To sustain user trust, systems expose transparency and explainability artifacts—concise, human-readable rationales that link sensor inputs to chosen actions and illuminate key trade-offs or constraint margins [2, 8].

At the same time, human authority is preserved through graded control modes, time-boxed confirmations, and escalation ladders that guarantee a human can intervene at tactically relevant latencies [3].

Robust accountability and audit machinery underpins the whole stack: tamper-evident, hash-chained logs record inputs, model versions, constraint checks, and overrides, enabling deterministic post-incident forensics and clear liability allocation.

Because autonomy cannot be ethical if it is easily hijacked or leaks sensitive data, stringent security and privacy safeguards—cryptographic authentication, least-privilege data handling, and privacy-preserving learning— are mandatory.

Continuous bias and fairness controls monitor slice-level error parity and domain drift, then trigger mitigation (e.g., reweighting or calibrated thresholds) before disparate impact reaches safety-critical thresholds.

Finally, every layer must emit verifiable evidence for compliance and certification so that regulators and insurers can trace requirements to tests and run-time assurances, satisfying emerging AI air- and space-worthiness standards [1,6,7].

2.3 Runtime Features (How it Looks in Applied Practice)

At run time, an ethically aware autonomy stack must exhibit four observable capabilities. First, an ethical governor executes in the highest-privilege loop: it evaluates every candidate action against formalized hard constraints—crew-safety bounds, ROE geofences, propellant reserves—and issues an immediate veto when a violation is predicted, even if the mission optimizer proposes the action. Second, the decision logic is inherently risk-aware: each option is scored by an explicit utility function that balances quantified risk (e.g. probability of collision, thermal margin consumed) against mission value (scientific return, schedule, fuel efficiency) while respecting the thresholds approved in the Value & Risk Charter. Third, the system supports graceful degradation: on detecting sensor faults, model uncertainty spikes, or integrity-loss alarms, it shrinks the autonomy envelope, falls back to safe modes, and—where latency permits—summons human confirmation rather than persisting with high-risk autonomy. Finally, every cycle produces an auditable rationale bundle that answers "why now, why this?" by hashing inputs, logging the active model and constraint versions, recording the utility scores for the top-K alternatives, and embedding the governor's pass/fail verdicts. These tamper-evident records enable flight controllers, investigators, and regulators to replay decisions deterministically, attribute accountability, and feed near-misses back into continual-learning pipelines.

2.4 Accountability Across the Stack and the Problem of Opacity

True accountability requires a clear chain of evidence that spans the entire socio-technical stack. At the data and sensing layer, asset owners and sensor vendors must attach provenance metadata, calibration certificates, and bias-assessment reports to every measurement; signed lineage hashes ensure later investigators can prove the readings were neither tampered with nor mislabeled. The model[1] owner—typically the prime contractor or AI supplier—must produce training and validation artifacts, hazard and threat analyses, fairness test results, immutable version hashes, and a formal change-control log that ties each update to pass/fail evidence. Moving up, the systems integrator is responsible for interface specifications, fail-safe design patterns, end-to-end verification & validation, cyber-hardening measures, and periodic safety-case refreshes as hardware or software evolves. During deployment and operations, the mission authority must enforce Rules-of-Engagement, maintain a live override policy, monitor real-time risk thresholds, and execute an incident-response plan that can quarantine or roll back unsafe autonomy. Finally, at the governance tier, regulators, insurers, and original-equipment manufacturers require traceable conformance to air- or space-worthiness regulations, contractual audit rights, and a RACI matrix that unambiguously assigns liability—each element bound to signed artifacts in a tamper-evident repository.

Opacity anywhere in this chain severs accountability: if model internals are black boxes, certification authorities cannot see how hazards are mitigated; if sensor provenance is missing, investigators cannot reconstruct root cause; and if override actions are not logged, liability becomes unclear. Hence transparency, versioned evidence, and cryptographic integrity mechanisms are not administrative afterthoughts but safety-critical requirements.

2.5 Why Black Boxes Block Trust and Forensics

Certification bodies base air- and space-worthiness on a hazardmitigation argument: every credible failure mode must be traced to a design or procedural control with quantified residual risk. A deep network whose internal logic is opaque fails that evidentiary test—no auditor can see how collision risk is reduced or how an ROE constraint is enforced. The impact radiates outward. Operators lose the ability to anticipate failure modes or to calibrate trust, a well-known driver of mode confusion and over-reliance in humanautomation teaming [3]. Investigators cannot replay an accident without a reconstruction of internal state; absent that, root cause degenerates into speculation, corrective actions are delayed, and "unknown software error" becomes a catch-all finding. Security analysts face a

[1] Throughout we use "model" to include pre- and post-processing code.

blind spot: tampering, adversarial drift, or dataset poisoning can lurk undetected because no invariant ties input changes to decision logic. Finally, insurers and regulators cannot apportion liability—was it data corruption, design negligence, or operator misuse? Premiums rise or coverage is denied.

Hence, interpretability, rationale logging, and data/decision provenance are not user-interface niceties; they are first-order safety properties. An ethically aware system must record why now, why this: hashed inputs, model version and hyper-parameters, constraint evaluations, utility scores for the top-K alternatives, and the ethical governor's veto verdicts. Only with such evidence can certification authorities sign off, operators build appropriate mental models, investigators perform deterministic forensics, and insurers underwrite the residual risk [2,8] (Fig. 1).

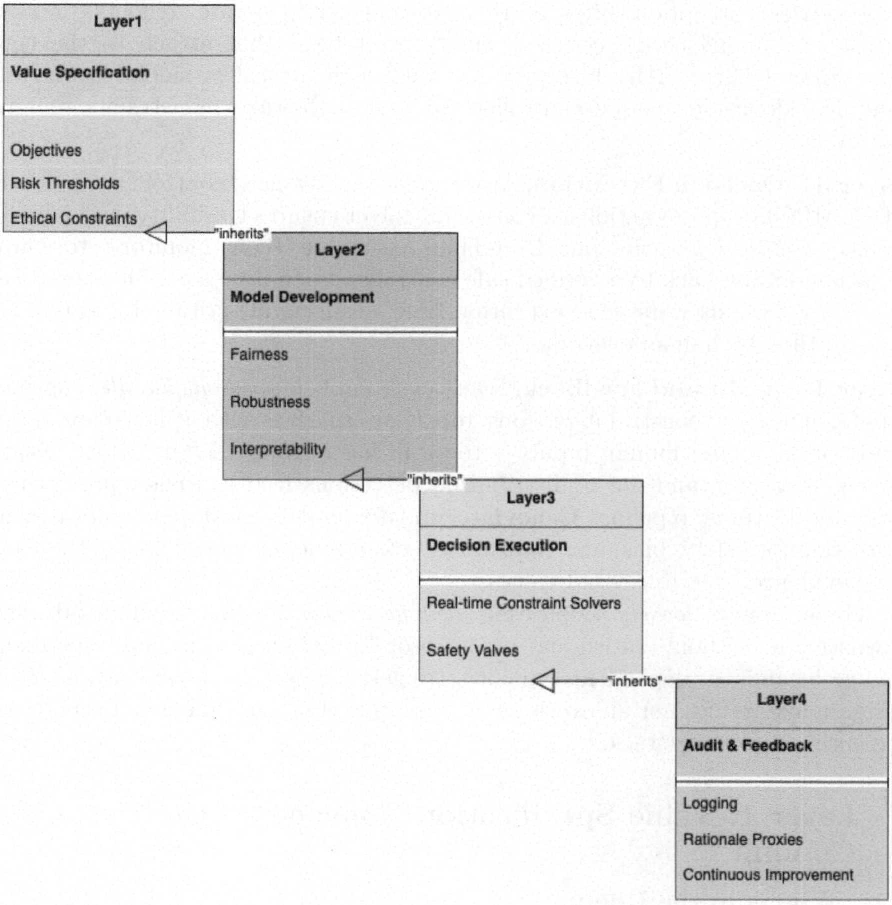

Fig. 1. Four-Layer Architecture

3 Architecture Overview

We operationalize ethical principles through a *four-layer architecture* that threads values all the way down to real-time software and back again.

Layer 1—Value Specification. Stakeholders produce a signed *Value & Risk Charter* that codifies a lexicographic objective hierarchy (e.g., *crew safety* > third-party safety > mission > efficiency), enumerates *hard constraints* such as ROE geofences and authenticated-command rules, and sets quantitative risk bounds (probability-of-collision thresholds, propellant minima, thermal margins). Each requirement is given a testable ID so that later stages can trace evidence back to intent.

Layer 2—Model Development. Data curation, training, and validation are performed under explicit fairness, robustness, and interpretability targets. Slice-level metrics, corruption suites, and red-team attacks generate artifacts (dataset datasheets, model cards, certified worst-case tables) that attach to the corresponding Charter IDs. Interpretable veto logic or safety-shield layers are compiled alongside opaque controllers so that high-stakes constraints remain auditable.

Layer 3—Decision Execution. At run time, an advanced controller (e.g., deep RL or MPC) proposes actions; a constraint solver ensures feasibility; and a high-assurance *ethical governor* plus Run-Time Assurance (RTA) monitor vetoes any violation, falling back to a verified safe controller when necessary. Deterministic scheduling bounds worst-case execution time, ensuring life-critical loops remain pre-emptible by human overrides.

Layer 4—Audit and Feedback. Every cycle emits a *rationale bundle*—hashed inputs, model and constraint versions, top-K alternatives with utility scores, governor verdicts, and human inputs—stored in hash-chained WORM logs. Near-misses, overrides, and out-of-distribution detections feed a privacy-preserving, federated-learning pipeline. Candidate update models must pass digital-twin regression for safety, bias, and robustness before redeployment, closing the loop from evidence back to revised values.

The layers are *loosely coupled but evidence-locked*: artifacts cannot advance downstream without satisfying predecessor constraints, and any upstream change invalidates dependent evidence, triggering selective re-verification. This design makes ethics not an overlay but a compile-time and run-time property of the entire autonomy stack.

4 Layer 1: Value Specification Convene → Codify → Commit

4.1 Who is in the Room

Ethical autonomy begins with a cross-functional design review that mirrors traditional Systems Requirements Reviews (SRR) yet adds explicit value stakeholders. The panel includes: Mission authority & flight ops, safety & human factors, systems/ML engineers & integrator, cybersecurity & privacy, legal/-compliance/insurer, and ethics/stakeholder representatives.

4.2 Process

Prepare (1–2 weeks): circulate mission concept and top risks; collect use-cases and "nightmare scenarios;" draft a value–objective tree and hazard list; propose initial metrics (pLOC/pLOM targets, separation minima, ΔV reserves, latency, ROE confidence).

Workshop (0.5–1 day): confirm lexicographic order (e.g., *Crew safety > third-party safety > mission > efficiency*); set hard constraints (crew-safety first, ROE conformance, cyber rules); define risk bounds (collision probabilities, resource minima); fix the authority model (autonomy envelope, time-boxed confirmations, escalation ladder and hard override); and agree on a forensic/audit plan (tamper-evident logs, rationale snapshots, lineage, clock sync, retention).

Ratify & trace (1 week): publish a signed *Value & Risk Charter* (objective hierarchy, constraints catalog with acceptance criteria, risk-threshold matrix, autonomy/override policy, and an evidence plan mapping each item to tests/twins/red-team cases). Track RACI; every model/logic change updates the charter.

4.3 Example Requirements

HC-001 (Hard Constraint): *Crew Safety First.* Reject any action whose predicted $\Delta p\text{LOC} > 0$ or that reduces breathable-air time below the minimum safe egress; trigger SAFE_MODE and notify Flight within 1 s.

ROE-003: Kinetic effects require dual human confirmation with positive ID $\geq 99.9\%$, geofence compliance, and a recorded rationale bundle (inputs, model hash, constraint set, options considered).

CA-THR-02 (Risk Bound): If $P_c \geq 10^{-4}$ within 72 h and $\Delta V \leq 5\%$ reserve, execute; else escalate with two ranked alternatives and fuel/time trade-offs.

5 Layer 2: Model Development Fairness, Robustness, Interpretability

Layer 2 turns stakeholder values into *model guarantees* that survive contact with real data and operational stressors. Concretely, we (i) measure and mitigate *fairness* issues across operational slices, (ii) test and harden for *adversarial robustness* and off-nominal conditions, and (iii) ensure *interpretability and uncertainty* are available at run time for operators and investigators [2,8].

5.1 A. Fairness Checks (Measure → Mitigate → Monitor)

We define operational *slices* that reflect the mission envelope (e.g., day/night, weather bands, sensor modality, geography, altitude, link state, crew vs. cargo operations). For each slice s, we track error and calibration statistics and bound disparity:

$$\Delta_{\mathrm{TPR}}(s) = \big|\mathrm{TPR}(s) - \mathrm{TPR}(\mathrm{all})\big|, \tag{1}$$

$$\Delta_{\mathrm{FPR}}(s) = \big|\mathrm{FPR}(s) - \mathrm{FPR}(\mathrm{all})\big|, \tag{2}$$

$$\mathrm{ECE} = \sum_{b=1}^{B} \frac{|S_b|}{n} \big|\mathrm{acc}(S_b) - \mathrm{conf}(S_b)\big|. \tag{3}$$

We set maximum allowed disparities ($\Delta_{\mathrm{TPR}}, \Delta_{\mathrm{FPR}} \leq \tau$) and perform *counterfactual tests* by altering nuisance factors (lighting, background clutter) while preserving ground truth to detect spec gaming or Goodhart effects. When violations occur, we mitigate using reweighting or data augmentation, balanced sampling, per-slice decision thresholds, post-hoc calibration, and targeted data collection. In operations, drift detectors (e.g., population-stability index, KS tests) trigger re-audits when slice distributions shift.

Artifacts and Traceability. Each model revision ships with: (i) a *dataset datasheet* (provenance and known biases), (ii) a *model card* (intended use, limitations, slice metrics), (iii) a *slice report* (parity and calibration tables), and (iv) a *threshold rationale* that links slice thresholds to mission risk tolerances [8]. All artifacts reference Requirement IDs from the Value & Risk Charter.

5.2 Adversarial Robustness Tests

We formalise a threat model covering: RF/GNSS spoofing, packet delay/duplication and reordering, sensor saturation/glare, lossy compression, bit-flip faults, and timing jitter. Evaluation includes standard corruption suites, OOD/domain-shift checks, and *hardware-in-the-loop* (HIL) fault injection. Hardening combines adversarial or expectation-over-transforms (EOT) training, domain randomization, input sanity checks (bounds, temporal consistency), anomaly detectors, and *graceful degradation* pathways to safe modes.

Evidence. We report worst-case performance tables under corruptions, certified bounds (e.g., randomized smoothing radius for perception models), ablation results for sanity checks, and *red-team logs.* Robustness acceptance criteria are tied to mission risk (e.g., minimum separation or pLOC margins).

5.3 Interpretable Components and Rationale Monitors

For high-stakes veto logic we embed constraint layers (the *ethical governor*) and, where feasible, simple or monotone submodels that preserve directional consistency with safety rules. Post-hoc explanations (e.g., feature attributions

Algorithm 1 Robustness Test Protocol (condensed)

Input: Model $\mathcal{M}$, clean set $\mathcal{D}$, threat classes $\mathcal{T}$
For each $t \in \mathcal{T}$: generate perturbed $\mathcal{D}_t$ at graded severities
Evaluate metrics (error, calibration) and safety margins on $\mathcal{D}_t$
If OOD detectors fire $\Rightarrow$ route to abstain/override path
Log worst-case over severities; compute certified bounds if applicable
Produce robustness report $\rightarrow$ Requirement IDs (VRC) & gates

Algorithm 2 Run-Time Assurance Loop (simplified)

$a \leftarrow$ AdvancedController(x)
if Monitor.Safe(x, a) **then**
  Execute(a)
else
  $a' \leftarrow$ BaselineController(x)
  Execute(a')
end if
Log(RationaleBundle(x, a, checks))

or prototypes) are provided where they do not mislead operators; the UI surfaces *top-K alternatives with utilities* and the active constraints that fired [2]. Uncertainty is exposed via ensembles or conformal prediction, enabling *abstain* when confidence falls below an approved threshold with coverage guarantees $(1 - \alpha)$.

Forensics: The Rationale Bundle. Every decision emits a tamper-evident bundle containing: hashed inputs, model and code digests, constraint-set IDs, utilities for top-K options, uncertainty estimates, governor verdicts with margins, and human inputs/overrides. These records support deterministic replay, liability assignment, and feedback into Layer 4 learning pipelines.

5.4 Safety Valves and RTA

A high-assurance monitor vetoes any candidate action violating invariants (crew safety, ROE/geofence, reserves). Checks include control barrier functions $h(x) \geq 0$, reachability/collision bounds, and auth/integrity gates that reject stale or unauthenticated telemetry. If violated, the system routes to a verified fallback controller (hold/loiter/abort).

Run-Time Assurance (Simplex). Three parallel elements: (i) an advanced controller (e.g., ML/MPC) proposes; (ii) a safety monitor evaluates; (iii) a baseline controller executes if risk exceeds threshold. Deterministic execution (bounded WCET, priority scheduling) isolates life-critical loops and records rationale bundles with pass/fail checks.

6 Layer 3: Decision Execution Constraint Solvers, Ethical Safety Valves, and Run-Time Assurance

Layer 3 turns model predictions into *actions* that are provably safe, lawful, and auditable *in real time.* It binds an optimization layer (constraint solvers) to a high-assurance *ethical safety valve* and a *Run-Time Assurance* (RTA/Simplex) architecture, all under deterministic scheduling and worst-case timing guarantees.

6.1 Problem Formulation (Receding Horizon)

Let $x_t \in \mathbb{R}^n$ be the state, $u_t \in \mathbb{R}^m$ the control, and $x_{t+1} = f(x_t, u_t)$ the (learned or certified) dynamics. Over horizon H, the solver chooses $U = \{u_t, \dots, u_{t+H-1}\}$ to minimize mission cost subject to *hard invariants*:

$$\begin{aligned} \min_{U} \quad & \sum_{k=0}^{H-1} \ell(x_{t+k}, u_{t+k}) + \ell_T(x_{t+H}) \qquad (4) \\ \text{s.t.} \quad & x_{t+k+1} = f(x_{t+k}, u_{t+k}), \quad k = 0 \dots H-1 \\ & g_i(x_{t+k}, u_{t+k}) \leq 0, \quad i = 1 \dots p \quad \text{(safety/ROE)} \\ & (x_{t+k}, u_{t+k}) \in \mathcal{S} \quad \text{(resources: } \Delta V\text{, thermal, link)} \\ & x_{t+k} \notin \mathcal{X}_{\text{no-go}} \quad \text{(geofence/keep-out)} \end{aligned}$$

Typical instantiations include convex QP for linear f and quadratic ℓ, or MILP for mixed discrete–continuous choices (e.g., mode switches $m \in \{0,1\}^K$). Temporal logic (LTL/SMT) can encode sequencing and dwell-time ROE.

6.2 Constraint Solvers (Real-Time Tactics)

We use **MPC/QP** for continuous control with state/input bounds, **MILP** for mode selection and resource scheduling, and **SMT/LTL** planners for temporal/logic constraints. Real-time feasibility is achieved via:

- *Receding horizon & warm starts*: initialize from the previous solution.
- *Anytime solving*: return the best feasible plan within a time budget.
- *Precomputed autonomy envelopes*: an offline feasibility set $\mathcal{E}$ (invariants satisfied) for fast on-line membership tests.
- *Convexification/sequential QP*: local linearization to keep QP timing bounded.

6.3 Ethical Safety Valve (Runtime Shield)

The *ethical governor* vetoes any candidate action $\hat{u}_t$ that would violate an invariant. One practical construction uses control-barrier-function (CBF) constraints for each safety property $h_j(x) \geq 0$:

$$\underbrace{\nabla h_j(x_t)^\top f(x_t, u)}_{\dot{h}_j(x_t, u)} + \kappa\, h_j(x_t) \;\geq\; 0, \quad \kappa > 0. \qquad (5)$$

Algorithm 3 RTA Loop with Timing Budget

Given: sample time T_s, budgets $(t_{\text{sense}}, t_{\text{est}}, t_a, t_m, t_b, t_{\text{exec}})$
$z_t \leftarrow \textsc{Sense}()$ ▷ $\leq t_{\text{sense}}$
$x_t \leftarrow \textsc{Estimate}(z_t)$ ▷ $\leq t_{\text{est}}$
$\hat{u}_t \leftarrow \mathcal{C}_a(x_t)$ ▷ $\leq t_a$ (anytime allowed)
if $\mathcal{M}.\textsc{Safe}(x_t, \hat{u}_t)$ **then** ▷ $\leq t_m$
    $u_t \leftarrow \hat{u}_t$
else
    $u_t \leftarrow \mathcal{C}_b(x_t)$ ▷ $\leq t_b$ (deterministic)
end if
$\textsc{Execute}(u_t)$ ▷ $\leq t_{\text{exec}}$
$\textsc{LogRationale}(x_t, \hat{u}_t, u_t, \text{margins}, \text{constraints})$
require $t_{\text{sense}} + t_{\text{est}} + \max(t_a{+}t_m,\ t_b{+}t_m) + t_{\text{exec}} \leq T_s$

At each step we solve a minimal-deviation QP to *project* the advanced controller's proposal $\hat{u}_t$ back into the safe set:

$$\begin{aligned} u_t^\star = \arg\min_u \|u - \hat{u}_t\|_2^2 \\ \text{s.t. CBF/LTL/ROE constraints (e.g., (5))} \\ \text{Auth/integrity gates (fresh, signed telemetry)} \end{aligned} \tag{6}$$

If (6) is infeasible, the valve *vetoes* and triggers the baseline controller (safe hold/loiter/abort). This guard runs in the highest priority task and has bounded worst-case execution time (WCET).

6.4 Run-Time Assurance (RTA/Simplex)

RTA combines three elements executed every control tick:

1. **Advanced controller** $\mathcal{C}_a$ (e.g., DL/MPC) proposes $\hat{u}_t$.
2. **Safety monitor** $\mathcal{M}$ applies the ethical valve (invariants, ROE, resources).
3. **Baseline controller** $\mathcal{C}_b$ (verified) executes when risk exceeds threshold.

6.5 Determinism, Scheduling, and Graceful Degradation

We allocate timing budgets so the life-critical loop remains schedulable (Table 1). Safety-critical tasks (monitor, baseline controller) run at higher priority/partition than ML inference. When uncertainty rises or resources fall, we *shrink the autonomy envelope*: tighten constraint margins, increase human-confirm thresholds, and enter safe modes that reduce actuation aggressiveness while maintaining separation and thermal/propellant reserves.

Table 1. Illustrative WCET budget (per control tick of T_s ms).

Stage	Symbol	WCET (ms)
Sensing/I/O	t_{sense}	2
State estimation	t_{est}	1
Advanced proposal	t_a	4 (anytime)
Safety monitor	t_m	1
Baseline control	t_b	1
Actuation	t_{exec}	1
Total (worst branch)		$\leq T_s$ (e.g., 10)

6.6 Evidence and Acceptance Criteria

Layer 3 produces machine-checkable evidence:

- **Constraint-solver reports:** feasibility rates, minimum margin-to-constraint, and regret vs. optimal under time budgets.
- **Valve coverage:** fraction of hazardous proposals vetoed in twin scenarios; minimum CBF/LTL margin at execution.
- **RTA proofs:** schedulability analysis, WCET measurements, and partitioning arguments (no ML pre-emption of safety threads).
- **Forensic logs:** per-tick rationale bundle (hashed inputs, model/constraint versions, utilities for top-K options, veto reasons, human inputs).

Acceptance examples: (i) zero invariant violations across the hazard library; (ii) >99.9% of injected hazards intercepted by the valve with $\geq$ specified margin; (iii) all control ticks meet T_s under worst-case load; (iv) successful, deterministic replay of decisions from logs.

7 Layer 4: Audit and Feedback Logs, Rationale, and Safe Learning

Layer 4 closes the loop between *what the autonomy did* and *how the system improves* without compromising safety or privacy. It produces tamper-evident evidence for certification and forensics, makes the "why" legible to operators, and routes curated signals into privacy-preserving learning and controlled redeployment.

7.1 Rigorous Logging and Provenance

Every control cycle emits a **rationale bundle** with the minimum needed to reconstruct and explain the decision. We store entries on a write-once, append-only medium (WORM) with hash chaining and synchronized clocks where time is stamped by a monotonic clock cross-checked with PTP/GPS. Access is controlled via role-based policies and hardware-backed signing keys (per role, per vehicle). Personally identifiable information (PII) is minimised (hashes or tokens preferred) and retention windows are explicit.

Forensic Usability. Logs must support *deterministic replay* and *timeline queries* (by event ID, constraint ID, model version). Reconstruction scripts are versioned and tested; any missing artifact (e.g., missing model binary) fails the replay test.

Table 2. Minimal rationale-bundle schema (illustrative).

Field	Type	Purpose
`ts`	int64	Monotonic tick + UTC snapshot
`inputs_hash`	bytes32	Hash of preprocessed sensors/telemetry
`model_id`	string	Model weights/version hash
`code_digest`	bytes32	Git/CI digest of decision code
`constraints`	list	IDs + pass/fail + margins (CBF/ROE/resources)
`alts`	list	Top-K alternatives considered
`utilities`	list	Scores for each alternative
`uncertainty`	float/list	Calibrated confidence or interval
`human_act`	enum/meta	HOLD/PROCEED/ABORT + operator ID (signed)
`chain`	bytes32	Hash link per (??)

7.2 Rationale Proxies (Operator-Facing "Why")

Operators need *compact, faithful* explanations at the moment of action. We surface: (i) feature attributions or prototypical exemplars where applicable, (ii) salient frames/telemetry spans, (iii) the *top-K alternatives* with utility deltas and constraint margins, (iv) rule/constraint firings (which guardrail triggered), and (v) *confidence/abstain* flags when uncertainty is high. These proxies are tightly coupled to the logged bundle so that what the crew sees mirrors what the auditors replay.

7.3 Learning Under Guardrails (Federated/Continual)

Layer 4 converts operational signals into safer models without leaking sensitive data or destabilizing certified behavior.graph*Signals & triage We curate: false alarms, near-misses, out-of-distribution (OOD) detections, vetoed actions, and human overrides. Each item is de-duplicated, labeled, and linked to its constraint context (which requirement, which margin failed).

Algorithm 4 Safe Feedback Pipeline (Layer 4)

1: **Collect** signals $\mathcal{S}$ (near-miss, veto, OOD, override) $\leftarrow$ logs
2: **Triage** & label: attach constraint IDs, slices, environment tags
3: **Sanitize** with DP: (ε, δ)-DP transforms; secure aggregation
4: **Train** candidate $\mathcal{M}'$ (federated/continual, abstain-aware)
5: **Validate** in twin: safety $\rightarrow$ margin $\geq \gamma$; fairness $\rightarrow \Delta \leq \tau$; robustness $\rightarrow$ worst-case $\geq \rho$
6: **Red-team** targeted attacks; record failure modes
7: **Gate** via canary/shadow; monitor guard metrics; **rollback** on breach
8: **Attest** provenance (sig/ledger); **Deploy** if all checks pass

Privacy and Aggregation. Updates are computed with secure aggregation and (ε, δ)-differential privacy; per-domain privacy budgets are tracked and enforced. Raw telemetry stays on-vehicle or on-prem; only encrypted statistics or gradients leave the trust boundary.

Gates Before Deployment. Every candidate model passes through a *digital-twin regression battery* (hazard coverage, fairness parity by slice, adversarial robustness), a red-team exercise, and a canary/shadow rollout with automatic rollback on safety triggers. Provenance of each update (author, data domains, training recipe, eval reports) is signed; optionally, a zero-knowledge attestation anchors the origin to an auditable ledger without revealing sensitive inputs.

7.4 Metrics and Acceptance Criteria

Layer 4 produces *verifiable* outcomes:

- Forensic completeness: 100% of safety-significant actions reconstructable end-to-end.
- Latency to insight: median time to replay and explain an incident $\leq$ target (e.g., 1 h).
- Privacy budget: per-domain (ε, δ) within policy over period T.
- Feedback quality: fraction of near-misses that yield measurable safety-margin improvement in twin.
- Update safety: zero invariant violations in regression suite; canary shows non-inferior safety and fairness.

Why it Matters. Without Layer 4, evidence decays into ad hoc screenshots and unverifiable claims. With it, *every* action is explainable, traceable, and useful for controlled learning—turning day-to-day operations into a certifiable improvement engine.

8 Case Study A: LEO Collision Avoidance Fuel vs Schedule

8.1 Scenario, Inputs, and Hard Constraints

A conjunction data message (CDM) indicates a close approach in 48 h with $P_c = 2 \times 10^{-4}$, exceeding the mission threshold $P_c^{\max} = 10^{-6}$. The vehicle carries a remaining ΔV_{res} budget with a policy reserve of $\geq 8\%$. Hard constraints for the decision engine are: (i) post-maneuver collision risk $P_c(u, t_b) \leq P_c^{\max}$, (ii) propellant after burn $\geq \Delta V_{\text{reserve}}$, (iii) thermal/link/geofence limits satisfied, and (iv) schedule slip within the authority's window unless explicitly approved. Here u is the planned maneuver (magnitude and direction) and t_b is its epoch.

We treat $P_c(u, t_b)$ as provided by the flight dynamics service using a standard encounter-plane covariance method; the solver need not symbolically differentiate $P_c(\cdot)$ so long as it can query it for candidate actions. A safety slack σ_{Pc} may be enforced to maintain a margin to $P_c^{\max}$.

8.2 Two Safe Options

The flight dynamics system returns two *feasible* options that satisfy all hard constraints:

- **A (immediate burn):** $\Delta V = 5$ m/s, schedule slip = 0 min.
- **B (later detour):** $\Delta V = 2$ m/s, schedule slip = 40 min.

8.3 Multi-objective Scoring With Normalization

To make the trade-off explicit and auditable, we scalarize fuel and schedule costs with operator-approved weights ($w_{\text{fuel}}, w_{\text{sched}}$) and simple normalizers (10 m/s and 60 min):

$$J(u, t_b) = w_{\text{fuel}} \cdot \frac{\Delta V}{10} + w_{\text{sched}} \cdot \frac{\text{delay (min)}}{60}. \tag{7}$$

8.4 Execution Path (RTA and Governor)

Both A and B satisfy invariants; the constraint solver ranks them by J. Before actuation, the *ethical governor* rechecks: (i) updated P_c with fresh covariance, (ii) resource margins (propellant, power, thermal), (iii) link state for commanding, and (iv) geofences/ROE. If any check fails, the governor blocks the maneuver and falls back to a safe hold until human review or a recompute is available. The RTA loop guarantees a bounded worst-case decision time and logs all checks.

Algorithm 5 LEO CA Decision (per CDM update)

$\{(u_i, t_i)\} \leftarrow$ GENERATECANDIDATES() ▷ A, B, etc.
$\mathcal{F} \leftarrow \{(u_i, t_i) : P_c(u_i, t_i) \leq P_c^{\max},\ \text{margins} \geq 0\}$
if $\mathcal{F} = \emptyset$ **then**
  Escalate (human + replan)
end if
$(u^\star, t^\star) \leftarrow \arg\min_{(u_i,t_i)\in\mathcal{F}} J(u_i, t_i)$
if GOVERNORSAFE$(u^\star, t^\star)$ **then**
  EXECUTE$(u^\star, t^\star)$
else
  Hold and **Recompute** (or human confirm alternative)
end if
LOGRATIONALE($\{u_i, t_i, J_i\}$, weights, margins, verdicts)

8.5 Operator UI and Rationale Bundle

The mission display shows: (i) top-K options with ΔV, delay, and post-maneuver P_c; (ii) active weights $(w_{\text{fuel}}, w_{\text{sched}})$; and (iii) constraint margins (propellant reserve, thermal/link, ROE). Crew can HOLD, PROCEED, or select an ALTERNATIVE; a physical override remains available. The *rationale bundle* records inputs (CDM fields hashed), solver type and horizon, candidates and scores, the chosen action, and the governor's pass/fail results with margins.

8.6 Sensitivity and What-Ifs

Because J is linear in the weights, sensitivity to priority shifts is transparent. For any two safe options (A, B),

$$J_A \leq J_B \iff w_{\text{fuel}}\left(\frac{\Delta V_A - \Delta V_B}{10}\right) + w_{\text{sched}}\left(\frac{\Delta t_A - \Delta t_B}{60}\right) \leq 0.$$

Mission authority can sweep $(w_{\text{fuel}}, w_{\text{sched}})$ to *trace the indifference curve* where the preferred option flips, then lock weights for the current ops phase (e.g., post-anomaly fuel conservation).

8.7 Acceptance Criteria

A maneuver recommendation is acceptable if and only if: (i) $P_c \leq 10^{-6}$ with the configured safety slack, (ii) all margins (propellant, thermal, link, geofence/ROE) are non-negative, (iii) the RTA loop meets its tick budget, and (iv) the rationale bundle is complete and passes deterministic replay. Under *Ops priority* weights the system shall recommend A; under *Fuel-scarce* it shall recommend B (Table 2), unless a margin regression occurs between compute and commit, in which case the governor blocks and requests re-evaluation or human direction.

9 Case Study B: Crewed Depressurization Priority Sequencing and Overrides

9.1 Scenario and Hard Invariants

A rapid cabin depressurization is detected when the pressure rate exceeds a mission-specific threshold (e.g., $\Delta P/\Delta t > 3$ kPa/s) over a short window. The autonomy stack must satisfy the following *hard invariants*:

$$\begin{aligned} &\textbf{Crew-first:} && \mathrm{pLOC} \leq \mathrm{pLOC}_{\mathrm{target}} && (8)\\ &\textbf{Breathable-air time:} && T_{\mathrm{air}}(t) \geq T_{\mathrm{min}} && (9)\\ &\textbf{Structural/thermal:} && \sigma(x) \leq \sigma_{\mathrm{max}}, \quad T(x) \leq T_{\mathrm{max}} && (10)\\ &\textbf{ROE/comms integrity:} && \text{only authenticated, fresh commands} && (11) \end{aligned}$$

where T_{air} is the predicted time-to-threshold for safe breathing and pLOC is the predicted probability of loss of crew given the evolving state.

Breathable-Air Time Model (Simplified). Let $P(t)$ be total cabin pressure, $\dot{P}_\ell$ the estimated leak rate, and P_{min} the minimum safe pressure (accounting for O_2 partial pressure). Assuming approximately linear decay over the next horizon,

$$P(t+\tau) \approx P(t) - \dot{P}_\ell\,\tau, \qquad T_{\mathrm{air}} \approx \frac{P(t) - P_{\mathrm{min}}}{\dot{P}_\ell}. \tag{12}$$

A more complete model augments (12) with O_2 fraction dynamics and crew metabolic consumption; we conservatively take the minimum of the pressure and O_2-based estimates.

9.2 Sensing and State Estimation

Two independent pressure sensors must concur (*2-of-2* voting) before declaring a depressurization. A leak-rate estimate is computed via a robust derivative:

$$\dot{P}_\ell = \mathrm{median}\left(\frac{P_k - P_{k-1}}{\Delta t}\right)_{k \in \mathcal{W}}, \tag{13}$$

over a short sliding window $\mathcal{W}$; outliers are rejected by a Hampel filter. Fault hypotheses (sensor bias/dropout) are tested against IMU/vibration/valve telemetry to avoid false isolations.

9.3 Priority Sequencing (T+0 to T+120 s)

T+0–2 s: Detect and Classify. Dual-sensor confirmation; dismiss sensor-fault hypothesis; auto-alert crew and Flight.

T+2–10 s: Isolate and Stabilize. Close nearest bulkheads/valves; auto-seal candidate breach zone; run barrier checks on (10); update T_{air} via (12).

T+10–20 s: Life-Support Bias. Maximize O_2 delivery to the crew zone; depressurize non-essential volumes to reduce leak flux; switch to suit loop as needed.

T+20–60 s: Crew Routing and Localization. Compute safest compartment; present AR cues; confirm headcount; stream medical telemetry.

T+60–120 s: Vehicle Safing and Abort Prep. Repoint for comms/thermal; constrain thrusters to protect propellant margins; arm deorbit/abort if thresholds persist.

Discussion. This case study illustrates how pre-authorized fast actions, enforceable invariants, and time-boxed human control produce both responsiveness and assurance. By logging margins and decisions, the same incident also becomes training signal for Layer 4, improving leak localization and T_{air} prediction in twin-based regression before any software redeploy.

10 Related Work and Certification Pathways

Trustworthy-AI guidance emphasizes human agency, transparency, and accountability [1]. XAI and social-science insights argue for explanations aligned with operator cognition [2,8]. Human–automation research details pitfalls in mode awareness and trust calibration [3]. Digital twins provide evidence for V&V [4,5]. Recent work surveys and proposes certification frameworks for AI in aviation [6,7]. Assurance-case construction patterns for autonomy provide structure for claims, arguments, and evidence [9].

11 Related Work and Certification Pathways

Trustworthy-AI principles. Foundational guidance emphasizes human agency, transparency, accountability, and robustness as preconditions for the safe deployment of AI in society [1]. For aerospace, these principles must be *operationalized*: agency becomes meaningful human control and override authority; transparency becomes operator-facing explanations and replayable logs; and robustness spans fault tolerance, cyber integrity, and distribution shift resilience.

Explanations aligned with operator cognition. Explainable AI (XAI) initiatives argue that explanations are most effective when they match the end-user's mental models and decision timelines [2,8]. In flight operations, this favors concise, contrastive "why this/why not that" rationales, calibrated confidence or coverage bounds, and visualization of constraint margins (e.g., geofence distance, fuel/thermal reserves), rather than generic feature attributions detached from actionable choices.

Humanautomation teaming lessons. Decades of research highlight mode confusion, automation surprises, and miscalibrated trust as primary failure modes when humans supervise complex systems [3]. The Layer 3/4 mechanisms in this work (graded authority, time-boxed confirmations, and auditable rationale bundles) directly target those pitfalls by making automation intent legible and by preserving tactically relevant human authority.

Digital twins for V&V at scale. Digital-twin methodologies enable evidence generation under rare or hazardous conditions by coupling high-fidelity simulation with live or recorded telemetry [4,5]. Twins support requirements-based testing, coverage of edge-case scenarios (e.g., LEO conjunctions, depressurization, ROE escalation), robustness/corruption sweeps, and regression of bias/-fairness metrics across operational slices—producing artifacts suitable for certification audits.

Emerging certification approaches for AI in aviation. Recent work surveys pathways for certifying AI-based functions, proposing documentation structures, hazard analyses tailored to data-driven components, and runtime assurance patterns that fence advanced controllers with simpler, verifiable guards [6,7]. A recurring theme is *evidence continuity*: each lifecycle stage (requirements, data/-model development, integration, and operations) must emit artifacts that link back to intent and forward to verification and monitoring—precisely the chain our four-layer architecture enforces.

Assurance-case patterns for autonomy. Assurance-case methodologies provide a disciplined way to argue system safety by structuring *claims*, *arguments*, and *evidence* in a traceable graph (e.g., GSN-style) [9]. For ethically aware autonomy, top-level claims such as "crew-safety-first is enforced at run time" are decomposed into subclaims about constraint encoding (Layer 1), model behavior (Layer 2), run-time veto and fallback (Layer 3), and immutable rationale logging (Layer 4), each backed by test, analysis, and operational evidence.

11.1 Mapping Principles to Certification Evidence

Table 3 summarizes how prior work informs concrete artifacts emitted by our architecture. This mapping can seed a compliance matrix in a safety case or certification package.

11.2 Integrating into an Assurance Case (Sketch)

A top-level claim (C0): *"Mission autonomy is ethically aware and safe for intended use."* is supported by:

- **C1 (Values enforced).** Constraints and risk bounds are encoded and traced to tests (evidence: Value & Risk Charter, constraint acceptance tests).
- **C2 (Model fitness).** Fairness/robustness targets met across slices and threats (evidence: slice reports, corruption tables, red-team logs).
- **C3 (Run-time assurance).** Safety valve and RTA prevent invariant violations with bounded WCET (evidence: monitor coverage, WCET analysis).
- **C4 (Accountability).** Immutable logs enable deterministic replay; human decisions are recorded (evidence: rationale-bundle replays, hash-chain audits).

Table 3. From principles in related work to certifiable evidence in this paper.

Principle/Insight	Evidence Artifact in Our Approach
Human agency, accountability [1]	Autonomy envelope; override policy; signed rationale bundles with human actions logged
Operator-aligned explanations [2,8]	Top-K options with utilities and constraint margins; calibrated confidence/abstain flags
Trust calibration & mode awareness [3]	Time-boxed confirmations; escalation ladders; UI status chips for constraints and integrity
Twin-based V&V [4,5]	Scenario libraries; robustness/bias regression; near-miss replay and coverage reports
Certifiable AI in aviation [6,7]	Layered safety case: value charter, model cards, robustness/bias reports, RTA/WCET proofs
Assurance-case construction [9]	Claimargumentevidence graph linking requirements (IDs) to tests and logs

Each claim references concrete Requirement IDs and artifacts, yielding a living safety case that evolves with software updates rather than a static snapshot.

The literature provides *what* we must achieve (agency, transparency, robustness) and *how* to argue it (assurance cases). Our architecture supplies the *plumbing*—specific artifacts and run-time checks—so those arguments can be assembled into a certifiable package that regulators and operators can evaluate.

12 Conclusion

Ethical autonomy in aerospace is achievable *by design*, not as an afterthought. By encoding stakeholder values as machine-checkable constraints and objectives (Layer 1), building models with measurable guarantees for fairness, robustness, and interpretability (Layer 2), binding decisions to constraint solvers and run-time safety valves under a Simplex/RTA pattern (Layer 3), and closing the loop with immutable rationale logs and guarded learning (Layer 4), we obtain systems that are safer, more certifiable, and operationally effective. The case studies show that when safety and ROE are *hard invariants*, trade-offs become transparent, human authority remains tactically relevant, and every action is reconstructable for investigation and continuous improvement.

Cybersecurity is not a parallel concern; it is the *enabler of ethics in practice.* Without strong cyber controls, the very properties that make autonomy "ethical" collapse:

Hard constraints are only meaningful if inputs and commands are authentic and fresh. Spoofed GNSS, forged sensor packets, or replayed telemetry can make a safe maneuver look unsafe (or vice versa). Cryptographic authentication, anti-replay, and freshness checks (age bounds) ensure the ethical governor and RTA monitor evaluate *reality*, not an attacker's narrative. In our LEO case, this prevents a spoofed conjunction from draining fuel; in depressurization, it blocks a false leak alarm; in contested airspace, it stops effects delivery based on tampered PID. ROE gates and dual-confirm workflows depend on identity and non-repudiation. Role-based access control, hardware-backed keys, and signed confirmations make "dual human confirm" a cryptographically enforceable rule rather than a UI convention. Loss of link integrity triggers automatic de-escalation—an ethical outcome implemented by cyber checks.

Tamper-evident, hash-chained logs with synchronized clocks transform "explanations" into admissible evidence. Secure boot, signed binaries, and a software bill of materials (SBOM) preserve the provenance of the model/logic that made a decision. Without these, post-incident forensics become speculation and liability assignment is untenable.

Fairness and robustness guarantees assume a benign data pipeline. Cyber brings supply-chain scanning, dataset signing, and poison detection to protect training and continual-learning flows. Differential privacy, secure aggregation, and policy-bound privacy budgets let Layer 4 learn from near-misses without leaking sensitive telemetry, aligning ethics with law.

Ethical guards only help if they always run. Time/space partitioning, priority scheduling, WCET analysis, and zero-trust boundaries ensure non-critical ML cannot starve safety monitors. Secure inter-partition messaging makes the RTA hand-off dependable even under attack or overload.

Cyber disciplines operationalize "graceful degradation": detect compromise, shrink the autonomy envelope, rotate keys, quarantine models, and roll back to a known-good baseline. Ethics requires fail-secure behavior; cyber provides the playbook and mechanisms to execute it at machine speed.

Ethics without cyber is unenforceable; cyber without ethics is misdirected. Embedding cybersecurity from the Value & Risk Charter onward is what makes value-aligned constraints *binding*, explanations trustworthy, and learning safe. This inseparability is why our architecture treats integrity, identity, and provenance as first-class, cross-layer requirements—so that ethical autonomy remains ethical under real-world faults, drift, and adversaries.

References

1. High-Level Expert Group on Artificial Intelligence: Ethics Guidelines for Trustworthy AI (2019). https://digital-strategy.ec.europa.eu/en/library/ethics-guidelines-trustworthy-ai. Accessed 2025
2. Gunning, D.: Explainable Artificial Intelligence (XAI) (2017)
3. Endsley, M.R.: From here to autonomy: lessons learned from human–automation research. Hum. Factors **59**(1), 5–27 (2017)
4. Boschert, S., Rosen, R.: Digital twin—the simulation aspect. In: Hehenberger, P., Bradley, D. (eds.) Mechatronic Futures, pp. 59–74. Springer, Cham (2016). https://doi.org/10.1007/978-3-319-32156-1_5

5. Grieves, M., Vickers, J.: Digital twin: mitigating unpredictable, undesirable emergent behavior in complex systems. In: Kahlen, F.-J., Flumerfelt, S., Alves, A. (eds.) Transdisciplinary Perspectives on Complex Systems, pp. 85–113. Springer, Cham (2017). https://doi.org/10.1007/978-3-319-38756-7_4
6. Gariel, M., Shimanuki, B., Timpe, R., Wilson, E.: Toward a framework for certification of ai-based systems. arXiv preprint (2023) arXiv:2302.11049 [cs.SE]
7. Bello, H., Geißler, D., Ray, L., Müller-Divéky, S., Müller, P., Streit, A.: Certification of ai in aerospace: landscape, challenges, and opportunities. arXiv preprint (2024). arXiv:2409.08666 [cs.SE]
8. Miller, T.: Explanation in artificial intelligence: insights from the social sciences. Artif. Intell. **267**, 1–38 (2019)
9. Porter, Z., Habli, I., McDermid, J., Kaas, M.: A principled approach to the construction of assurance cases for ai and autonomous systems. arXiv preprint (2022). arXiv:2203.15370 [cs.SE]

A Novel LLM-Assisted Educational Framework for SQL Language Learning

Jaykumar Tandel(✉), Rohan Bopardikar, and Jia Zou

Arizona State University, Tempe, USA
{jrtandel,rbopardi,jia.zou}@asu.edu

Abstract. Structured Query Language (SQL) has been widely used for data science and data management, integrated with relational database systems, big data management systems, and data science tools. However, there is a lack of educational platforms for practicing how to solve SQL problems in real-world or industrial contexts and receiving real-time feedback. To address the issue, this work provides an LLM-assisted educational framework for learning SQL. Our framework is novel in three aspects: (1) Unlike traditional teaching that only provides a plain English description of the problem to be solved by SQL, we use examples to illustrate the patterns of the target table expected to be output from students' SQL programs to make the problem design process automatic, scalable, and easily integrated with complex industrial and real-world scenarios. (2) We use LLM to generate the code to produce the ground-truth target data for automatic grading. (3) We use LLM to automatically generate annotations to enrich the SQL problem metadata information, including a plain English description, difficulty level, and the learning objective of the problem, to enable efficient search and recommendation of problems for different students. Our evaluation showed that LLM with zero-shot prompting achieves accuracy competitive to existing automatic data transformation tools while saving a significant amount of labeling and supervised learning efforts.

Keywords: SQL Language Learning · Large Language Model · Educational Platform · Automatic Data Transformation

1 Introduction

Structured Query Language (SQL) is one of the most widely taught and applied languages for working with data. It has remained the standard for relational database systems for decades, and continues to be essential in big data ecosystems and modern data science pipelines. Beyond database administrators, SQL proficiency is now expected of data scientists, engineers, and business analysts across industries such as finance, retail, healthcare, internet, education, and so on. Surveys have shown SQL to be one of the most in-demand skills for data-related careers [9,13–15]. Consequently, SQL is a staple in computer science,

J. R. Barr et al. (Eds.): ERWCSA 2025, ACSAR 4, pp. 193–202, 2026.
https://doi.org/10.1007/978-3-032-18230-2_14

information systems, and data science curricula, often introduced in early undergraduate courses and revisited in advanced topics. Despite its perceived declarative simplicity, SQL poses significant learning challenges. Students struggle with mapping natural-language problem statements into relational algebra, reasoning about joins and aggregation, and understanding the correctness of their queries [20]. For this reason, educational technologies that provide scaffolding and practice opportunities for SQL are considered crucial in supporting effective learning.

Over the years, a variety of educational platforms have been developed to help students practice SQL. Interactive tutorials such as SQLZoo [1], Mode Analytics SQL Tutorial [2], and DataCamp [3] offer guided lessons with progressively harder queries. Problem-based learning systems such as LeetCode [4] and HackerRank [5] include SQL exercises alongside programming problems, while research-oriented platforms such as SQLator [6], DBTutor [7], and SQLify [17] provide automated grading and feedback tailored for classroom use. These systems typically evaluate correctness by comparing the results of a student's query against the output of an instructor-authored reference query, sometimes with query canonicalization or test data variations to detect equivalent solutions.

Despite their contributions, existing platforms face several limitations. First, SQL problem creation is largely manual: instructors must craft natural-language descriptions, design datasets, and write reference queries, which is labor-intensive and difficult to scale to industrially realistic scenarios [10,16]. Second, evaluation pipelines often rely on a single ground-truth query, which can fail to capture semantically equivalent alternatives, leading to false negatives and discouraging students [11,12]. Third, metadata about problems, such as difficulty levels, learning objectives, and cognitive skills targeted, is typically missing or inconsistently annotated, making it difficult for instructors to personalize problem sets or for platforms to recommend exercises adaptively [22]. As a result, while current SQL platforms are effective for drill-based practice, they provide limited support for scalable, realistic, and adaptive SQL pedagogy.

To address these challenges, we propose an LLM-assisted educational framework for SQL learning. Our framework introduces three novel contributions:

(1) Scalable, Accurate, and Realistic Target-Based Problem Creation. Given real-world datasets, it requires expert knowledge and tremendous manual efforts to derive meaningful and realistic queries on the datasets and generate corresponding plain English descriptions without ambiguity and mistakes. Compared to the textual description of the problem, we found it is much easier to obtain a few examples that illustrate the patterns of the target data expected to be output from the SQL queries to be developed by the students. Note that the examples do not need to correspond to any of the tuples in the given source datasets. Therefore, we can easily obtain a small number of examples from historically transformed datasets. For example, the AutoPipeline Github benchmark dataset [8] provides the source datasets and transformed datasets for 700 real-world data transformation pipelines crawled from Github repository. Therefore, instead of relying solely on textual descriptions, we use example-based specifications of target outputs to automatically generate diverse and complex SQL problems, making problem creation scalable and easily adaptable to real-world data transformation scenarios.

(2) LLM-Based Generation of Ground-Truth Target Data for Automatic Grading. Existing SQL learning platforms rely on manual efforts to generate reference answers. To automate the process, given the source datasets and a few examples of the target data, we leverage large language models (LLMs) to generate the ground-truth transformation code that produces expected results based on our prior works about automatic data transformation [18, 19], enabling reliable and automatic grading without requiring extensive manually authored solutions.

(3) LLM-Based Metadata Generation for Personalized Adaptive Learning. Our framework further uses LLMs to enrich SQL problem metadata by automatically generating plain-English problem descriptions, estimated difficulty levels, and learning objectives, thereby supporting personalized problem recommendation and adaptive curriculum design.

We evaluated our framework on a diverse collection of SQL transformation tasks. The results show that zero-shot prompting of LLMs achieves grading accuracy comparable to specialized transformation tools, while substantially reducing the need for manual labeling and supervised training. Moreover, the automatically generated problem metadata was judged to be of high quality, demonstrating the potential of our approach for scalable SQL pedagogy. Taken together, these results highlight how LLM-assisted methods can augment traditional SQL education platforms by improving scalability, adaptability, and alignment with industrial problem-solving contexts.

2 System Overview

As illustrated in Fig. 1, our proposed system consists of the following components:

(1) LLM-Based Code Generation for Data Transformation. Given a set of input source tables and a small number of examples that illustrate the target output patterns, we employ large language models (LLMs) to automatically generate the transformation logic, leveraging LLM's zero-shot reasoning capabilities. The LLM produces SQL programs that convert the source data into the desired target form. This component enhances our prior works SQLMorpher [18] and DataMorpher [19] by introducing a multi-step reasoning strategy, a hint-based critique strategy, and a serial model ensemble strategy, as detailed in Sect. 3.2.

(2) Ground-truth Target Data Generation. Once the LLM has generated candidate transformation code, the system executes the code on the provided source tables to produce ground-truth target datasets in a sandbox. These target datasets serve as the expected outputs against which student submissions can be evaluated, ensuring robustness in grading and reducing false negatives due

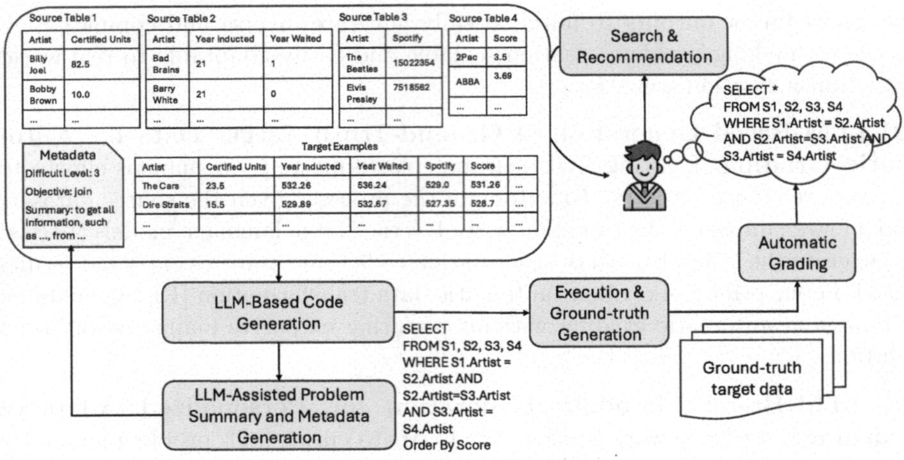

Fig. 1. System Overview.

to semantically equivalent query formulations. In addition, false positives could also be detected by using variations of source datasets and the corresponding ground-truth target dataset.

(3) LLM-Based Code Summary and Metadata Generation. To enrich each automatically generated SQL problem, we further use LLMs to produce high-level plain-English description of the problem. In addition, we analyze the generated SQL query to extract the following metadata (i) a difficulty rating derived from the complexity (i.e., number of operators) of the generated transformation, and (ii) identification of occurrences of each relational operator, such as joins, aggregations, subqueries, or window functions. These annotations enable instructors to better align problems with pedagogical goals and allow the system to support adaptive learning by tailoring problem recommendations to students' skill levels.

(4) Automatic Grading. Students submit SQL queries in response to a given problem. The system executes their submitted queries on the same source datasets and compares the outputs against the previously generated ground-truth targets. The grading engine evaluates correctness by checking equivalence in data values, schema consistency, and ordering when appropriate. In addition, with the assistance of LLM, the system provides diagnostic feedback, such as identifying missing tuples or incorrect aggregations, thereby helping students understand their mistakes and refine their reasoning.

(5) Problem Search and Recommendation. The system also supports efficient retrieval and recommendation of problems. Using the metadata generated in component (3), problems are indexed by description, difficulty, and targeted SQL constructs. This enables students to search for problems by keyword or concept (e.g., "aggregation with GROUP BY" or "join queries"), and allows instructors to assign personalized assignments. Moreover, the system also has the feature of recommending new problems to students adaptively using a two-tower model. In the student tower, a student's normalized skill gap for each type of relational operator, such as join, aggregation, filter, union, subquery, with clause, etc., will be estimated. A skill gap for an operator is estimated as the total of full scores of problems involving the operator subtracting the student's total score over those problems. Then, the normalized skill gaps over different relational operators form a feature vector. At the same time, in the problem tower, the normalized occurrences of different operators in the LLM-generated reference query also form a feature vector that describes the problem. Finally, the cosine similarity of the two vectors will be computed as the recommendation score.

Together, these five components form a closed-loop pipeline that generates high-quality SQL problems from real-world data, automatically produces ground truth for grading, and enriches problems with pedagogical metadata. This integration of LLM-based generation with educational workflows allows the system to scale beyond manually curated platforms and to align SQL learning with industrial data practices efficiently.

3 LLM-Based Code Generation for Data Transformation

3.1 Problem Definition

The input of a data transformation problem include: (1) a set of source datasets $\mathcal{T}^{in} = \{T_1^{in}, ..., T_m^{in}\}$; (2) a schema of the ground truth target dataset $\hat{\mathcal{T}}^{tgt}$, denoted as S^{tgt}; and (3) a collection of target examples, which do not need to correspond to any tuples from the source datasets, denoted as $\mathcal{T}_0^{tgt}$. The problem is to search for a sequence of operators, $\mathcal{O} = \{o_1, ..., o_k\}$, with each $o_i \in \mathcal{O}$ is of one of the relational operators, so that the transformed data, represented as $\mathcal{T}^{tgt} = o_k(...(o_1(\mathcal{T}^{in})))$, satisfies that $\mathcal{T}^{tgt} = \hat{\mathcal{T}}^{tgt}$.

3.2 Multi-step Reasoning Strategy

To leverage LLM to solve the above problem, we developed an iterative multi-step strategy. In each iteration, there are two steps:

(1) We use LLM to select the next operator from a list of candidate operators, such as equi-join, union, groupBy, aggregate, pivot, unpivot, filter, projection, NMP (i.e., no more operators);

(2) We use LLM to configure the operator selected in the previous step. Taking `equi-join` for example, the model will predict the tables to be joined and the join attributes.

It repeats these two steps until the first step returns `NMP`. Then, we send all the history of operator configurations to LLM and ask LLM to generate an SQL program following the sequence of operators.

3.3 Hint-Based Critique

We also applies LLM to validate the responses obtained by the multi-step reasoning strategy using a hint-based critique prompt that includes the following example domain-specific rules described in natural language:

1. If the resulting data generated by the failed Python script has the same schema with the target data, but has more rows, it may indicate three things (1) a Group By operator and Aggregate operators are missing. We would suggest adding a Group By operator using the left-most non-float, and unique attributes from the given target examples as GroupBy attributes and choosing the Aggregation operator such as count, average, medium, sum, etc., based on the range of valuesfor each of other columns. (2) If OUTER join is used, it should be replaced by INNER join. (3) We shall remove rows that contain NaN values.
2. If multiple source tables share the same schema while the target table (i.e., target examples) also has the same schema, UNION must be used. However if m source tables share the same schema consisting of k non-key columns, but the target table has renamed each non-key column shared into k different columns, and thus consists of $k \times m$ non-key columns, JOIN should be applied to join all source tables on the primary key.
3. Group By columns are never float types. These Group By columns correspond to columns that are UNIQUE and non-float in the target examples, which are usually at the leftmost part of the columns of the target examples.
4. JOIN is usually applied to two tables sharing the same primary key, or applied to two tables where one table has a column (i.e., foreign key) referencing to the primary key of the other table.

3.4 Cost-Effective Serial LLM Ensemble

Different LLM models incur different monetary costs, e.g., OpenAI's gpt-5-mini API costs \$0.25 for 1 million input tokens and \$2.00 for 1 million output tokens, while its reasoning API o4-mini costs \$1.10 for 1 million input tokens and \$4.40 for 1 million output tokens. Assuming there exists a light-weight verifier to determine whether the generated code is correct, our cost-effective serial LLM ensemble strategy will first apply the cheapest LLM model to all cases, and only send the failed data transformation cases to the second-cheapest LLM models. It will repeat the process until all cases have been verified successfully or all candidate LLM models have been explored. The lightweight verifier could be a human domain expert or a soft scorer that checks whether the functional dependency, key constraints, and column mapping discovered in the generated target dataset are consistent with those found in the target examples.

4 Experimental Evaluation

4.1 Exepriemntal Setup

We used the 400 real-world data transformation cases organized in Level 1–3 and 9 from the AutoPipeline Github benchmark [8] as testing workloads. Level-

k represents that the corresponding data transformation query consists of k SQL operators. Level-9 represents that the corresponding data transformation query consists of 9+ SQL operators. We compare our proposed LLM prompting approach to the following baselines:

Chain-of-Thoughts (CoT) Zero-shot [21]. We also implemented an LLM-based pipeline using zero-shot CoT planning, which prompts the LLM to generate the data generation code in multiple steps, and run these steps one by one.

Auto-pipeline [24]. This system automatically synthesize multi-step data transformation pipelines based on source datasets and target examples. In their paper, they provided three approaches, search-based, supervised-learning-based, and reinforcement learning (RL)-based. We focus on comparing to the RL-based approach, since it achieved the best accuracy. Their RL approach used three types of 32 convolutional filters followed by 2D max-pooling and average-pooling and two final Multi-Layer Perceptron (MLP) layers in each of sub models. These sub models corresponding to FD, Key, operators, and column-mapping prediction tasks.

Auto-suggest [23]. It trains one relatively complicated model that involves embedding layers, recurrent neural network (RNN), and MLP, to predict the next operator. In addition, it trains five simpler models to predict join columns, join types, groupby columns, pivot index/header split, and columns to unpivot.

We considered OpenAI's gpt-5-mini, gpt-4.1-mini, and o4-mini as candidate models, while using a naive verifier based on ground-truth target data, which is available from the AutoPipeline Github benchmark.

4.2 Experimental Results

In Table 1, Auto-Pipeline and Auto-Suggest results are extracted from their paper [24], since these two systems are not publicly available. We have no way to compare their latency and costs, e.g., training time, so we show these results for Auto-Pipeline and Auto-Suggest as not available (-).

As shown in Table 1, our proposed LLM-driven methods consistently exceed or at the very least remain close to the performance of learning-based AutoPipeline. CoT-zeroshot provides a strong baseline for LLM-based reasoning, but the introduction of Multi-Step reasoning, hint-based critique, and our ensemble strategy yields significant improvements. The comparison between gpt-5-mini and gpt-o4-mini highlights that more reasoning-capable (and costlier) models generally perform better across all levels, motivating the ensemble approach: when a cheaper model fails, a stronger model is invoked. This ensures that most simple cases, solvable by lightweight models, remain cost-efficient, while complex cases benefit from the enhanced reasoning of larger models. Notably, in L1 and L9 the ensemble achieves the best results, with o4-mini ranking second, which underscores certain irregularities in LLM performance across levels. In L2 and L3, the AutoPipeline remains competitive, but our ensemble approach keeps pace; more importantly, in larger and more complex transformations where it struggles, our approaches significantly outperform it. Note that Auto-Pipeline and Auto-Suggest both rely on the training of numerous ML models to configure and select operators, which requires training data preparation, while our approach is zero-shot, and thus significantly more convenient, without any training overhead.

Overall, for these 400 cases, our ensemble approach achieved an overall accuracy of (83.5%), outperforming Auto-Pipeline (79.5%) and Auto-Suggest (43%).

Table 1. Overall Results over Level 1–3 and 9 in Github Benchmark. Each Level has 100 cases. In total, we have 400 cases. The best results are highlighted in bold and the second best results are underlined. Both AutoPipeline and AutoSuggest are based on supervised learning, while our approaches are based on zero-shot without any training overheads.

	L1			L2			L3			L9		
Methods	Auc	Lat	Cost	Auc	Lat	Cost	Auc	Lat	Cost	Auc	Lat	Cost
CoT-zeroshot w/ gpt4-turbo	66%	27 s	$0.06	24%	25 s	$0.08	38%	38 s	$0.08	53%	50 s	$0.12
Our Approach w/ Serial Ensemble	**94%**	50 s	$0.01	82%	35	$0.02	81%	208	$0.07	**77%**	241 s	$0.08
Our Approach w/ gpt-5-mini only	76%	55 s	$0.01	74%	71 s	$0.01	68%	115 s	$0.02	62%	238 s	$0.04
Our Approach w/ gpt-4.1-mini only	86%	15 s	$0.005	66%	12 s	$0.006	64%	25 s	$0.01	72%	82 s	$0.02
Our Approach w/ o4-mini only	90%	43 s	$0.03	75%	54 s	$0.04	73%	154 s	$0.10	74%	178 s	$0.11
Auto-Pipeline	89%	-	-	**89%**	-	-	**86%**	-	-	54%	-	-
Auto-Suggest	44%	-	-	11%	-	-	18%	-	-	49%	-	-

5 Conclusion and Future Works

We introduced an LLM-assisted educational framework for SQL learning that automates problem creation, grading, and metadata generation through multi-step reasoning, hint-based critique, and a cost-efficient ensemble of LLMs. Our evaluation on real-world benchmarks shows that the LLM-Assisted reference answer generation approach achieves accuracy on par with or better than existing learning-based systems, while offering scalable and adaptive support for SQL pedagogy. In future work, we plan to extend the framework with more complex relational operators and query constructs and add an LLM-assisted counterexample generation component to improve the accuracy of data transformation code generation. We also plan to integrate with large-scale learning platforms to enhance accessibility and impact further.

References

1. https://sqlzoo.net/wiki/SQL_Tutorial
2. https://mode.com/sql-tutorial
3. https://www.datacamp.com/category/sql?page=1

4. https://leetcode.com/problemset/database/
5. https://www.hackerrank.com/domains/sql
6. https://www.sqlator.com/index.html
7. https://www.dbtutor.com
8. https://gitlab.com/jwjwyoung/autopipeline-benchmarks
9. 365DataScience: The data analyst job market in 2024 [research on 1,000 job postings] (2024). https://365datascience.com/career-advice/the-data-analyst-job-market/, Accessed 19 Aug 2025
10. Aerts, W., Fletcher, G., Miedema, D.: A feasibility study on automated SQL exercise generation with chatgpt-3.5, pp. 13–19. DataEd '24, Association for Computing Machinery, New York, NY, USA (2024). https://doi.org/10.1145/3663649.3664368
11. Bhangdiya, A., et al.: The XDa-TA system for automated grading of SQL query assignments. In: 2015 IEEE 31st International Conference on Data Engineering, pp. 1468–1471 (2015). https://doi.org/10.1109/ICDE.2015.7113403
12. Chu, S., Li, D., Wang, C., Cheung, A., Suciu, D.: Demonstration of the Cosette automated SQL prover. In: Proceedings of the 2017 ACM International Conference on Management of Data, pp. 1591–1594. SIGMOD '17, Association for Computing Machinery, New York, NY, USA (2017). https://doi.org/10.1145/3035918.3058728
13. Cobloom: the top in-demand data science skills of 2025 (2025). https://www.cobloom.com/careers-blog/in-demand-data-science-skills, Accessed 19 Aug 2025
14. Coursera: 7 in-demand data analyst skills to get you hired in 2025 (2025). https://www.coursera.org/articles/in-demand-data-analyst-skills-to-get-hired, Accessed 19 Aug 2025
15. of Labor Statistics, U.B.: Database administrators and architects job statistics. https://www.bls.gov/ooh/computer-and-information-technology/database-administrators.htm, Accessed 19 Aug 2025
16. Pirttinen, N., Hellas, A., Leinonen, J.: Experiences from learnersourcing SQL exercises: do they cover course topics and do students use them? In: Proceedings of the 25th Australasian Computing Education Conference, pp. 123–131. ACE '23, Association for Computing Machinery, New York, NY, USA (2023). https://doi.org/10.1145/3576123.3576137
17. de Raadt, M., Dekeyser, S., Lee, T.Y.: Do students sqlify? improving learning outcomes with peer review and enhanced computer assisted assessment of querying skills, pp. 101–108. Baltic Sea '06, Association for Computing Machinery, New York, NY, USA (2006). https://doi.org/10.1145/1315803.1315821
18. Sharma, A., et al.: Automatic data transformation using large language model: an experimental study on building energy data (2023). https://arxiv.org/abs/2309.01957
19. Sharma, A., et al.: DATAMORPHER: Automatic data transformation using LLM-based zero-shot code generation. In: 2025 IEEE 41st International Conference on Data Engineering (ICDE), pp. 4536–4539. IEEE Computer Society, Los Alamitos, CA, USA (2025). https://doi.org/10.1109/ICDE65448.2025.00346, https://doi.ieeecomputersociety.org/10.1109/ICDE65448.2025.00346
20. Taipalus, T., Seppänen, V.: SQL education: a systematic mapping study and future research agenda. ACM Trans. Comput. Educ. **20**(3) (2020). https://doi.org/10.1145/3398377

21. Wei, J., et al.: Chain-of-thought prompting elicits reasoning in large language models (2023). https://arxiv.org/abs/2201.11903
22. Xu, J., Wei, T., Lv, P.: SQL-DP: a novel difficulty prediction framework for SQL programming problems. In: Proceedings of the 15th International Conference on Educational Data Mining (EDM 2022), pp. 86–97. International Educational Data Mining Society, Durham, United Kingdom (2022). https://doi.org/10.5281/zenodo.6852986
23. Yan, C., He, Y.: Auto-suggest: Learning-to-recommend data preparation steps using data science notebooks. In: Proceedings of the 2020 ACM SIGMOD International Conference on Management of Data. p. 1539–1554. SIGMOD '20, Association for Computing Machinery, New York, NY, USA (2020). https://doi.org/10.1145/3318464.3389738
24. Yang, J., He, Y., Chaudhuri, S.: Auto-pipeline: Synthesizing complex data pipelines by-target using reinforcement learning and search (2021). https://arxiv.org/abs/2106.13861

Enhancing Security and Privacy in Web Applications: A Focus on Children's Data and Health Information

Preethi Santhanam and Catalina Aranzazu-Suescun(✉)

Embry-Riddle Aeronautical University, Prescott, AZ 86301, USA
{santhanp,aranzazc}@erau.edu

Abstract. The rapid growth of web applications has significantly transformed the way individuals interact with technology, offering different levels of convenience, on-demand access to a wide range of services, and highly personalized user experiences. However, this growth has also brought challenges, particularly in the areas of data security and user privacy. These concerns are especially critical when applications handle sensitive and personal user data, including health information and, most importantly, data related to children.

As digital services increasingly integrate into everyday life, ensuring the responsible handling of such data becomes not only a technical necessity but also a legal and ethical imperative. In response to these challenges, this project focuses on investigating key security and privacy concerns in web applications, with a particular emphasis on safeguarding children's data and health-related information.

To address this, the project leverages advanced machine learning techniques, specifically transformer-based natural language processing (NLP) models such as BERT and Legal-BERT, to systematically analyze and interpret application privacy policies. These models are used to classify sections of privacy policies for compliance with major regulatory frameworks, including the Children's Online Privacy Protection Act (COPPA) and the Health Insurance Portability and Accountability Act (HIPAA). By identifying and categorizing mentions of children's data and health information, the models help highlight whether an application's policy adequately addresses relevant legal protections.

In parallel, we also examine whether web applications follow through on the promises made in their privacy policies. This part of our work involves analyzing app behavior such as when and how permissions are requested, whether secure data transmission is used, and what kind of third-party services are integrated. Often, we find a disconnect between the language in a privacy policy and what the app actually does, especially in web apps aimed at children or those that deal with health data.

Our early findings suggest that while many web apps use the right terminology, they often fall short when it comes to clarity, completeness, or meaningful transparency. For example, some policies mention COPPA compliance but do not explain how consent is obtained or how long data is stored. Others mention HIPAA but omit any description of how data is encrypted or accessed. These gaps can create real risks not only for end

J. R. Barr et al. (Eds.): ERWCSA 2025, ACSAR 4, pp. 203–214, 2026.
https://doi.org/10.1007/978-3-032-18230-2_15

users, but also for app developers who may unknowingly expose themselves to legal and ethical consequences.

By combining legal knowledge, machine learning, and a user-centered perspective, this research aims to build tools that help make privacy protections more visible and enforceable. Ultimately, we hope our work supports a more trustworthy app ecosystem—one where users can feel confident that their most sensitive information is handled with care and compliance.

Additionally, through this analysis, uncover gaps in privacy policies and determine whether applications are complying with legal requirements that protect children's online privacy and safeguard health data.

Keywords: Children's data · Health data · Machine learning · Privacy policies · Sensitive data · Web applications

1 Introduction

Web applications have become primary access points for a wide range of essential services, including healthcare, education, and communication. While these technologies offer significant convenience and accessibility, many operate with limited transparency regarding their data collection, storage, and sharing practices. In some instances, privacy policies are incomplete, complex, or difficult for users to interpret, leaving individuals uncertain about how their personal information is being handled. This lack of clarity is particularly concerning when it involves sensitive categories of data, such as children's personal information or health-related records, where the potential consequences of misuse or unauthorized disclosure can include identity theft, targeted tracking, discrimination, and reputational damage.

In the United States, certain federal laws provide enhanced protections for these types of data. The Children's Online Privacy Protection Act (COPPA) establishes strict requirements for the collection and use of personal information from children under the age of 13, while the Health Insurance Portability and Accountability Act (HIPAA) sets standards for safeguarding the privacy and security of health information. However, compliance is not universal, and enforcement challenges persist, leaving gaps in protection. These realities highlight the importance of stronger regulatory oversight, clearer communication from service providers, and the integration of privacy-by-design principles into the development of web applications to ensure that users can engage with digital services securely and with confidence.

This study focuses on identifying whether and how web applications fulfill their legal obligations in handling such sensitive data. The rest of the paper is organized as follows. Section 2 presents the related works done in the field. Section 3 presents an overview of the regulatory framework for this project. Section 4 presents the methodology used to extract the information from the privacy policies of web applications to identify compliance with the laws. Section 5 shows the analysis of the results. Finally, Sect. 6 states the conclusions of the project.

2 Related Works

Authors of [1] present a methodology combining static analysis, dynamic analysis, and machine learning to assess whether Android applications comply with Google Play's privacy guidelines. The approach checks if applications have a compliant privacy policy and whether they access sensitive user data only after policy acceptance. It also evaluates third-party libraries for compliance. Implemented in a tool called 3PDroid and tested on popular Google Play apps, the study found that over 95% access sensitive data, but only about 1% fully comply with the guidelines.

Continuing on this focus on privacy policy evaluation, authors of [2] present PermPress, a machine-learning system that checks if Android app privacy policies fully disclose the use of dangerous permissions. Using the annotated MPP-270 dataset, PermPress achieves high accuracy (AUC 0.92) in predicting permission-completeness. In a study of 164,156 applications, only 31% fully disclosed all dangerous permissions, while 60% omitted at least one. The findings reveal significant gaps in transparency and the need for standardized privacy policy checks.

Extending the discussion to a broader regulatory context, authors of [3] offer a comprehensive review of automated privacy risk analysis in mobile applications and social networks, focusing on tools and methods that use machine learning and natural language processing to evaluate compliance with regulations like GDPR. Using the PRISMA methodology, the study systematically analyzes key research and finds significant advancements in applying automated techniques to assess privacy risks. Similarly, authors of [4] trace the evolution of e-health from paper records to sophisticated Electronic Health Record (EHR) systems, and highlight the transformative role of AI in cybersecurity. It emphasizes how AI-driven technologies—such as continuous monitoring, anomaly detection, real-time threat response, predictive analytics, and adaptive learning—enhance threat detection and resilience in e-health systems. The review also looks ahead to emerging research directions, including quantum-resistant encryption, regulatory compliance automation, blockchain-enabled interoperability, and ethical AI development, all pivotal for building secure, scalable, and trustworthy digital health infrastructures.

In a related line, authors of [5] present a study that highlights how AI and machine learning improve mobile app security by enabling faster, more accurate vulnerability detection through automated code analysis, anomaly detection, behavioral monitoring, and simulated attacks. These adaptive technologies continuously learn from new data, providing ongoing protection against evolving threats in frequently updated applications.

Turning attention to discrepancies between stated policies and actual behavior, authors of [6] analyze over 68,000 Android apps and reveal widespread contradictions between privacy policies and actual data practices. Many apps share data without disclosure, falsely claim secure transmission, or misrepresent their target audience. The findings expose the failure of the notice-and-consent model, showing it often misleads users and cannot ensure informed privacy choices.

To further understand how privacy policy content varies by organization, authors of [7] use advanced NLP and ML techniques to explore how organizational characteristics, like company size and headquarters location, relate to GDPR compliance claims in privacy policies. The researchers developed five high-precision ($\geq .908$) classification models to detect GDPR-related promises, and applied them to a dataset covering 8,614 EU organizations. Their analysis revealed that small and medium-sized enterprises are less likely to include two core GDPR requirements in their privacy policies, while organizations based in Denmark are more likely to disclose such requirements, in contrast to those headquartered in Spain, Italy, and Slovenia, which showed negative correlations with multiple GDPR disclosures.

Continuing this trajectory of using automation for privacy assessments, authors of [8] propose a system that uses NLP and code analysis to assess mobile app privacy compliance. Examining nearly 18,000 Android apps, it found that many lacked required privacy policies, and those with policies often had discrepancies, such as undisclosed data collection or sharing. The study shows automated tools can expose widespread privacy noncompliance in apps.

3 Regulatory Framework

When it comes to privacy for health and children, especially in the U.S., several important laws and regulations safeguard how personal health data and children's data are collected, used, stored, and shared.

3.1 Regulation for Health Information

The Health Insurance Portability and Accountability Act (HIPAA) [9] in the United States applies to "covered entities," which include healthcare providers, health plans, and healthcare clearinghouses, as well as their "business associates." It establishes a Privacy Rule that limits how protected health information (PHI) can be used or disclosed without patient authorization, and a Security Rule that requires technical, administrative, and physical safeguards to protect electronic PHI (ePHI). Additionally, HIPAA's Breach Notification Rule mandates that affected individuals, the U.S. Department of Health and Human Services (HHS), and, in certain cases, the media must be notified if a data breach occurs.

The Health Information Technology for Economic and Clinical Health Act (HITECH) [10] strengthens HIPAA's enforcement and privacy and security requirements. It increases penalties for violations, encourages the secure adoption and meaningful use of electronic health records (EHRs), and imposes stricter breach notification procedures to ensure that individuals are promptly informed when their health information is compromised.

42 CFR Part 2 [11] protects records related to substance use disorder treatment from disclosure without the patient's consent, often imposing stricter requirements than HIPAA. This regulation is designed to encourage individuals to seek treatment without fear of stigma, discrimination, or legal consequences, thereby promoting greater access to care and safeguarding patient confidentiality.

Many U.S. states have their own medical privacy laws that go beyond the protections provided by HIPAA. For example, California's California Consumer Privacy Act (CCPA) [12] and California Privacy Rights Act (CPRA) [13] expand privacy rights for residents, although data already covered by HIPAA is generally exempt. The Texas Medical Privacy Act [14] offers broader coverage than HIPAA by applying to a wider range of entities, while New York's Stop Hacks and Improve Electronic Data Security (SHIELD) Act [15] establishes specific data security requirements to safeguard personal information.

In the European Union, the General Data Protection Regulation (GDPR) [16] applies to any organization that handles the personal data of EU residents, even if the organization is located outside the EU. Under the GDPR, health data is classified as a "special category" of information, receiving heightened protections. The regulation requires explicit consent for processing health data and grants individuals significant rights over their information, including the right to access, correct, and erase their data—often referred to as the "right to be forgotten."

3.2 Regulation for Children's Data

The Children's Online Privacy Protection Act (COPPA) [17] applies to websites, apps, and online services that are directed toward children under the age of 13, as well as those that knowingly collect personal data from them. It requires parental consent before collecting, using, or disclosing a child's personal information, and gives parents the right to review and delete their child's data. COPPA also mandates that operators provide clear and comprehensive privacy policies. The law covers a wide range of personal information, including names, addresses, geolocation data, photos, videos, voice recordings, persistent identifiers, and more.

The Family Educational Rights and Privacy Act (FERPA) [18] applies to educational institutions that receive federal funding and grants parents—and eligible students—the right to access and request corrections to education records. In most cases, schools must obtain written consent before releasing a student's records. FERPA covers a variety of information, including grades, disciplinary records, health information maintained by the school, and special education records, ensuring that student data is kept private and secure.

Some U.S. states have enacted child privacy laws that extend protections beyond federal requirements. California's California Consumer Privacy Act (CCPA) and California Privacy Rights Act (CPRA) provide special safeguards for the personal information of minors under the age of 16. The Delaware Online

Privacy Protection Act [19] expands COPPA protections to cover minors under 18, offering broader online privacy rights. Additionally, New York Education Law 2-d [20] imposes extra safeguards for student data shared with third-party vendors, ensuring stronger security and transparency in the handling of educational information.

3.3 Regulation Used in This Project

In this project, privacy disclosures were analyzed in the context of COPPA and HIPAA. COPPA requires parental consent and transparency in data collection for children under 13, while HIPAA mandates secure handling of electronic protected health information. These laws serve as benchmarks to assess the sufficiency and clarity of privacy policies and supporting implementation practices.

4 Methodology

We employ a multi-phase NLP pipeline using transformer models such as BERT and Legal-BERT. These models are fine-tuned on annotated privacy policy datasets to extract and classify sections mentioning children's data and health information. We supplement this with rule-based pattern matching for regulatory compliance indicators. Policies are scored based on the presence and specificity of disclosures related to consent, data sharing, retention, and user rights.

LegalBERT [21] is a family of domain-specific BERT models trained on large datasets of legal texts such as legislation, court rulings, and contracts. This specialized training equips the models with a deeper understanding of legal language, terminology, and syntax, leading to significantly higher accuracy on legal NLP tasks compared to general-purpose BERT models.

Multiple variants have been developed to address different sub-domains, for example, CONTRACTS-BERT focuses on contractual language, EURLEX-BERT on EU legislation, and ECHR-BERT on human rights cases. Lighter, more efficient versions are also available, offering faster performance with minimal trade-offs in accuracy. Like other BERT models, Legal-BERT supports transfer learning and can be fine-tuned on smaller, task-specific datasets to further enhance its performance.

In practice, Legal-BERT powers a range of legal tech applications, including contract analysis, legal research, e-discovery, document review, and even judgment prediction based on historical legal data. The Legal-BERT ecosystem has also expanded beyond English, with models like ITALIAN-LEGAL-BERT and InLegalBERT tailored to the Italian and Indian legal systems, respectively, enabling more accurate and localized NLP applications in diverse legal contexts [22].

Regarding the data collection, we started with a set of children's app privacy policies that were available as PDF files. To work with them, we developed a Python script to extract the text from privacy policies and split it into sentences. The goal was to create a dataset where each sentence could be analyzed on its own. During this process, we noticed a lot of irrelevant fragments like formatting noise or broken lines, so we integrated NLP (Natural Language Pipeline) for cleaning the sentences to filter those out. Each document was saved into a CSV file with one sentence per row.

Since privacy policies are long and repetitive, we also tried a simple keyword filter to flag sentences more likely to be COPPA-related (terms like parental consent, child, advertising, and delete). This made the review process faster, but we also kept an eye on other sentences, because we didn't want to bias the dataset too early.

For labeling, we defined three options: compliant (1), non-compliant (0), and skip if the sentence wasn't relevant. For example, a clear reference to parental consent would be compliant, while vague or misleading language about data use could be non-compliant. Anything like generic marketing or EU-specific legal text could be skipped.

Rather than labeling everything at once, we used an active learning approach implemented in our script. We first labeled 50 sentences manually with human intervention. The model was trained on these, then it picked out the sentences it was most unsure about. Labeling those uncertain cases gave the biggest "learning boost" to the model. We repeated this process until we had about 500 labeled sentences.

We used LegalBERT as our base model, since it was already pre-trained on legal text. That seemed more appropriate than a general BERT model. Each cycle followed the following steps:

- Once we have the model, we select 50 uncertain sentences (initial seed set) using a least-confidence strategy. These are labeled by a human annotator, and then we retrain the model.
- Training was lightweight: 2âĂŞ3 epochs, batch size 8, and a learning rate of 2e-5. This made the iterations fast enough to repeat multiple times.
- Finally, after we had 500 sentences labeled by human, we considered the model stable enough to try auto-labeling. At that point, our machine learning model would label everything else automatically.
- To avoid losing track of what was done by humans, we did not overwrite any labels. Instead, the script added extra columns to the CSV: one for the model's prediction and one for the probability scores. For sentences already labeled by human, the model's prediction was kept in a parallel column so we could compare the two.

For evaluation, we used the manually labeled set as ground truth. We looked at precision, recall, F1, and accuracy. Because the validation set was small, the metrics were a bit unstable at times, but overall, the results suggested the model was picking up the difference between compliant and non-compliant statements. Figure 1 shows a diagram of the methodology used in the project. Algorithm 1 presents the psceudocode for the active learning process for COPPA and HIPAA compliance.

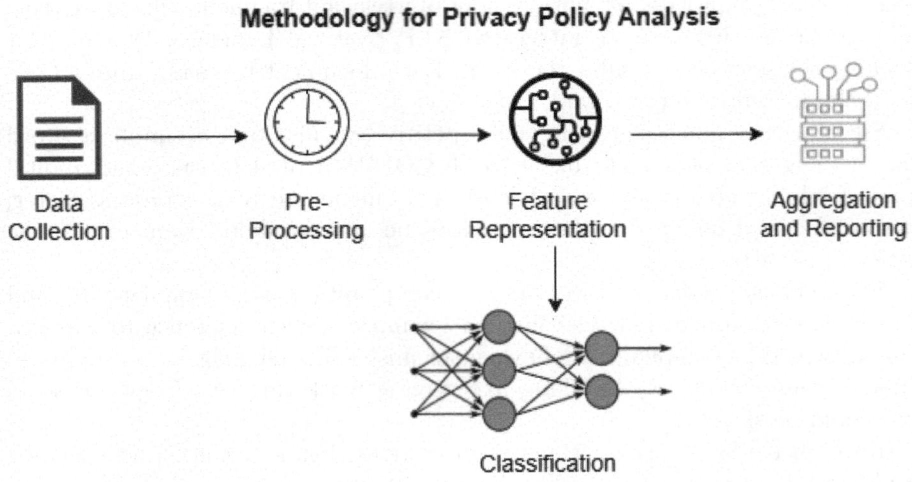

Fig. 1. Methodology used in the project.

Algorithm 1. Active Learning for COPPA and HIPAA Compliance

```
df ≤ read_csv(input_csv)
if 'label' ∈ df: df['label'] then
    ≤ NaN
end if
if no labeled rows then
    seed ≤ sample(SEED_SIZE from unlabeled)
    df[seed]['label'] ≤ HUMAN_LABEL(seed)
end if
for t in 1..ITERATIONS do
    (train, val, unlabeled) ≤ SPLIT_DATA(df)
    if |train| < MIN_SIZE then
        extra ≤ sample(QUERY_SIZE from unlabeled)
        df[extra]['label'] ≤ HUMAN_LABEL(extra)
        continue
    end if
    tokenizer ≤ LOAD_TOKENIZER(MODEL)
    trainer ≤ TRAIN_MODEL(MODEL, train, val, tokenizer)
    probs ≤ PREDICT_PROBA(trainer, unlabeled)
    query ≤ SELECT_UNCERTAIN(probs, QUERY_SIZE)
    df[query]['label'] ≤ HUMAN_LABEL(query)
    SAVE(df, output_dir, t)
    if count_nonNaN(df['label']) ≥ MAX_LABELS or unlabeled empty then
        break
    end if
end for
SAVE_FINAL_MODEL(trainer, tokenizer, output_dir)
SAVE_FINAL_DATASET(df, output_dir)
```

5 Analysis of Privacy Policies

Figure 2 presents the results of the sentence-level labeling of the model after completion of the learning process. Our findings reveal that many web apps inadequately address their responsibilities. For example, references to COPPA or HIPAA may be present, but lack supporting details about how data is protected or shared. Ambiguous policy language and incomplete permission disclosures are common. Using our model, we can quantify the frequency and quality of such disclosures at scale across app categories.

text	pred_label	pred_label_name	prob_non_compliant	prob_compliant
Since we don't collect directly identifiable personal information and use identifiers in a way that is not able to be linked to a directly identifiable person, children are not able to make their personal information publicly available nor the functionalities of our Apps and Services do not allow such disclosure.	1	compliant	0.2986	0.7014
Children can access many parts of the App/Services and its content and use many of its features without providing us with personal information.	1	compliant	0.312713	0.687287
Our Practices for Disclosing Children's Information https://www.bubadu.com/privacy-policy/ 9/40 8/2/25, 4:45 AM Bubadu Privacy Policy We do not share, sell, rent, or transfer children's personal information other than as described in this section.	1	compliant	0.398583	0.601417
This type of advertising is precluded by the Children's Online Privacy Protection Act and its implementing regulations under the Children's Online Privacy Protection Rule (collectively <<TERM_COPPA>>) for children under 13 without prior, verifiable parental consent, as well as by the existing self-regulatory advertising groups, including DAA and the Network Advertising Initiative (NAI).	1	compliant	0.424454	0.575546
We do not use advertising cookies or similar technologies in areas where students or children are logged in to the Services, or on the ClassDojo Website where a student or child user is directed to login to the dedicated child or student login page.	1	compliant	0.314178	0.685822

Fig. 2. Results of the model: compliant labeled.

Another common issue is the lack of clarity regarding the data lifecycle. Policies tend to decline to address how data is stored for how long, how deletion requests are handled, or whether there are limits on storage. Rather, they make vague pronouncements such as"data can be stored as long as necessary," which offer little practical information to users.

We also found that sharing data with third parties is rarely talked about in specifics. Policies will mention that data can be shared with "partners" or "service providers," but few will say who these are or what they do. Without this specificity, it is difficult for users to know where their data is going or why.

Readability is also a problem. Policies are composed at a level too advanced for the typical reader, and useful information is generally buried in dense legal terminology. So even where disclosures exist, they are not presented in language most users can easily comprehend.

Finally, the tone of the language is softer than it is suggestive of concrete commitments. The words "we may," "we might," or "as needed" recur, with the user left uncertain about specific practices being performed.

In summary, our research detects several common shortcomings in privacy policies, including vague references to legislation, poor descriptions of data handling, lack of disclosure about third-party sharing, low readability, and the use of evasive language. These shortcomings mean that a majority of policies fall short of their intended role as a tool for accountability and user protection.

Table 1 shows the performance of our model. The model reached an accuracy of about 72%, where two out of three predictions were correct. More importantly, it achieved a recall of 97%, showing that it was able to identify almost all of the relevant sentences in the dataset. The F1-score of 79% highlights a good balance between accuracy of positive predictions and the ability of the model to find all the relevant instances.

Table 1. Model Performance Results

Metric	Score
Accuracy	71.8%
Recall	97.2%
F1-score	78.7%

These results demonstrate that the learning approach helped the model steadily improve and reach strong coverage of important sentences, which is particularly valuable in the regulatory context. The trade-off between precision and recall is expected in such text-heavy tasks, and the current results show a solid foundation for further refinement.

6 Conclusion

Our research highlights that many privacy policies fail to meet their core purpose of ensuring accountability and protecting users. The prevalence of vague legal references, unclear data handling practices, undisclosed third-party sharing, and evasive language significantly reduces their effectiveness, pointing to a critical need for clearer, more transparent, and user-centric policy design.

By integrating legal analysis, natural language processing (NLP)-driven policy evaluation, and comprehensive technical security assessments, this work aims to provide a scalable approach to audit privacy practices and protect vulnerable populations.

The tools and findings developed in this research help bridge the gap between privacy regulation, user understanding, and technology design. They offer practical support for regulators working to enforce compliance, provide clearer insights to users trying to navigate complex privacy policies, and guide developers in building apps that are not only legally compliant but also respectful of users' rights and needs.

References

1. Verderame, L., Caputo, D., Romdhana, A., Merlo, A.: On the (un)reliability of privacy policies in android apps. In: 2020 International Joint Conference on Neu- ral Networks (IJCNN), United Kingdom (2020). https://doi.org/10.1109/IJCNN48605.2020.9206660
2. Rahman, M.S., Naghavi, P., Kojusner, B., S. Afroz, B.W., Rampazzi, S.: Permpress, machine learning-based pipeline to evaluate permissions in app privacy policies. IEEE Access 10 (2022). https://doi.org/10.1109/ACCESS.2022.3199882
3. Blanco-Aza, D., et al.: Privacy analysis in mobile apps and social networks using ai techniques. In: 2024 4th Intelligent Cybersecurity Conference (ICSC), Spain (2024). https://doi.org/10.1109/ICSC63108.2024.10895037
4. Nankya, M., A. Mugisa, Y.U., Upadhyay, A., Chata, R.: Security and privacy in e-health systems: a review of ai and machine learning techniques. IEEE Access 12 (2024).https://doi.org/10.1109/ACCESS.2024.3469215
5. Bhimanapati, V.B. R., Jain, S., Pandian, P.K.G.: Security testing for mobile applications using AI and ML algorithms. J. Quantum Sci. Tech. **1**(2), (2024). https://doi.org/10.36676/jqst.v1.i2.15
6. Okoyomon, E., et al.: On the ridiculousness of notice and consent: contradictions in app privacy policies. In: Workshop on Technology and Consumer Protection (ConPro 2019), in Conjunction with the 39th IEEE Symposium on Security and Privacy (2023)
7. Aberkane, A.-J., Broucke, S., Poels, G.: Factors related to GDPR compliance promises in privacy policies: a machine learning and NLP approach. IJISPM **13**(2) (2025)
8. Zimmeck, S., et al.: Automated analysis of privacy requirements for mobile apps. In: The 2016 AAAI Fall Symposium Series: Privacy and Language Technologies Technical Report FS-16-04. (2017). https://doi.org/10.14722/ndss.2017.23034
9. U.S. department of health human services - health information privacy. https://www.hhs.gov/hipaa/index.html
10. U.S. department of health and human services - HITECH act enforcement interim final rule. https://www.hhs.gov/hipaa/for-professionals/special-topics/hitech-act-enforcement-interim-final-rule/index.html

11. Code of federal regulations - title 42 CFR. https://www.ecfr.gov/current/title-42
12. California consumer privacy act (CCPA). https://oag.ca.gov/privacy/ccpa
13. The california privacy rights act of 2020. https://thecpra.org/
14. Texas state law library - privacy and personal information. https://guides.sll.texas.gov/privacy-and-personal-information/medical-records
15. 2023 new york statewide civil legal aid technology confer- ence - 2A agents of the SHIELD - data privacy and security. https://www.nycourts.gov/LegacyPDFS/accesstojusticecommission/tc/2023/2A-Agents-of-SHIELD-CLE-Resources.pdf
16. Intersoft consulting - general data protection regulation GDPR. https://gdpr-info.eu/
17. Federal trade commission - children's online privacy protection rule (COPPA). https://www.ftc.gov/legal-library/browse/rules/childrens-online-privacy-protection-rule-coppa
18. U.S. department OD education - FERPA - 34 CFR PART 99—FAMILY EDUCATIONAL RIGHTS AND PRIVACY. https://studentprivacy.ed.gov/ferpa
19. The delaware code online - TITLE 6. https://delcode.delaware.gov/title6/c012c/index.html
20. New york state education department - data privacy and security - fact sheet for parents. https://www.nysed.gov/data-privacy-security/fact-sheet-parents
21. Hugging face - nlpaueb/legal-bert-base-uncased. https://huggingface.co/nlpaueb/legal-bert-base-uncased
22. Neelamegam, P., Nirmala, S, J.: Recent trends in legal AI: a comprehensive review. In: 2025 Third International Conference on Augmented Intelligence and Sustainable Systems (ICAISS) (2025). Trichy, Indihttps://doi.org/10.1109/ICAISS61471.2025.11042154

Author Index

J. R. Barr et al. (Eds.): ERWCSA 2025, ACSAR 4, p. 215, 2026.
https://doi.org/10.1007/978-3-032-18230-2

The manufacturer's authorised representative in the EU is Springer
Nature Customer Service Centre GmbH, Europaplatz 3, 69115 Heidelberg,
Germany. If you have any concerns regarding our products, please
contact ProductSafety@springernature.com

Printed and bound by CPI Group (UK) Ltd, Croydon, CR0 4YY
05/10/2026
02228031-0004